CAREERS AND FAMILY

Volume 121, Sage Library of Social Research

RECENT VOLUMES IN
SAGE LIBRARY OF SOCIAL RESEARCH

CAREERS
and FAMILY
Sex Roles and
Adolescent Life Plans

Carol Kehr Tittle

Volume 121
SAGE LIBRARY OF
SOCIAL RESEARCH

 SAGE PUBLICATIONS   Beverly Hills   London

HD
6057
.9
.T58
1981

For information address:

SAGE Publications, Inc.
275 South Beverly Drive
Beverly Hills, California 90212

SAGE Publications Ltd
28 Banner Street
London EC1Y 8QE, England

Printed in the United States of America

Library of Congress Cataloging in Publication Data

Tittle, Carol K   1933-
    Careers and family.

    (Sage library of social research ; v. 121)
    Bibliography: p.
    Includes index.
    1. Vocational guidance for women. 2. Sex role.
3. Social values. 4. Family. 5. Vocational interests.
I. Title.
HD6057.9.T58   305.4'3   81-2015
ISBN 0-8039-1352-4   AACR1
ISBN 0-8039-1353-2 (pbk.)

FIRST PRINTING

CONTENTS

PREFACE

The present work had its origins in an unlikely circumstance: a study of the sex-fairness of tests used in education, particularly measures of occupational interests. There were fewer scales and often different occupational scales available to help girls and women make career-related decisions. Similarly, discussions of theories of career development and career decision-making focused narrowly on the development of the career paths of men. There were no discussions of plans and values related to marriage and parenthood because they did not appear related to career decisions for men. For women, these other, traditionally sex-related adult roles were and are highly salient, leading to "contingency" planning and delaying or "stalling" in career development, commitment, and work plans. For many women, a full commitment to undertaking the adult role of worker is delayed until children are well into their school years, leading to the phenomenon in both higher education and work that has been labeled as the reentry or returning woman.

The importance of the relationship of adult roles of wife or husband and mother or father to career development may be examined more fully with the growth of the field of life-span development. This perspective on growth and development over the entire life span should encourage career development theorists to integrate the adult roles and patterns of participation of both men and women into their theoretical frameworks. The study described here attempts to begin such a framework in a particular way—by expanding the consideration of values in career and life planning to include not only occupational values but also values related to marriage and parenthood.

The study follows the general idea of the occupational values that appear in the computer-based System of Interactive Guidance and Information (SIGI) developed by Martin Katz and his colleagues. SIGI focuses on occupational values and information. We added the ideas of values that might be related to an individual's decisions to become a husband or wife and to become a parent—the marriage and parenthood values. The reasoning was as follows. The clarification of values assists in the consideration of occupations. The examination of values thought to be related to the decision to marry or become a parent, in conjunction with occupational values, should assist students to identify the values that may be satisfied in these three different adult roles. Perhaps most people will find that satisfaction of different values predominates in these three contexts. For example, women particularly might find that needs for the occupational value, Helping Others, would be predominantly satisfied in the parental role, and other values are satisfied in the roles of worker and wife. For men, conversely, it may become apparent that the world of work may not satisfy some of their important values and needs.

The underlying thesis in formulating values for marriage and parenthood is that considering all three value sets together may assist individuals to recognize that they will make decisions for each adult role. Any single role is unlikely to satisfy their full range of values or needs. Planning for education and the adult roles of worker, marriage partner, and parent may or may not follow sex-stereotyped views of these roles. The many options open to individuals of each sex should be considered at early ages, and the values here are intended to facilitate that process for adolescents.

The values in the areas of marriage and parenthood were developed the first year of the project and revised definitions were used in the main study, as part of an individual interview schedule. The main study was concerned with the responses of eleventh-grade urban students to the values, and their experiences and plans related to occupations, education, work, and family. The participants represented equally students of both sexes, two socioeconomic levels (middle and low), and three ethnic groups (white, black, and Hispanic).

The chapters that follow present a brief description of the data on women's employment and earnings patterns that underscore the need for research in this area and an overview of the study (Chapter 1). Chapter 2 describes the background for the study, drawing upon the research literature in several related areas. Chapter 3 gives the definitions of the major variables: the values sets, SES, ethnicity, and the two scales developed by Lolagene Coombs, one examining level of involvement with respect to work and family, and the other job versus child orientation. Chapter 4 describes the procedures used to identify the sample and carry out the data collection, the major sections of the interview schedule, and characteristics of the students in the samples and their parents.

The major findings for the study are set out in four chapters. Chapter 5 describes the eleventh-grade students in terms of their plans and expectations for education, occupation, and work. Work decisions and analysis of a role model question are included. The focus is on the 12 cells in the sample design (sex, SES, and ethnic groups) and the similarities and differences among these groups on this initial set of questions.

Chapter 6 contains the findings for several major questions related to the three sets of values: How do adolescents respond to the values for occupational, marriage, and parenthood decisions? Do responses differ by the three main factors of the sample: sex, SES, and ethnic group? How overlapping or independent are the values, both within each set of values and among all three sets? The answers to these questions are important for both practice and theory. Counselors and career educators need to know if students can differentiate among the values and if they tap different dimensions or are largely redundant. For future research it is also important to know the answers, so we can decide whether to change the values and how to test their further use.

In Chapter 7 the values and other independent variables are examined for their relationship to several family planning variables: the number of children desired, the score on the job-child orientation scale of Coombs, and the variable number of years of full-time work before age 41. In Chapter 8 student perceptions of sex-role variables are described. The relative importance of work, marriage, and children is examined, as well as the timing of plans for education, marriage, children, full- and part-time work participation. Direct allocation of responsibilities of men and women for activities of families with children are included. Chapter 9 presents case studies of the values. Transcripts of student interpretations of the values add to an understanding of the values.

The final chapter summarizes the findings from the study and draws implications for school career education programs, for the evaluation of interventions in career education and guidance programs, and for future research on adolescents, their career-related decisions and work plans, and their perceptions of sex roles.

There is currently widespread concern for high school youth and their career and work plans, and for women and equal opportunity. It is hoped that this study will assist vocational guidance and career-education staffs and administrators to understand and plan these programs within an expanded view of life-span development. Counselors should find the many questions of interest, because informal observations indicated that students, after responding to the series of questions in the interview schedule, were frequently interested in pursuing the ideas further.[1] Researchers and college faculty in career education, guidance, adolescence, the psychology of women, sex roles, family planning, and counseling will also find the study useful as both a description of one urban sample at a particular time and, hopefully, as a stimulus to their own thinking in these areas.

NOTE

1. A copy of the complete interview schedule can be obtained by writing the author.

ACKNOWLEDGMENTS

The first note of appreciation is to the eleventh-grade students and their high school staffs who participated in the study. Students, with parental consent, voluntarily participated in the interviews. The high school principals, teachers, and guidance staff who kindly and helpfully permitted us to conduct interviews in their schools are dedicated, thoughtful, and concerned individuals. Without their commitment to students and a curiosity about the outcome of research studies, there would be no study to report.

Appreciation is also expressed to colleagues and staff at two institutions: the Center for Advanced Study in Education (CASE) at the Graduate Center of the City University of New York (CUNY), where the study originated and the data collection was completed, and the University of North Carolina at Greensboro, where the data analysis and report were completed. Administrators at both institutions helped to support the grant: Max Weiner, then Director of CASE, and Dave Reilly, Dean of the School of Education at UNC-G. The major support for the work was given by a grant from the National Institute of Education, under the Education and Work Program. As with all such support, the acknowledgment must indicate that, "contractors undertaking such projects under government sponsorship are encouraged to express freely their professional judgment in the conduct of the project. Points of view or opinions stated do not, therefore, necessarily represent official National Institute of Education position or policy." The Research Council of UNC-G has also supported the preparation of the final manuscript.

Special acknowledgments are due Deanna Chitayat and Elenor Rubin Denker, who worked together with me to prepare the grant and develop the values in the first year of the project. Elenor Rubin Denker and Joyce Block were invaluable associates during the second year of the project, in data collection, coding for computer analysis and developing a computer code book. Iris Cook, Barbara Mait, Linda Newman, Lynn Novick, and Robert Velen were also interested and reliable interviewers over a longer-than-anticipated data-collection period. Judith Cole assisted in the preparation of the final report.

Charlotte Fiske at CASE and Kathleen Martinek and Anita Hawkins at UNC-G patiently and competently coped with administrative and typing responsibilities for the project reports.

Michael Schlessinger at CASE and William A. Powers at UNC-G were programmers for the project.

Martin Katz was consultant to the project and was both knowledgeable and generous in suggesting adaptations of the occupational values, new items for the interview, possible data analyses, and reviewing the NIE final report. Lolagene Coombs of the University of Michigan kindly permitted the use of her then-unpublished scales of preferences for work and children and reviewed their presentation format.

Carol Kehr Tittle
October 1980

Chapter 1

EDUCATION AND CAREERS:
Understanding Adolescent Choices

In the midst of an uncertain economic future, today's youth make initial career-related decisions and have their own perceptions of what it will mean to move into adult roles of worker, long-term or permanent relationships with others, and parenthood. Whether examined consciously or not, there are many options available to both boys and girls. The need to develop a better understanding of these choices and perceptions is based on the premise that a knowledge of the values that direct these choices and perceptions can foster self-knowledge in the service of individual choice. Katz (1966) described the function and importance of defining individual values. Questions the individual needs to ask, in addition to What are my values? are, Where have my values come from? and then the individual will be better able to ask, Where are they taking me?

The need for understanding arises from the inequalities in the outcomes of career choices made by men and women. The present study was undertaken to examine choices in the areas of values and plans for education, work, marriage, and parenthood. This chapter describes the demographic data on women's employment and life cycle that emphasize the need for understanding, and presents an overview of the research study and its major questions.

The Status of Women

ECONOMIC STATUS

To the outside observer, there are important differences in where values take men and women and teenage boys and girls in making occupational choices and finding employment. The differences in employment patterns, occupations entered, financial returns, and unemployment rates are great. For example, compare the unemployment rates for adults and youth of each gender. In 1978, the unemployment rate was lowest for white adult males (20 and over) and highest for black teenage women ages 16 to 19 (Women's Bureau, 1979). The adult unemployment rate for white males was 3.7%, white women 5.2%, Hispanic men 6.3%, Hispanic women 9.8%, black men 9.1% and black women 11.1%. For youth, the unemployment rates are even worse: white males 13.5%, white females 14.4%, Hispanic males 19.5%, Hispanic females 22.0%, black males 36.5%, and black females 41.0%. The pattern of sex differences, regardless of racial or ethnic group, is remarkably consistent.

Similar differences exist in earnings and occupations. Women workers are concentrated in low-paying dead-end jobs (Women's Bureau, 1979). As a result, the average woman worker earns only about three-fifths of what a man does, when both work full-time year-round. The median wage or salary income of year-round workers in 1977 was lowest for minority-race women ($8,383) and for white women ($8,787). For minority men the income was $11,053 and for white men, $15,230. The median earnings of full-time year-round women farm workers were $1,635, for private household workers $2,714, for sales workers $6,825, and for clerical workers $8,601. Also, in 1977, fully employed women high school graduates (no college) had less income on the average than fully employed men who had not completed elementary school: $8,462 and $9,332, respectively. Women with four years of college also had less income than men with only an eighth-grade education: $11,134 and $11,931.

Another perspective on earnings data is given by an analysis over the last 25 years. In 1955 full-time women workers earned $.64 to men's $1.00. By 1960 this figure had dropped to $.61. In 1970 women's earnings were calculated to be 59.4¢ to men's $1.00. In 1977 the figure was 58.9¢ to men's $1.00. Women were 80% of all clerical workers in 1978 but only 6% of craft workers (and 3% of all apprentices as of June 1978). Women were 63% of service workers but only 43% of professional and technical workers. Women were 64% of retail sales workers and only 23% of nonfarm managers and administrators. They were also 95% of all private household workers.

These differences are examined in greater detail for minority groups and women in a report of the U.S. Commission on Civil Rights (1978). The data are based on national samples and are presented for seven minority groups, among them two of the groups with which the present research is concerned, blacks and Puerto Ricans (Hispanic). The data on high school completion, median earnings for college-educated persons, unemployment, occupational segregation, and average earnings increments are of particular interest.

The data on high school completion rate are given in terms of the percentage of each group's completion rate compared to that of majority (white) males as the base of 100 in 1976. The rates of completion for females were: white 99%, black 85%, and Puerto Rican 78%. For males the completion rates were: black 85% and Puerto Rican 78%. The sexes are alike in their rates of completion within each ethnic group, but the minority ethnic groups have lower high school completion rates. Rates for college completion are not similar, however, and differ for the sexes within ethnic groups. Completion rates for females, as percentage of white males, were: white 65%, black 32%, and Puerto Rican 12%. For males, the completion rates were: white 100%, black 32%, and Puerto Rican 18%. Rankings for median earnings in 1975 (i.e., some earnings) by 12-15 years of school completed were: majority males, black males, black females, and majority females. The same rankings of earnings in 1975 were found for four or more years of higher education.

The percentage of the labor force 16-19 years of age out of work and actively seeking work in 1976 was also analyzed in relation to the majority male base of 1.00. For females, the ratios were: white 3.25, black 8.69, and Puerto Rican 6.47. The ratios for males were: white 1.00, black 8.10, and Puerto Rican 9.36. The earnings were also examined in terms of the average earnings *increment* by age. Thus, in 1975, black males' average earnings increment by age was 49% as much as the earnings increment for majority males. In dollar amounts, this meant $185.30 compared to $357.75. For Puerto Rican males, the data were 26% and in dollars, $97.97. The data for females were:

	%	$
White	15	57.55
Black	8	29.95
Puerto Rican	-5	-20.00

The discrepancies in dollar amounts for male groups are large, but the differences for females are even greater, and are indicative of the extensive effects of level-of-education attained, occupational segregation and discrimination.

Of particular interest in terms of career decisions and occupational choice are the indicators of the extent to which each group would have to *change* occupations in order to have an occupational distribution identical to majority males. In 1976, these percentages were:

	Female	Males
White	66.1%	(base)
Black	69.3%	37.9%
Puerto Rican	78.9%	50.4%

Thus, within all the female groups a greater percentage would have to change occupations to achieve equity than would have to within the male minority groups.

Almquist (1979) has also reviewed data on labor force participation, occupations, and earnings for males and females and several of the minority groups, including blacks, Spanish-speaking, Asians, and native Americans. She cited data on the extent to which the jobs held by women have not been equally rewarded. Studies that have measured job characteristics, such as length-of-training required, autonomy, and freedom from supervision, found that nearly two-thirds of the difference between female and male earnings ($2,248) can be accounted for by the "fact that job characteristics translate into higher payoffs in men's work than in women's work" (p. 24). Spaeth (1977) has documented this effect in another analysis, using a college sample. He found, in a follow-up of 3,081 persons in the University of Illinois graduating class of 1961, that women reaped lesser returns in occupational status from advanced education.

Employment patterns of women differ from those of men. Men have long predominated in the labor force, but this status is changing. About 42 million women were in the labor force in 1978, and they constituted more than two-fifths of all workers. Fifty percent of all women ages 16 and over were workers, and for the usual working ages, 59% of all women 18 to 64 were workers in 1978, compared with 88% of men. The average worklife expectancy of women has increased by more than one-half over the two decades since 1950. In 1970, the average woman could expect to spend almost 23 years of her life in the work force. Today the average woman worker is as well educated as the average man worker; both have completed a median of 12.6 years of schooling (Women's Bureau, 1979).

LIFE CYCLE TRENDS

Most striking and indicative of changes in the actual behavior of women's adult roles is the change in work patterns of mothers. Fifty-three percent of all mothers with children under 18 were in the labor force in 1978. For the last 10 years over half of the mothers who lived with husbands and had only school-aged children have been employed (Hoffman, 1979). Now almost 42% of the mothers of preschoolers are also employed, and more than one-third of mothers with children under three and who live with their husbands are employed. Maternal employment *is* the modal pattern. Even more striking are data that suggest that as few as 19% of the households in the United States fit past normative expectations of women's adult roles; that is, are households in which the husband works, the wife is at home, and there are one or more children home. These are the statistics, yet an important concern and one examined by the research that follows is: To what extent are youth's expectations or normative views in agreement with the behavioral trends?

The rate of divorce in the United States has increased dramatically since 1965 (Hetherington, 1979). Estimates are that 40% of the current marriages of young adults will end in divorce. The severe negative economic consequences for women of marital dissolution have been well documented (Corcoran, 1979). Giele (1978) reported that present support laws do not work. One year after a divorce decree only 38% of the fathers were meeting support payments; after 10 years only 13% were in full compliance with the support order. These data are reflected in statistics on the heads of households and work. Among all families, about 1 out of 7 was headed by a woman in 1978, compared to 1 out of 10 in 1968 (Women's Bureau, 1979). Of all women workers, about 1 out of 8 was a family head. For black women workers, about 1 out of 4 was a family head. Among all poor families, 49% were headed by women in 1978. More than 2 of 3 poor black families were headed by women. Most women work because of economic need. As of March 1978, women in the labor force showed the following characteristics: never married, 25%; widowed, divorced or separated, 19%; married, husband's 1977 income under $7,000, 10%; married, husband's 1977 income $7,000-$9,999, 8%; married, husband's 1977 income $10,000-$14,999, 15%; and married, husband's 1977 income $15,000 and over, 23%.

These data on women as heads of households, combined with data on the economic need of women in the labor force, reflect changes in the life cycle of women and their marital and family statuses. Waite (1978a), Glick (1977), and Van Dusen and Sheldon (1976) have summarized recent changes. For example, women 18 to 24 years old in 1976 projected families of two children, somewhat fewer than those women in a follow-up study of a national survey of high school students (Peng, Wisenbaker, Bailey, & Marnell, 1978, Vol. 1) and the students in the present study. It is projected that the average young woman who marries in the 1970s will bear her first child when she is about 23 and her last child before she is 30. Women will be engaged in child bearing for about seven years of their adult lives and have preschool-age children for a little over a decade. The youngest child will be in school when the woman is 35 and she will have 30 years before retirement at age 65. The life expectancy of her children will be 81 years if the child is a girl, born in 1976, and 72 years for a boy child. For women born in the 1950s, who marry in the 1970s, the estimate of percentage ever married is 93% (correspondingly, only 7% will never marry) and only about 10% of all these women will be childless.

Many of these statistics promise increased education and labor-force participation by women, as is presently occurring. The status of women's educational attainment is improved: Currently about 75% of youth complete high school and about 45% (although 60% of the high school graduates) enter a degree-credit program in colleges or universities. Women are presently about as likely as men to enter college, and data from the follow-up of the National Longitudinal Survey of 1972 showed that for white females, 46% of those enrolled had graduated on schedule (within four years), compared to 36% of the males. For blacks, the number graduated also favored females, 32% versus 27% for males; for Hispanics, a slight difference also favored females in percentage graduated, 18% versus 14% for males (Eckland & Wisenbaker, 1979). Data on college majors, however, show that women are still underrepresented in business and management, engineering, biological and physical sciences, and first professional degrees, for example, dentistry, optometry, pharmacy, law, and veterinary medicine (1975-76 data, Grant & Lind, 1978).

Thus, many of the differences in occupational choice and earnings will persist. And, we can expect that present life-cycle trends will continue. The behavior of men and women will continue to depart from our earlier, now-stereotyped, views of the appropriate adult roles for men and women. Particularly for women, the difference between past normative views of marriage and family roles are not aligned with present behaviors. Part of any strategy to reduce these disparities in occupational and family statuses must include attempts to improve our understanding of the relationships between values, adult roles traditionally ascribed by sex, and the career-related choices and work perceptions of youth. This study is directed toward increasing such understanding.

Overview of the Study

Among the educational tasks of the school is the provision of knowledge about occupations and career planning. This knowledge is now being formally transmitted in the new curriculum area of career or occupational education. The career education curricula developed for use in elementary and secondary schools are based on approaches to career decision-making that focus on an independent decision maker whose occupational choice is a logical consequence of her or his occupational values and knowledge. This approach is increasingly criticized for neglecting a basic element for career decision-making for women: the traditionally defined adult sex roles of women. Both within sociology and psychology the development of approaches to occupational choice have used data on males as a point of reference.

The most serious omission in conceptualizing career choice is the consideration of the effects of sex role socialization on the decision-making process. Choices within a woman's world which include decisions about marriage, parenthood, and female-male responsibilities in homemaking are left unexamined in theory and often in research. These latter aspects of a woman's world are important parts of the adult woman's sex roles as defined in American culture. It has been argued by Psathas (1968) and Falk and Cosby (1978), in their reviews of sociological research on occupational choice and status attainment, that these aspects of sex roles have direct implications for the types of occupations women consider, for their labor-market entry and exit patterns, and, as a result, for women's career decisions. More recently Fitzgerald and Crites (1980) have suggested the importance of these aspects of women's roles for the development of a career psychology of women, acknowledging the deficiencies of theories of career choice and career maturity in providing sufficient understanding for counselors of women's career development.

The present study examined background and process variables that may relate to career decisions and attainment. More specifically, the study examined what we have called the sex-role values of an urban sample of eleventh-grade boys and girls. The study was designed to fit within a National Institute of Education framework for research on career awareness that specified: 1. background variables, such as ability, sex, cultural background, and socioeconomic status; 2. process variables, including self-assessment skills and decision-making skills, along with knowledge, values, preferences, and self-concept, as influencing the making of decisions; and 3. attainment variables, such as occupational attainment, educational attainment, earnings, mobility, and job satisfaction (National Institute of Education, 1976). The present study also had the long-range goal of providing sets of values in the areas of marriage and parenthood that could accompany occupational values in interventions designed to assist students to further their career exploration.

In order to examine the effects of sex-role-related values on the career decision-making process, the domain to be studied had to be explicitly identified. Occupational values, a major part of the adult role for males, previously had been studied, and models for the procedure of defining a value domain already were in existence. For example, the System of Interactive Guidance and Information (SIGI), developed after an extensive research effort by Martin Katz and his colleagues (1973), includes a set of occupational role-related values that are used in helping students define the needs or satisfactions they may find in an occupation. These occupation-related values are: High Income, Prestige, Independence, Helping Others, Security, Leadership, Interest Field, Leisure, Variety, and Early Entry. Katz, starting from past research and using a structured interview, was able to elicit from students the dimensions along which they construed occupations.

While occupation-related values had been identified through research, and, as a result, were in a system now in use by students, there was no similar set of terms and definitions identified and demonstrated to be useful to students in clarifying values related to major adult roles traditionally ascribed to women and traditionally believed to constitute their major satisfactions as adults: parenthood and marriage. The present research was the first step in the development of these sets of values and the attempt to relate them to career-related decisions. We sought to develop the values as part of an understanding of such decisions, or the apparently unexamined decisions, such as are found in studies of motherhood and a single woman's views of work: "I was 40 years old, says a suburban housewife, before it dawned on me that I really had had no choice about becoming a mother. Not that I didn't know all about contraception but that it had never occurred to me that anything else was possible" (Bernard, 1974, p. 24). Similar views were expressed in an interview of a 27-year-old single woman and her thoughts about work:

> I grew up thinking you get married. . . . So, for a long time . . . I sort of held my life in suspension, as if the real thing hadn't begun yet. Then one day about two years ago it hit me like a ton of bricks: while I was waiting around, life was passing . . . I wasn't really committing myself to the idea of a career either, because I kept thinking "this is temporary." [The woman had worked as a dental technician and then decided to go back to school to study nursing.] . . . I had a very good job that offered me excellent pay and with a tremendous amount of security. But at some point those things just weren't working any more. I may be working 40 more years, so it had better be work I like to do [*New York Times*, January 7, 1977].

Along with the development of the values thought to be part of the decisions to marry and to become a parent, the research was designed to examine the values in relation to a series of background characteristics of 600 eleventh-grade students and to their plans for education, work, family, and career. The orientation of the study is primarily descriptive with respect to these characteristics and plans, providing a view of the range of individuals who responded to the values and the other questions. The sample is representative of urban youth with respect to three character- istics: sex, ethnic group, and socioeconomic status. Both females and males are equally represented, as are black, white, and Hispanic youth, and both middle and low classifications of socioeconomic status.

While the research is based on a sample of individual interviews done at one point in time, 1977-1978, there is also a concern with the theoretical and practical implications of the findings. The development of an ex- panded view of the context and content of career decision-making as proposed here should encourage other researchers to examine values re- lated to occupational, marriage, and parenthood adult roles and to articu- late these ideas in describing and understanding how students choose careers and work settings. For the long term, there is an assumption implicit in the research that including these other, sex-role-related values in career education and decision-making approaches should affect the distri- bution of sexes in many occupations. By identifying the needs and values that can be fulfilled in major adult roles women should be free to explore their interests and make choices with a more conscious perspective on where their values are taking them. Men should also benefit from consider- ing these adult roles jointly.

Many of the girls and boys in the sample spontaneously expressed their feelings of interest, intrigue, and reflection when the interviews concluded. Indeed, one of the most striking observations of the interviews was the interest of students in responding to the questions and their expressions of the need for such discussion opportunities. A majority of the students were attending large public high schools, and questions on, "Who do you talk to about . . ." indicated that few have contacts with persons outside of their immediate family and close friends with whom to explore their values and plans (see Chapter 4). Few teachers or counselors assist students in this way. Although questions on this area had been included more or less routinely, we were surprised at the extent of the need expressed. In only a small number of low-enrollment parochial high schools were there examples of the relationships between school staff and students that exemplified the type of career education and guidance activities that are needed to help students make conscious choices about their futures.

Although much of the impetus for the study arises from a concern for sex-role-related values and their relationships to plans for education, occupations, work, and family, the implications of the study should not be viewed as limited to the domain of career education and career development approaches. Programs that are aimed at linking youth and work at a pragmatic level must also reach out to assist them in understanding and considering their options in all adult roles.[1]

The next chapter places the study within the perspective of areas of related research and develops a framework for criteria to be used in examining equity in career decision-making and career education for men and women. Chapter 3 describes the major variables and procedures of the study. The remaining chapters present the findings from the study, including case studies of students based on interview transcripts. The final chapter summarizes the main findings and draws implications for career education programs, the evaluation of intervention programs, and future research on adolescence, work, and sex roles.

NOTE

1. Data analyses on this project were carried out using SPSS and SAS programs: *Statistical Package for the Social Sciences* (2nd ed.). Nie, N H., Hull, C. H., Jenkins, J. G., Steinbrenner, K., & Bent, D. H. New York: McGraw-Hill, 1975. *SAS User's Guide, 1979 Edition.* Raleigh, N.C.: SAS Institute, Inc., 1979.

The descriptive statistics, cross tabulations, and discriminant analyses were done using SPSS. The MANOVAs, ANOVAs, regression and factor analyses were done using SAS. Factor analyses are principal components with varimax rotation.

Chapter 2

BACKGROUND

The need to understand the choices and behaviors of adolescents as they move from their high school experiences to the labor market and post-secondary education is made more critical by the influence of federal and state policies. These policies help direct the choices of students in subtle and as yet unanalyzed ways. For example, Nolfi et al. (1978) suggest that the analysis of the National Longitudinal Survey of the High School Class of 1972 (NLS) will guide policy in postsecondary education, vocational education, manpower training, and public employment, among other areas. Policies such as universal entitlements for high school graduates are being discussed, as well as plans for better integration of education and work for youth. Another major policy theme is concerned with the effects of race and sex. In their analysis of the NLS data, almost every finding includes references to these "highly sensitive variables." In fact, a major analysis of the relation between earnings and schooling for students who do not go on to postsecondary education is carried out only for males.[1] This latter analysis is the result of the neglect of females in the adolescent and labor market research literature.

Earlier research conducted by Douvan and Adelson (1966) included both boys and girls in their national interview survey of adolescent boys and girls in 1955 and 1956. The differences in the findings led Adelson to conclude that both sexes should always be included. Yet in 1979 Adelson commented on the forthcoming *Handbook of Adolescent Psychology* that there would be no chapter of the adolescent girl because of the paucity of research on which to base such a chapter. There is, however, more attention to both sexes in current research and this chapter reflects these attempts to define variables and collect data that will increase the understanding of career development, education and work plans, and life-span development of women as well as men. As Ginzberg and others (1966) recognized in a study of 300 women who pursued graduate education between 1945 and 1951, career development is a matter of options, decisions, and life styles for women. To a considerable extent this remains true today, but more as a psychological choice rather than a behavioral choice between homemaking and work. The costs of such choices are made clear in studies of dual-career families (e.g., Fogarty, Rapoport, & Rapoport, 1971) and in studies of women who return to education and work (e.g., Rubin, 1979; Tittle & Denker, 1980).

Whereas much of the research that is described here focuses on sex differences, analysis of sex differences often conceals as much as it reveals. The wide variability among women on almost all measures, and even increasingly on such status characteristics as marital status and type of occupation entered, is a reminder that most research examines modal occurrences and patterns. Not all women internalize the social, normative prescriptions of women's roles, nor do all women reject such ideals. The research is also limited by its conduct at a particular point in history. As Adelson (1979) reminds us, we focus on units of measurement and how we measure them, on particular populations of the young and aspects of their reality, but there are other aspects of the adolescent in the larger society we ignore or cannot perceive. Much of the more recent research includes attempts to define measures capturing aspects of adult roles that have traditionally been ascribed to women.

In this chapter four areas of research are examined. The first area includes the data on occupational status and choices of men and women. There are numerous studies that attest to the differences in the relationship of education and labor market experiences and expectations of minorities and women compared to the majority group of white males. The second area is concerned with sex roles, the views of both men and women on the appropriate adult roles and activities of women and men. Sex roles, their normative and behavioral aspects, are considered to underlie many of the sex differences in occupational expectations and decisions. The third area considers the fundamental nature of values and how values may be expressed in occupational choices. The fourth area is an examination of current psychological theories of career development and decision making. Related research is examined for its implications in expanding the scope of such theories to describe women's occupational and life-span development. The chapter concludes with a proposal for a set of criteria by which career programs can be evaluated.

Occupational Status and Choice

There have been several reviews of the research literature from the sociological perspective, analyzing the studies that have attempted to predict occupational status (prestige) or type of occupation. In the psychological literature there has been more concern with the origins of sex differences in type-of-occupation preferred or entered and with the variables that may distinguish between "innovators" or "traditionalists"—those young men or women who choose occupations that predominantly employ males or, conversely, those that predominantly employ females.

OCCUPATIONAL STATUS

Studies in the occupational status (prestige) area have often found few differences in overall status. Analyses, however, by Gottfredson (1978a) and England (1979), among others, provide the reason for this finding. Although women may appear to have similar occupational prestige distributions compared to men, women's incomes are vastly lower and prestige status does not equate to socioeconomic status. Furthermore, as Gottfredson indicates, the largest sex differences are not by level of work but by type of work within levels. Using Holland's type-of-work classifications, women are underrepresented in realistic occupations and overrepresented in social jobs at all levels. Similarly, the percentage black almost always decreases with increasing job level, and black males are underrepresented in all types of high level jobs. (Although black females are not as underrepresented in high-level work for their sex as are black males.) Occupational aspirations of women and blacks reflect the over- and underrepresentations found in occupational census data (Gottfredson, 1978b). Data from the National Assessment of Educational Progress 1973-1974 Career Assessment Survey were used to show that aspirations reflect the census data on types of occupations entered.

Levine (1976) summarized a series of studies on correlates of educational aspirations and achievements and occupational aspirations and achievements by pointing to the influence of social and economic origins, intelligence (ability), sex, and race found in most studies. The contingency plans of women in relation to marriage and presence, number and age of children for whom the woman is responsible add to the complexity of examining women's employment and earnings achievements.

For high school students, Marini and Greenberger's review (1978a) indicated that boys aspire to and expect to obtain a higher level of education than girls (although this may be changing, as noted below). Occupational choices are highly sex-stereotyped, and the main variables correlated with educational aspirations of both sexes are similar but show a stronger relationship to the plans of boys than girls. Occupational aspirations, socioeconomic background, academic ability, and parental encouragement have positive effects for boys, but there are either much smaller or no effects for girls. Educational aspirations are linked to occupational aspirations for boys, and their attainment plays an important role in the male stratification process, influencing the level of occupational achievement. This link is weaker for women, however. Further, a woman's socioeconomic status has been largely determined by her husband's occupation.

THE NATIONAL LONGITUDINAL SURVEY
OF YOUNG WOMEN (PARNES DATA)

Many of the research studies on occupational status and wages have been carried out on the National Longitudinal Survey of Young Women (Parnes data). Current analyses of these data have focused on particular groups of women, for example, vocational students (Richardson & Owings, 1979); career patterns of women aged 30-44 in 1967 (Vetter & Stockburger, 1977); examination of the effect of marriage and parenthood (Kerckhoff & Parrow, 1978); the early-adult roles of black and white women (de Almeida, 1977); and trends in the postponement of marriage (Cherlin, 1978). The Parnes data are based on follow-ups of women initially interviewed in 1968 and followed through 1975, with further interviews scheduled so that the group (one of four cohorts) will be followed up for 15 years (Mott, 1978).

Women vocational students gave their plans for age 35: more than half expected to be married, keeping house, or raising a family at age 35; just less than one-third planned to be working. Career patterns for women aged 30-44 were examined using a system based on milestones in life (leaving school, marriage, and first child) and Super's (1957) career patterns (Vetter & Stockberger, 1977). One major finding was that 80% of the sample were classified as noncontinuously working groups of women. Race differences were found: 18% of the white women and 30% of the black women had worked continuously or almost continuously since leaving school; 50% of the white and 33% of the black women had either no work experience or no work experience after marriage or the acquisition of children. About one-third of each group were currently employed. As noted in Chapter 1, these data on working women have changed in the past decade. Of interest is the analysis that attempts to be more specific about the labor market patterns of women; such patterns reflect wide situational differences among women, as well as perhaps individual motivations and personality variables.

Cherlin (1978) documented part of the shift in working patterns. Between 1969 and 1975 the proportion of women in their early twenties who planned to be housewives decreased sharply, and the decline was greater for women with more education. The percentage of white women planning to be housewives decreased from 1/2 to 1/4, and for black women from 1/3 to 1/5. Kerckhoff and Parrow (1978) showed depressing effects of early marriage and early parenthood on educational and occupational attainments. Females suffered greater educational and occupational losses than males due to marriage; males showed no loss due to parenthood. A series of studies by Moore and Hofferth have examined these effects for women in more detail. The consequences of age at first childbirth have been analyzed for educational attainment, labor force participation and earnings, family size, female-headed families and welfare recipiency, and marriage, separation, and divorce. These studies used both the Parnes data and the Michigan Panel Study of Income Dynamics. Moore and others (1978a) concluded that early marriage and early first birth results in a life-long loss of schooling. Hofferth and others (1978b) found that early first birth does not *directly* affect participation in the labor force, nor occupational status, hours of work, hourly wages or annual earnings. Initiation of parenthood during the teen years does, however, seem to be associated with considerably larger families later in life (Moore & Hofferth, 1978a). Early childbearing is not directly related to subsequent welfare dependency, although Moore and Hofferth (1978b) argue that it increases the probability indirectly because of larger family size and disrupted schooling, among other factors. Early marriages also were found to be less viable than later marriages and there was some relationship to indicate that teenage childbearing increases the risk of divorce (Moore and others, 1978b). A causal model examining all these variables indicated that the age at which a woman bears her first child does not have an inevitable effect on her later well-being, but that it can contribute or detract from such well-being (Hofferth & Moore, 1978).

Mott (1978) presented a series of analyses of data (from 1968 to 1973) on these young women. Analyses of college expectations and realizations appeared consistent with an economic investment model: College desires and attendance were positively related to parental education, family income, and mental ability, and negatively related to number of siblings. Low family income is associated with low attendance. Of great interest are the data showing changes in the traditional pattern of pregnancy, first child, and work activity. The average woman in the sample stayed in the labor force until three or four months before the birth of the first child and, in many instances (40% for white females and 60% for black females), was back in the labor force within five months. There are consistent differences between black and white females, with the average black females with 12 or more years of school only spending about eight months without a job due to the birth, compared to between 13 and 18 months for other race/education groups. Much of this disparity may be due to presence/absence of the husband and black husbands' lower earnings. Other things being equal, for example, the presence of an infant has a greater depressing effect on labor force participation of better-educated young white mothers. Implications for counseling women are clear: High school students need to be informed of the short-term work interruption and to be geared toward patterns of continuing lifetime employment. Analyses of wage differentials emphasize the importance of counseling and guidance to let young women know the importance of planning for lifetime work.

Brito and Jusenius (1978b) used the Parnes data to analyze sex segregation—young college women's occupational preferences in 1973. The number and types of occupations to which women aspire (regardless of sex-typing of the occupation) is limited, and about 75% expect to hold a stereotypically female occupation. In agreement with sex-role attitude findings cited below, the presence or expectation of children does not affect black females, although it negatively affects the likelihood that white college women expect to be in a male occupation. "This suggests that, unlike their white counterparts, black women do not perceive a trade-off between time commitments to a family and time commitments to the labor force" (p. 67).

Earlier studies by Waite and Stolzenberg (1976) and Stolzenberg and Waite (1977) had examined plans for childbearing and employment, also using the Parnes data on women in their midtwenties. They found that the number of children a woman planned to bear had only a small effect on the likelihood that she planned to participate in the labor force at age 35; however, the plans to participate in the labor force at age 35 had a substantial effect on the total number of children planned.

In summary, these studies of the Parnes data reflect a considerable difference in the labor market participation, earnings and plans for men and women, blacks and whites. The studies have also begun to analyze more systematically women's work patterns and the relationship between marriage, fertility, and work plans. Yet they are bound to some degree by their initial date of data collection, in the late 1960s. Studies with data collected in the 1970s are examined next, with some preliminary findings from the National Longitudinal Survey of the High School Class of 1972.

STUDIES OF HIGH SCHOOL STUDENTS

Smaller-scale studies have examined educational and occupational preferences and attainments for regional or state samples. One example is the Southern Youth Study which collected longitudinal data on 1,052 black and white rural youths of both sexes in five southern states. Data were collected in 1966, 1968, and 1972. Sanchez (1978) reported that achievement attitudes for women are significantly depressed by early marriage, and that marriage deferment was not determined by social class. Cosby and Charner (1978) edited a volume summarizing a number of these studies; relevant findings here are that sex differences in career preferences were found, as in other studies, and that it was harder for blacks to transmit advantages achieved at any stage to the next phase (see also Falk & Salter, 1978; Smith and others, 1976).

Moyer (1978) and Marini and Greenberger (1978a,b) have reported analyses using data from the Pennsylvania Educational Quality Assessment. Moyer reported that 52% of all female eleventh-grade students desired occupations requiring postsecondary formal education, and both studies reported highly differentiated occupational aspirations and expectations by sex. Another study used Illinois secondary schools (N = 15) and twelfth-grade girls: 95% of the girls expected to marry and of these girls, 91% also planned to work outside the home. New Educational Directions (1977) reported that, for 128 Indiana high school students, 80% planned to enter a traditionally sex stereotyped career choice.

Curry et al. (1978) interviewed tenth-grade girls in 14 Ohio high schools. The Wisconsin status attainment model was used (parental SES, mental or academic performance, and significant others' occupational and educational aspirations). The explained variance in occupational expectations was very weak for females (as in other studies), about 25% that of males and no variable had a direct effect that was significant for white females. Interestingly, home-career expectations did not improve prediction for girls. The authors noted, however, that the variance of home-career expectations was highly restricted in the data (presumably almost all expected to marry and to work). Very few girls planned only an occupation to the exclusion of home and family.

The data from the National Longitudinal Survey of the High School Class of 1972 are reported in several sources. The survey was initiated by and conducted for the National Center for Education Statistics. It began in spring 1972 with administrations of survey forms to a sample of 18,000 seniors. In the follow-up surveys an additional 5,000 students were added from the sample schools (National Center for Education Statistics, 1977). Follow-ups have been conducted in the falls of 1972, 1973, 1974, and 1976; the sample retention rate has been 88% (Eckland &Wisenbaker, 1979). Data on homemaker, marital, and childbearing statuses were collected (Peng et al., 1978). In October 1974, 29% of the women said they were homemakers. By October 1976, 42% of all women stated they were homemakers; some differences were reported by racial/ethnic groups, with black women reporting the lowest percentage. Homemaker status was more likely for low and middle SES women than high (percentages of 47, 38, and 23) and for women of low ability than of middle or high ability (percentages of 44, 39, and 26, respectively). Whereas 36% of the men reported being married in October 1976, the rate for women was 53%. The highest rates were for Hispanics, with 60% of the women and 47% of the men married; data for whites were 55% for white women and 36% for white men; and for blacks, 41% of the women and 33% of the men ever married. Divorce rates ranged from 16% to 7% over these sex and ethnic groups.

Data on at least one child showed that status varied greatly by race/ethnic group: 43%, 33% and 20% of the black, Hispanic, and white respondents, respectively, had at least one child. The mean number of children expected by October 1976 was 2.2 for whites and 2.4 for both the black and Hispanic groups. Further analysis by Nolfi et al. (1978) of the group of students who did not enter postsecondary institutions immediately examined predictions of work success. The influence of high school characteristics appeared to be minimal, whereas measures of family income or SES measurably affected student success (wages). And, a "pervasive characteristic of this sample is the higher aspirations and greater relative success of white males compared to those of blacks and women" (1978, p. 2). Career expectations were sex-role stereotyped: 90% of the females in the sample chose either clerical, sales, service, professional or homemaker, whereas 75% of the males chose to be craftsmen, laborers, operators, professionals, technicians, or protective workers (1978, p. 13). In terms of labor force participation there was further reinforcement of sex stereotypes: "the most striking difference between males and females (out of school) is the unimportance of ability and personality factors for women and their importance for men" (1978, p. 72). The authors question whether this results from the different mix of jobs offered women or different attitudes toward work. Although wage levels are examined, the

R^2 of .15 indicates relatively little of the variance for this group is explained by the series of independent variables used. As mentioned earlier, a regression analysis of schooling and occupational decisions is carried out only for men.

Lichtman, Rothschild, and Peng (1979) also used the NLS data to examine educational attainment for females and three ethnic groups. The Ns for groups used in analyses ranged from 94 (Hispanic females) to 3010 (white females). Educational attainment data are for 4½ years after high school (1976 follow-up). Different variables appeared as predictors for the three groups, as well as sex differences within the black and Hispanic groups. For blacks and Hispanics, the effects of parental education and occupation are minimal. For black males in the NLS sample educational expectations are not predictive of educational attainment, but occupational expectation and parental encouragement are. (For black females, parental encouragement has a negative regression weight.) The varying patterns of predictions make clear the limited generalizability of the general model used. Corder-Bolz (1979), in a study of high school students, also concluded that the variables influencing the occupational aspirations and expectations of males and females are different.

Osipow (1973), in summarizing the earlier research related to social class membership and careers, noted that both social class membership and sex are important situational determinants of career development. These variables affect attitudes and the economic resources available to implement career plans. In a critique of the literature examining minority group status, Osipow stated that, in general, research on career development for these groups has confounded race, social class, ethnicity, educational levels, and economic variables.

Picou and Campbell (1975) compiled a series of articles on career behavior of special groups. Among the special groups examined were American Indians, Asian Americans, and Mexican Americans, as well as women. Membership in these sociocultural groups appeared to influence career opportunities and choices. (See also Almquist, 1979, for more extensive documentation for minorities.)

Reviewing the studies here leads to the conclusions that there are probably few differences in the influences of the educational choice process for girls and boys as currently defined, but that there is little understanding of the occupational attainments (types of jobs and earnings) of women as gained from regression and causal modeling thus far. And, attainments for minority groups are not well explained. Before examining the related research on sex roles, it will be useful to indicate how early and pervasive are these sex-stereotyped views of occupations.

THE ORIGINS OF OCCUPATIONAL SEGREGATION

Data to illustrate the origins of occupational segregation patterns can be found in studies of children's occupational choices and adults' views of the appropriateness of occupations for females or males. Looft (1971) demonstrated that six- to eight-year-old children gave different responses according to their sex when asked what they wanted to be when they grew up. There was a striking variability in the boy's responses and near unanimity for girls (75% of the girls' responses were in two categories: teacher and nurse). A total of 18 occupational categories were given by boys and only 8 by girls. Iglitzin (1972) reported two studies of sex stereotyping with fifth grade school children in 1971-1972. As early as the fifth grade, boys provide a description of what it might be like on a typical day on a job, but girls emphasize details of family life rather than career activities.

Schlossberg and Goodman (1972) asked elementary school children to respond to a set of drawings representing work settings (six of feminine occupations and six masculine). Children were asked, "Could a man work here?" "Could a woman work here?" Children were more likely to exclude women from men's jobs than men from women's. A study by Entwisle and Greenburger (1972) examined ninth graders' attitudes toward women's work roles. Specific attitudes included whether women should work, what kinds of jobs women should hold, and whether women are intellectually curious. Middle-class boys of high I.Q. were more traditional; boys consistently reflected traditional sex-role stereotypes more than girls.

Using data collected about 1977, Frost and Diamond (1979) reported on both ethnic and sex differences in occupational stereotyping for fourth- to sixth-grade Los Angeles children. SES was not controlled in the study and black, Hispanic, and white students were included. Boys and girls in all three ethnic groups indicated preferences for careers stereotyped for their own sex, although apparently Anglo girls showed a greater tendency to cross sex-stereotyped lines.

Prediger, Roth, and Noeth (1974) reported on a nationwide study of eleventh-grade students. Over 50% of the girls selected vocational preferences that fell into three job families: education and social services, nursing and human care, and clerical/secretarial. Only 7% of the boys selected these occupations. Boys were much more likely than girls to prefer vocations in engineering, natural sciences, business management, and technologies trades.

Several studies have examined sex stereotyping of occupations. Shinar (1975) and Panek, Rush, and Greenawalt (1977) found both females and males stereotyped occupations in terms of the sex of employees usually associated with the occupation. Albrecht (1976) and Albrecht, Bahr, and Chadwick (1977) reported a study of 2,227 households in Utah. Age and social class, as well as sex differences, were examined in stereotyping of occupations. Greatest differences were found according to age and education, with younger, better-educated adults more egalitarian in perceiving occupations as available to both males and females. Medvene and Collins (1976) had psychotherapists and school counselors rate the prestige and appropriateness for women of a group of occupations. The samples of raters differed little in their rankings of occupational prestige, but differences in ratings were found for appropriateness for women. School counselors (female and male) were more likely to rate occupations as inappropriate for women.

The studies cited in this section have found early sex differences in occupational choice and continued sex-stereotyping of occupations through college-age and adult samples. The findings are consistent with a larger series of studies in sex-typed interests and activity preferences summarized by Maccoby and Jacklin (1974, pp. 280-283). They are also consistent with studies that have tried to predict women's career choices, studies that show the effect of both stereotyping of occupations and perceptions of appropriate adult roles for women. These studies have approached women's career choices from a different perspective than the status attainment and economic model studies.

Predicting women's career choices. Two studies, by Astin and Myint (1971) and Harmon (1970), are of particular interest because they are longitudinal and used measures of abilities, interests, personality and background. Astin and Myint (1971) followed up 5,387 women (tested in 1960 in the Project TALENT study) five years after high school.

Discriminant analyses showed that scholastic aptitudes, especially in mathematics, and high educational aspirations (college/advanced degree plans) were the best precollege predictors of a career orientation (sciences, social services, professions, and teaching groups). Interests and personality measures were not good predictors. A second discriminant analysis revealed that BA degree, college and graduate school attendance were important predictors separating natural sciences, social service/social sciences, and teaching from office work and housewife. Having an AA degree carried a large negative weight, and the variables married and children also had negative weights. A third discriminant analysis indicated that the most effective predictors in separating the career groups and noncareer (office work and housewife) groups were completing college and college attendance and selected aptitude variables. Expressed interests and personality measures were not predictive as they are for males.

Harmon (1970) followed up 169 women 10 to 14 years after college entrance (all had high scores on the social worker scale of the SVIB-W). Women were asked what their "usual career" was, and were categorized as career committed and non committed on this basis. The two groups did not differ on high school rank. The career committed group attended college longer, worked more years after leaving college, married later in life, had fewer children, more children at later ages, and more were unmarried.

Klemmack and Edwards (1973) also studied college women who indicated that the occupation that they would most realistically pursue was a feminine occupation and concluded that marriage and family plans serve a critical mediational function.

The findings of Astin and Myint, Harmon, and Klemmack and Edwards are consistent with the hypothesis that a woman's career commitment and occupational choice are related to her views of adult sex roles and life-style choices. Decisions about marriage, children and homemaking responsibilities appear to be predictors of career commitment. In contrast to these findings for women, Strong and Campbell (1966) reported a number of follow-up studies for males which indicated that expressed interests were a major predictor of career choice.

Almquist's study (1974) followed a class of college women over four years. Women choosing occupations with more males employed did not differ from women entering occupations predominantly female in either sociability experiences or in relationships with parents. Other studies have also pursued variables thought to be related to women's innovative or traditional occupational choices. Typical of these are Burlin (1976), Hawley (1972), Kotcher (1976), and Falk and Salter (1978) for the status attainment process of rural women. As these latter authors note, there have been relatively few studies of the status attainment process for women (although see Scanzoni, 1979a). This is particularly true for large scale status attainment studies attempting to account for women's entry into particular occupations, that is, traditionally male or female occupations. Major exceptions are the studies by Hofferth (1980), Brito and Jusenius (1978b), and the NLS data (Nolfi et al., 1978). Hofferth also used the Parnes data for women ages 14 to 24 in 1968 and followed through interviews in 1975. Her analyses show smaller proportions of women than men employed 3, 5, and 10 years after high school; that family size does not affect whether or not men are working but that women with large families are less likely to be working in any given year; and that neither marital status nor number of children are related to the sex-typicality of the occupations in which young men and women were employed 3, 5, and 10 years after high school. There are sex and race differences in mean number of years worked by 10 years after high school (9.61 years for white males, 9.60 for black males, 4.65 for white females and 4.52 for black females).

As with the psychological studies of career choice and development, studies to date have primarily focused on majority males with the exceptions noted earlier. Among other reasons, this focus has been reinforced by the different labor force participation patterns of women, typically with multiple entries and exits due to childbearing (see also Falk & Cosby, 1978). The apparently greater complexity of women's career development patterns should not deter research, however. Many of the studies summarized above provide evidence that aspects of sex roles appear to be important determinants of women's occupational choices and career patterns,[2] and Waite (1978b) suggested that a large rise in female labor force participation could be anticipated if there is a continued trend toward acceptance by individuals of work roles for women. There is evidence that changes in sex-role attitudes are occurring. Studies in sex roles and sex-role attitudes are examined next, particularly for evidence of sex, ethnic, or SES differences. It is important to note that unless SES is specifically mentioned for a study, there has been no attempt to control or estimate its effect. This is particularly important for studies of ethnic groups, because there is often a failure to control for SES. Any ethnic group comparisons must be viewed cautiously, although they are reported here when available. Research studies that link sex roles and career decision-making more directly are discussed in the section on theories of career development and career decision-making.

Sex Roles and Sex-Role Attitudes

Viewed historically, the development of sex roles appears to have proceeded in different, even contradictory directions. Bloch (1978) has posed the history of sex roles in terms of definitions of the social relations of the sexes which on the one hand stress the similarity and on the other the distinctiveness of the sexes.

In the sixteenth and seventeenth centuries, Bloch views the rise of Protestantism, the centralized state, and early commercial capitalism as reinforcing the conjugal family unit and patriarchal dominance within family life. In the seventeenth century in the U.S., there was a delayed emergence of this pattern of increased sexual hierarchy and diminished differentiation of roles due to the imbalance in the sex ratio and the prevailing shortage of labor. During the eighteenth and nineteenth centuries, however, sexual definitions diverged widely again and along different lines: "Male and female imagery and activities became more distinct and increasingly associated with contrasting 'rational' and 'affective' styles" (p. 245). In particular, childrearing became more exclusively the province of the mother: "As the dominant feminine ideal of the nineteenth cen-

tury, moral motherhood evolved in sharp contrast to the masculine ideal
of individual worldly success" (p. 252). These changing patterns have
become what Block has so aptly called our contradictory legacy of
equality and inequality, flexibility and rigidity, commonality and separate-
ness. The legacy is realized in current research on sex roles and views of
the importance of motherhood in sex-typing.

The status of research on sex roles was reviewed by Lipman-Blumen
and Tickamyer (1975). Women are typically socialized to receive their
total gratification through family roles, whereas men can look to both
occupation and family roles for fulfillment. Huston-Stein and Higgins-
Trenk (1978) have reviewed studies related to the development of feminine role orientation. Although there are changes in women's life patterns
over the past 30 years, there are still many social barriers to changes in
women's roles. As noted in Chapter 1, the modal pattern for women is
employment *and* maintaining the homemaking and motherhood roles.

Angrist (1974) also indicated that learning the adult sex role is seen
primarily as occupation-directed for males and family-directed for females.
She hypothesized that flexibility in the future roles of women was built
into the socialization process as *contingency* training and that this contingency orientation is reflected in personality development, belief systems,
and choices. At least some support for her position is to be found in the
lack of predictability for women's career choices, as opposed to those of
men. Katz (1979) has reinforced these ideas in her description of three
levels in the development of sex roles for females and males. As she
describes development for women, the vocational role is not clearly
established by age 20-35 (or is delayed in commitment). For many
women, it is not until middle adulthood (age 35-50) that the vocational
interests area is fully developed and self identity completed. (See also
Rubin, 1979, for a description of the socialization practices that typically
result in a highly ambivalent adult woman, and Chodorow, 1978, for a
psychoanalytic view of why the cycle remains unbroken). Nettles (1979)
tested the hypothesis that sex-role conceptions were associated with level
of ego development (Loevinger's levels). Using a sample of 107 married
couples, she found higher levels of ego development (personal maturity)
were associated with nonstereotypic sex-role conceptions ($r = .42$ for men
and .47 for women).

As a result of linking socialization practices and sex-role norms some
psychologists, for example, Russo (1976), argued that,

Motherhood is chief among the prescriptions of sex-typing. . . .
[T]he major goal of a woman's life is to raise well-adjusted children. . . . As long as this situation exists for the vast majority of

women in Western society and the world in general, prohibitions
may be eliminated and options widened, but change will occur only
insofar as women are first able to fill their mandate of motherhood.
(p. 144)

The U.S. Census reported in 1972 that over 90% of the women above the
age of 25 were married and over 90% of that group had children (cited in
Russo, 1976; see also Russo, 1979).

CRITICAL ASPECTS OF WOMEN'S SEX ROLES

Several writers have discussed sex roles and their relationships to
women's occupational choices and careers. Among the definitions of sex
and gender roles which have appeared in the literature are those of
Lipman-Blumen and Tickamyer (1975). Gender roles are considered useful
when viewed as mediating factors between gender identity (male or female) and sex role. It is via gender roles that develop out of gender
identity that males and females are funneled into what is societally defined
as sex-appropriate behavior. "The study of sex roles concerns roles within
all structured settings, the norms and rules governing role performance in
these settings, the correlates of role location and performance, the special
situation of deviant roles and those who occupy them, and the mechanics
of role change" (p. 303). Sex roles are based on assigning personality traits
on the basis of sex, allocating activities on the basis of sex, and, in our
culture, assignment of higher value to the male than the female. Method-
ologically, there is also work attempting to separate the ideological versus
the situational responses to items describing activities that tend to be
assigned by sex (Duncan, 1979).

Bernard (1976) usefully distinguished two components in the concept
of role: expectations or norms including beliefs and cognitions, and
enactments or conduct. These are two key distinctions, much like the
distinction that is made below for values; that is, there is a normative,
strongly pervasive, socially influenced, and reinforced set of beliefs, and
the reflection of these beliefs in actual conduct or behavior. A key aspect
of roles is that they are part of patterns. Bernard provided a reminder,
largely ignored thus far in research, that: Change in one part (of the
pattern) calls for change in the others. That is, change in the role of the
wife requires change in the role of the husband. Much of the research that
follows is concerned only with women's roles as homemaker, marital
partner, and parent (mother).

What factors or aspects of sex roles are critical in the definition of sex
roles for women in relationship to occupational choice and career decision
making? Two critical factors can be identified: marriage (and the role of

wife) and motherhood (parenthood). A review essay on marriage and the family was published in *Signs* (Lopata, 1971) and a number of articles have tried to clarify these areas, by defining terms or by calling attention to neglected aspects of these roles. The central importance of a role, role ambiguity, role strain, and role proliferation are among the concepts that are evolving.[3]

Bernard (1976) called beliefs about women's place the linch pin of the traditional female role. Data from a 1972 study of entering college women showed about one-fourth of them believed that the woman's place was in the home. This belief persists in subtle ways despite actual evidence of increasing labor force participation by married women and women with children under six years of age. The discrepancy between the belief and the actuality could be viewed as a plus for women, a tolerance for deviations from an anachronistic norm. Bernard, however, suggested that it also has dysfunctional consequences for women: "Life is organized and decisions are made as though the norm were actually a genuine and functional adjustment to a current situation" (p. 212).

Darley (1976) discussed the differences in achievement between males and females and provided an analysis of role behavior, particularly the ambiguity and lack of clarity within roles. She argued that it may not be only the kinds of behavior demanded by different sex roles that lead to differences in achievement, but also differences in the clarity and consistency with which these sex role demands are defined: "The obligations and responsibilities of wifehood are not validly depicted in movies and popular magazines nor are they clear simply from observing the behavior of one's parents, especially when such observations are made from the perspective of a child" (Darley, 1976: 86). And on the role of mother,

> The explosion of books, articles, and television talk shows on the subject of motherhood suggest that the expectations for this role are almost without limit, stunningly unclear, and highly variable. Is a good mother permissive or firm or both? Is she a friend to her children or an advisor or both? . . . Note that what is expected of a good father is also unclear, but the parent role is not generally taken to be as salient for a man as it is for a woman. (pp. 87, 89)

Emphasis on motherhood has led psychologists to begin to study attitudes toward motherhood (Hare-Mustin & Broderick, 1979).

A major series of studies on sex, career, and family have been carried out in Britain. Fogarty, Rapoport, and Rapoport (1971) presented reports that included examination of the special problem of women's promotions to top jobs, experience in both Eastern and Western European countries, and studies of families and work careers. They suggested that currently highly qualified women experience the same complexities as men (e.g., fitting together personal, interpersonal and social influences in the choice and development of an occupational career) *plus* the additional set of complexities associated with child rearing.

A valuable analysis of the dilemmas faced by "dual career families" is provided in case studies (Fogarty, Rapoport, & Rapoport, 1971). The dilemmas faced by such families included what these authors called dilemmas arising from sheer overload; dilemmas rising from the discrepancy between personal and social norms (for example, work after childbirth); dilemmas of identity—one cannot be a good woman and a working woman, because work is seen as masculine; social network dilemmas with family and inlaws; and role-cycling dilemmas. This latter dilemma occurs in two ways: between the occupational roles of husband and wife and family roles, and between the occupational role of the husband and the occupational role of the wife. Johnson and Johnson (1976) have presented a similar analysis of role strain and role proliferation in the two-person career couple. Komorovsky (1976) and Garnets and Pleck (1979) have also elaborated the concept of sex-role strain. For Garnets and Pleck low or high sex-role strain is a function of such variables as the sex-typed real and ideal self and sex-role salience. Studies have also examined the tradeoff in child care and income for males and females (e.g., Thomas & Neal, 1978). Further detailed analysis of male sex roles needs to accompany the study of women (e.g., Pleck, 1976).

A framework for problems faced by families in which both partners are committed to work may be part of the analysis required to assist theorists and practitioners to understand the relationship between sex-role values and career decision-making for women because it is not only professional women who face role proliferation. The goal in career decision theory is not to understand or predict only occupational satisfaction, but more generally, satisfaction with work as it fits into a life pattern. One small-scale study indicates that marriage and a career is becoming expected (Rand & Miller, 1972). Almost all of 60 junior high, 60 high school, and 60 college women both desired and expected to get married (97%) and to work (95%). For the urban sample in the present study, 94% of all students expect to marry and 92% expect to have children. All but 2 of the 600 students expect to work for pay after completing school.

Other analyses that emphasize the importance of sex roles to career development are those that examine the stages of women's lives. For example, there are the life-style patterns cited by Ginzberg et al. (1966) and the British pattern reported in Fogarty, Rapoport, and Rapoport (1971). Bernard (1975) discussed stage theories of development and proposed that for women a more useful analysis may consist of examining developmental discontinuities, that is, the sharp changes that occur at critical points in life. The discontinuities are: about age 8, when little girls are deflected toward *dependency* rather than independence; *marriage,* where the woman finds out that she will have to supply the dependency needs of her husband; at *motherhood,* where she has sole responsibility for the care of a dependent infant; and the two later stages, when the last child enters school, the stage of *middle-motherhood,* and finally, *late-motherhood.* These stages are very different from those proposed for male adult development (e.g., Levinson, 1978) and the analyses of male sex roles (Pleck, 1976). And they are not related to the woman's age or labor force experience, which may well be important determinants of later labor force participation and fertility expectations (Waite & Stolzenberg, 1976; Stolzenberg & Waite, 1977). Falk and Cosby (1978) elaborated upon a typology of women's possible marital/familial statuses (extending the earlier perspective on the occupational choice of women provided by Psathas [1968]). These analyses of statuses included such categories as, never married-without children; never married-with children; married-without children; married-with children; and so on. Within the children categories Falk and Cosby have subgroups such as children are preschool at home, children are preschool in day care, children are in school, and children have left home. These numerous combinations, which are not limited narrowly by age, appear to preclude age-defined stages for women, unless broad age spans are used.

CHANGES IN SEX-ROLE ATTITUDES

All writers agree that traditional sex roles are in the process of change. Lipman-Blumen (1976) cited demographic data to illustrate behavioral changes, for example the increasing participation of women in the labor force, later ages of marriage, fewer children, and decline in the fertility rate. A major study illustrating the change in traditional sex-role attitudes was conducted by Mason, Czajka, and Arber (1976). These authors used data from five sample surveys between 1964 and 1974 and analyzed common items. More egalitarian role definitions were endorsed, with the change occurring about equally for higher status and lower status women. Attitudes about rights in the labor market were more strongly related to attitudes about roles in the home. Education and employment were the two variables that were most important in predicting women's attitudes. The well-educated, especially those completing college, were less support-ive of traditional norms. Those who were more recently employed were also less supportive of traditional norms. Examples of the types of items analyzed are: A preschool child is likely to suffer if his (sic) mother works;

men should share the work around the house with women such as doing dishes, cleaning, and so forth; and, men and women should be paid the same money if they do the same work.

Mott (1978) provided data from the Parnes study (NLS) showing a change between 1968 and 1972 in the attitudes of young women toward the propriety of work for mothers of young children. Comparing 18 to 21 year olds in 1968 to the same age group in 1972, respondents indicated it was all right to work if:

	% positive response	
	1968	1972
(1) economic necessity[4]	91	94
(2) husband and wife agree	66	80
(3) even if husband disagrees	12	24

Similar percentage were found for ages 21 to 24 at these two measuring points.

In addition to changes in women's attitudes, sex differences in sex-role attitudes have been found. Entwisle and Greenberger (1972) included three questions on women's work role for a sample of Maryland ninth-grade students in 1968. Males were consistently more traditional than females. Angrist, Mickelsen, and Penna (1976, 1977) reported sex differences in high school students. In data collected in 1975 females had a more egalitarian attitude as expressed on items such as: raising children is more a mother's job than a father's; a wife should work only if there is a definite economic need; and married women should not work once they have children. There was a small subsample of black students in the study, and they tended to have more conservative attitudes than the white students. It was "easier" to explain the sex-role ideology scores of females: women who had higher school grades, from higher SES backgrounds, and whose mothers worked were "clearly socialized with more 'liberated' and equalitarian attitudes" (p. 185). Male sex-role ideology scores were harder to explain (R^2 for females was .24; for males, .16). Family background was not important and the only significant beta was for type of school (boys at a more elite school were less traditional).

Izenberg (1978) reported that 499 adolescents in the metropolitan New York area also showed sex differences in attitudes toward women's roles: boys had more traditional attitudes than girls in each of three grade levels (8, 10, and 12). Corder-Bolz (1979) also found females had less traditional sex-role attitudes than males, for a sample of eighth-to twelfth-grade students in the Souuthwest. Herzog, Bachman, and Johnston (1980) surveyed a national sample of high school seniors. There was a slight trend from 1976 to 1979 toward increased sharing of duties in preferences for allocation of work and family duties within their own prospective marriages. Group differences were that whites and males tended to be somewhat more conservative on attitudes towards wives with preschool age children.

One survey of high school students (23,200 of the 355,000 juniors and seniors listed in *Who's Who Among American High School Students*) found a change on some items toward a more traditional view of sex roles. For example, 8% of those surveyed in 1979 said they favored couples living together before marriage, whereas in 1971 the response was 47%. The 1971 survey found 43% of students agreeing that a woman should experience both career and marriage to be fulfilled, but only 32% of students in 1979 agreed (*New York Times,* December 5, 1979).

Gackenbach (1978) administered two sex-role inventories to black and white and female and male undergraduate students: Attitudes Toward Women Scale and the Women as Managers Scale. The analysis was based on 96 students (12 per cell) in a sex by race by career goal (business or helping professions) design. The only difference on the WAMS was a main effect for sex. Females favored expanded roles for women in the business world more than males. For the AWS scores, race and sex main effects were significant and two interactions: sex X race and sex X career goal. Males were more traditional in attitudes toward women's roles at home, and blacks were more sex-role traditional than whites. The interaction for sex X race showed white females had more liberal sex-role attitudes than the other groups. The interaction for career goal showed that males in the helping professions were more sympathetic to expanding roles for women at home than were males whose career goals were in business. For women it was reversed: Those with business-related career goals were more liberal toward women's expanding sex roles at home than those with career goals in the helping professions.

Thus, recent studies have generally shown that attitudes toward womens's roles in the home, as mothers, and as workers are becoming more egalitarian. The trend is most pronounced for females, particularly those with more education and labor-force experience. Males are more traditional, as a few studies have shown, and perhaps black men and women are also more traditional in some aspects of their views of women's roles than are white men and women. (Although Mason and Bumpass, 1973, found that some areas of sex-role attitudes for blacks were less traditional.)

SEX-ROLE ATTITUDES AND OTHER VARIABLES

A study by Hawley (1972) examined the relationship between the careers college students chose and their beliefs about men's views of the feminine ideal. Teachers in preparation (mean age 26) believed that significant men in their lives dichotomized attitudes into male/female categories. Only 18% said they would pursue their present goals and career plans over the objections of husbands. Mason (1974) related the goals of 360 senior high school girls (from 11 states) to three items on sex role attitudes. Girls with less traditional views of sex roles expected to have fewer children.

Wrigley and Stokes (1977) examined sex-role orientations for 388 white non-Catholic high school seniors from seven suburban public schools in the South. (A nine-item measure of sex-role ideology was used.) Girls with a contemporary sex-role ideology had higher educational aspirations and lower family-size preferences. They concluded that the number of children born during marriage was likely to become less a function of age at marriage and education and more the result of the number wanted in relation to other socially desired roles.

A number of studies have examined the relationships between sex roles, family size preferences and other variables for married women. Thornton and Camburn (1979), for example, used data from a 1970 national fertility study of 5,981 ever-married women under 45. Four sex-role indices resulted from a factor analysis of 18 questions: home orientation, job prerogatives for men, women passive, and opposed special privileges. These four indices correlated .12, .08, -.02 (n.s.), and .09 with total number of intended children. Correlations with home orientation and labor force participation were about -.27. Thus, the index for home orientation showed some correlation with both fertility and labor force participation. Beckman (1979) interviewed 583 women aged 18-49, currently married and living with spouse in Los Angeles. The sample was 61% white, 23% Hispanic, and 9% black. Sex-role attitudes showed different correlations with total number of children wanted for the three groups: the $r = .21$ for white women; $r = .05$ for Hispanic women (N = 136); and $r = .41$ for black women (N = 53). (The more traditional the attitudes the more children wanted.)

Scanzoni has examined the relationship of sex-role attitudes and birth intentions for college students and for married women. Data on college students (Scanzoni, 1976) compared changes in sex-role attitudes in samples of white undergraduate students at a large Midwestern university in 1971 and 1974. For these cross-sectional samples, both men and women had become less sex-role traditional, although the change was less for men.

Again, less traditional sex-role attitudes were related to lower birth intentions and the relationship was stronger for women than for men. Sex-role attitudes were examined in terms of the Traditional Wife Role, Wife Self-Actualization, Problematic Husband Alterations, Institutionalized Equality, Traditional Husband Role, Religious Legitimization of Mother Role, and Traditional Mother Role. Items per category ranged from two (THR, IE, RLM) to eight (TWR).

Of particular interest are data reported on married women who worked between 1971 and 1975, and for whom status attainment, income, level of education, and sex-role measures are available (Scanzoni, 1979a). A sample of 427 white women aged 18-29, married and husbands present, was interviewed in a regional (10-state Midwestern) sample. A high-work-involvement group was identified (N = 127). For this group 1975 job status was predicted by level of education and a more egalitarian position on the Traditional Wife Role measure. Conversely, 1974 income levels were best predicted by 1970 income and a more egalitarian rating on the Wife Self-Actualization measure (highest betas). Both of these regression equations differed from those of males by the addition of the sex-role preference measures, which showed an independent contribution to the prediction.

Thus, as much of the earlier writings on sex roles of women suggested, these preferences or attitudes appear to provide independent contributions to explaining a number of work, fertility, and occupational decisions or plans for women. The measures used in such studies have varied widely, from single- or few-item scales, to measures such as the Attitudes Toward Women scale and Personal Attributes Questionnaire of Spence, Helmreich, and Stapp, and now operationalized definitions of sex-role strain. These measures will need to be compared and refined further because the increasing number of married working women, despite family status, will shift the focus from general attitudes about whether women should put family first, to how to cope with the primacy of worker *and* parent roles (Johnson & Jaccard, 1979). A better understanding and assessment of male attitudes will also become important. We should also note here that broader conceptions of personality or stages of development should be considered for their theoretical contributions. White (1979) and Richardson (1979) and others have suggested that, for example, defining social competencies and social maturity will be more useful than concepts and measures of "masculinity" and "femininity." Nettles (1979) study is relevant here; she reported a correlation between higher levels of ego development and less stereotyped conceptions of sex roles (see also Loevinger, 1976, 1979, 1980).

ROLE MODELS

One other related area is examined in this section. It has often been suggested that role models are important for the educational and occupational aspirations of youth. Oberle, Stowers, and Falk (1978) reported a study in which place of residence (urban/rural) in Texas was examined in relation to type of role model for black youth. The question was posed in forced choice form: "Think of a person whom you would most want to fashion your life after" (p. 16). Alternatives included Teacher or School Counselor, Father or Mother, Older brother or sister, Relative not in immediate family, Close friend-not relative, and Glamour (TV or movie star, famous athlete, important government figure). Students did not have the option of naming "no one."

An earlier study conducted by Oberle (1974) had compared white and black youth from rural areas. In that study black boys and girls preferred different types of role models than whites, both when sophomores and seniors in high school. Glamour figures such as famous athletes were popular especially for black youth. In the study of rural black youth as sophomores, place of residence was significant. Black rural boys preferred glamour figures (49.4 vs. 39.6% for urban blacks) and Father or Mother (25.8% vs. 17.8%). Urban boys chose Relative not in immediate family and Close friend more frequently than did rural youth. Black girls differed in their role models from the boys, naming Teacher or School Counselor more frequently and Relative not in the immediate family. The Glamour figures were less frequently chosen by black girls (14.9% of urban girls and 26.0% of rural girls). Thus, variables related to type of role models between these two studies included year in high school, sex, age, ethnic group and place of residence. These differences imply different aspects of a role model's life may have salience for youth. These studies differ from some of the "role model" research by direct questioning of students (rather than making assumptions about same-sex parent and the like). The next section is concerned with values, the important needs and satisfactions that individuals seek to obtain.

Values

A major part of the present study is the development of the marriage and parenthood values. These are conceived to be terms (and definitions) that may be important to individuals in making decisions to marry or to become a parent. The rationale for the focus on values is described through definitions of values and the importance of values in guidance.

DEFINITIONS OF VALUES

Maslow (1954) defined values in relation to his hierarchy of needs: "The gratification of any such need is a 'value' " (p. 6). One reason for knowing the individual's values is to be aware of the influence of values on perception. Another reason for knowing values is to know the individual's nature, "Many problems simply disappear—others are easily solvable by what is in conformity with one's own nature" (Maslow, 1971, p. 111). Maslow's well-known hierarchical theory of motivation (1954) included needs such as safety, security, love, self-esteem, and self-actualization.

Margenau (1959), like Maslow, did not distinguish between value and need: "A value is the measure of satisfaction of a human want" (p. 38). He acknowledged that this brief definition did not convey the significance that attaches to the word *value,* noting that it left aside the ideas of intrinsic worth and that it was also an awkward approach to the appraisal of abstract and ideal things such as honesty or friendship. Margenau placed a different perspective on the idea of value by listing the entities that carry values or to which value is said to adhere. These are first, ordinary physical objects; second, processes in human activities designed to secure such objects; and then, on a scale of increasing abstractness, actually experienced relations or conditions (e.g., fellowship, parenthood, freedom) and finally ideals such as truth, goodness, and beauty. These entities are held together by a common bond: They can be desired or spurned by human beings.

Margenau also identified two kinds of values, one that he labeled factual and the other normative. The difference is that factual values are observable preferences and desires of a given people at a given time. Normative values are the ratings, in some sense, which people *ought* to give to valued objects. These two aspects of values are like the two aspects often distinguished for sex roles. Bernard (1976), for example, discussed changes in stability in sex roles in terms of norms and behaviors, using the idea of norms as expectations or beliefs and behavior or conduct as two aspects of a definition of role.

Rokeach (1973), in a brief review of earlier definitions, identified two perspectives from which values have been viewed. In the first, all objects have a one-dimensional property of value (or valence) ranging from positive to negative. The second perspective is the person approach represented by Vernon and Allport (1931) and their *The Study of Values.* According to Rokeach, a *value* is an enduring belief that a specific mode of conduct (instrumental value) or end-state (terminal value) of existence is personally or socially preferable to an opposite or converse mode of conduct or end-state of existence. A *value system* is an enduring organization of beliefs concerning preferable modes of conduct or end-states of existence along a continuum of relative importance (p. 5). Values, like beliefs, have cognitive, affective, and behavioral components. A value has a behavioral component in the sense that it is an intervening variable that leads to action when activated.

What are the functions of values and value systems for Rokeach?: "values as standards that guide ongoing activities, and of value systems as general plans employed to resolve conflicts and to make decisions. Another way is to think of values as giving expression to human needs" (p. 12).

Attitudes are distinguished from values because an attitude refers to an organization of several beliefs around a single object or situation. Conversely, "A value . . . refers to a single belief of a very specific kind. It concerns a desirable mode of behavior or end-state that has a transcendental quality to it, guiding actions, attitudes, judgments, and comparisons across specific objects and situations and beyond immediate goals to more ultimate goals" (p. 18). This latter, expanded definition fits the type of values related to sex roles with which the present study is concerned. The definition also fits the level of abstraction at which the occupational values developed by Katz (1973) are located. Terms such as Leadership, Major Interest Field, Leisure, Independence, and Early Entry are at a level of abstraction which permits them to be used to evaluate different occupations, but they are, in the main, not as abstract as the instrumental and terminal goals described by Rokeach. There are some obvious overlaps, but Rokeach has included terminal values such as national security, salvation, wisdom, a world at peace, and a world of beauty, among others. These are at a different level and more removed from everyday experience.

VALUES IN GUIDANCE

Within the guidance framework, Katz (1973) also describes *needs* or motivating forces, "the inner psychological and physiological drives for which satisfaction is sought" (p. 16). *Values*, however, "may be regarded as characteristic outer expressions and culturally influenced manifestations of needs. . . . *Interests* apply to the differentiated means by which the valued goal may be reached" (p. 16). In terms of the roles individuals may take on, values are primary:

> Although the role of an individual may be composed of and described in terms of many attributes, the individual's values are the mediating force that binds the attributes together, weights them, organizes them, and enables them to be activated in an organismic way in decision-making. . . . Thus values mediate the organization of

attributes within the individual's self-concept and muster them for
decision making. (p. 17)

Because values play this primary part in decision making, guidance must be
concerned with the student's exploration and examination of values. It
was this perspective that led to the inclusion of occupational values in the
System of Interactive Guidance and Information (SIGI) described by Katz
(1973).

Norris, Katz, and Chapman (1978) provide a more detailed summary of
sex differences in values. Here the focus is on sex differences in the Norris,
Katz, and Chapman study. Norris, Katz, and Chapman reported a unique
study of the process of career decision making based on data collected
during student use of SIGI (the System of Interactive Guidance and
Information, Katz, 1973). College students (N = 433) were observed in six
colleges in the act of career decision-making and data were collected
unobtrusively by the computer during actual use of SIGI. (The majority of
data on career decision-making and values are collected through surveys, as
is the present study.) In using SIGI, students rate the occupational values
and, among other processes, are able to examine occupations in their field
of interest that are classified by the values and meet the students' most
important values.

Age differences, sex differences, and "sex typical/sex atypical groups"
were examined for the occupational values in SIGI, as well as indicators of
process variables in using SIGI (e.g., consistency/inconsistency of value
weights, number of occupations requested for examination, and so on).
Age differences on the values were small and infrequent in their sample.
Sex differences tended to confirm the stereotype of the active, striving
male and the passive nurturant female. For males the top three values were
Security, High Income, and Work in a Major Field of Interest; for females
the top three values were Work in a Major Field of Interest, Security, and
Helping Others. The direction of the sex differences were: Helping Others,
F > M; Early Entry, F > M; Leadership M > F; Independence, M > F; and
Work in a Major Field of Interest, F > M. No significant sex differences
were found for the remaining occupational values of Prestige, Security,
Variety, or Leisure.

Although there were sex differences in average ratings of the occupational values, there were overlapping distributions on all variables examined. In an effort to "account for" the mean sex-differences, sex-typical,
and sex-atypical groups were formed using the main values that predicted
the dependent variable sex in a regression analysis (Helping Others, Leadership, Early Entry, and High Income). Each individual could then be
classified into one of four groups: female typical (actual and predicted sex

the same), female atypical, male typical, male atypical. Differences on several variables were then examined by two-way ANOVAs. One such variable examined was the predominant sex membership of occupations chosen by sex-typical and sex-atypical groups. The base rate for occupations in SIGI are that 60% of the occupations are predominantly male (33% or fewer women in the occupation), 22% are predominantly female (66% or more women in the occupation), and 18% are neutral (between 33% and 66% women in the occupation).

The expected difference in sex-typical and sex-atypical groups occurred. For example, 83% of typical males chose male occupations; and 41% of the typical females chose female occupations. However, 54% of the atypical females chose male occupations versus 30% for the typical females. As Norris, Katz, and Chapman point out, the SIGI system is in one sense "sex blind" and an individual who wants to escape from sex stereotypes of occupations can do so. Individuals themselves, however, are "sex blind" to different degrees, as the differences in sex-role attitudes demonstrate. The research described in the following chapters is concerned with clarifying the extent to which individuals may be able to make "sex blind" choices, and to consider whether entering other sets of values in the career decision-making process may assist in reducing the sex-based differences in occupational and earnings distributions.

The small though significant and persistent sex differences in the occupational values have been found in several other studies. Mahoney, Heretick, and Katz (1979) found distinct factor structures for each sex with a form of the Rokeach value survey (mentioned earlier). Although the sample sizes were small, the data are consistent with Katz's work and the findings in this study with eleventh graders (Chapter 6). Tuck and Keeling (1980) and Lybarger (1978) have found sex differences in factor structure of the Self Directed Search and another occupational interest survey.

Whereas the sex-role preference or attitude measures provide one indication of values attached to marriage, parenthood and work, another approach to these values is a more direct weighting or rating of the importance of these roles. Johnson and Jaccard (1979) have examined the career-marriage orientations in females and males. College students (N = 69) completed an open-ended questionnaire designed to elicit the perceived consequences and normative pressures for three life structure alternatives: emphasizing a career; emphasizing marriage; and placing equal emphasis on career and marriage. With regard to making career the top priority, considerations most frequently mentioned were ultimate career success, personal satisfaction and enjoyment, and money for a prosperous life style. Males were more likely to mention social recognition and health strain concerns; females were more likely to mention concerns related to what is best for raising children and self-reliance and autonomy. For the decision of marriage as the top priority, females and males differed on one category: self-reliance and autonomy was mentioned more frequently by women.

In a second study Johnson and Jaccard (1979) presented 9 aspects of life structure and asked 50 female and 50 male undergraduate college students to rank order them, as well as giving their priorities for the 3 life-structure alternatives and ratings to the 24 concerns identified in the first study. The nine life aspects were: sibling relations; parent relations; marriage; being a parent; work/career; friends/friendship; leisure; civic concerns; and religious concerns. Of the three life structures students were more likely to emphasize marriage or both, rather than career only (sex differences were not significant).

Values for marriage and parenthood, that is, the needs or satisfactions that individuals may take into account in making the decision to get married or to become a parent remain largely unexplored, however. Sometimes the reasons people give for getting married (e.g., Kirkpatrick, 1963) or for having children (Hoffman & Hoffman, 1973) are reported. Informal sources call attention to these values, as when the *New York Times* provides journalistic articles: "What the doctors' wives expected, they said, was prestige, security, happiness, pride and the satisfaction of performing as loyal helpmate to a man of service. What many of them got instead was disappointment" (Bennetts, 1979). Similarly, the *New York Times* has reported on possible changes in male views of parenthood (Brozan, 1980). As men may no longer assume that they will be the sole breadwinner and that wives will single-handedly raise children, arguments arise, such as:

> Having a child will jeopardize my career advancement. How can I become executive vice president of the agency if I regularly take time off for school plays and pediatrician appointments?
>
> Having a child will trap me in a job where I can earn sufficient money to support a family rather than taking one that gives me personal satisfaction.
>
> Having a child will curtail my freedom, to travel, to go out whenever I want.
>
> Having a child entails a lot of dreary physical work, fatigue, boredom.
>
> But if I choose not to have one, will I forever regret it?

These arguments also suggest that the values individuals express will vary with life stages.

Although economists (e.g., Sawhill, 1977) and sociologists (e.g., Bernard, 1974, 1975) also provide hints of the values important in decisions on career, marriage, and parenthood, few systematic studies were located. Sawhill provided a particularly useful summary of the economist's perspective on marriage and parenthood in relation to earnings and the economist's assumption that scarce resources are the constraint on people's freedom to choose from among alternative courses of action. Economists have devoted attention to analyses of fertility, marriage and divorce, and the division of labor within the home and its effects on labor force participation and earnings. Sawhill questions whether economists have done more than to describe the status quo in a society where sex roles are "givens." In the past marriage was often an economic necessity for women and a product of social norms. Children were also the result of social norms and unintended outcomes of sexual relations. If the earnings differential narrows, Sawhill foresees that:

> In the future, economics and technology are likely to ensure that the act of having a child and the decision to share life with another adult are freely and consciously chosen for the personal satisfactions they entail rather than as a means to some other end. Personal values and psychological needs met by marriage, children, and family life will be the final arbiters of choice. (p. 124)

To this statement can be added the needs met by work, which together with the others will permit an understanding of educational, occupational, marriage and parenthood patterns. The psychological approaches to understanding career choices are discussed next, in a section on the present status and findings of career development and career decision-making.

Career Decision-Making Approaches

Earlier in this chapter, selected research on women's occupational status and choice was reviewed. Part of the research is influenced by sociological approaches to defining the variables that predict status, and part by the economist's views of the variables that define tastes or preferences for work or amount of earnings. Another part of the research is influenced by psychologists' views of the career or vocational development process. In this section the views of the psychologist are examined briefly. First, general theories are identified for both career development and life-span development. Second, specific studies on career decision making approaches are described, and, finally, criteria for evaluating the process and outcomes of future career decision-making studies are suggested.

GENERAL THEORIES

Psychologists' theories of career development tend to be personality-based. Roe's (1956) theory emphasizes the importance of child-rearing practices as forming the needs and motivations that influence the type of career chosen. Careers are broadly categorized as oriented toward other persons or not toward other persons. Holland (1973) also theorizes that individuals enter occupations according to their personality, and has grouped occupations and personalities into six types: realistic, investigative, social, conventional, enterprising, and artistic. Super (1957, 1963) has proposed that career development follows the development or is the implementation of the self-concept of the individual, and there are stages of career choice: crystallization (ages 14-18); specification (18-21); implementation (21-24; stabilization (25-35); and consolidation (35 and over). Ginzberg (1972; Ginzberg et al., 1951) also proposed a stage theory of career development, with stages such as fantasy, tentative, and realistic. Occupational choice is seen as a decision-making process that is open-ended, in which the individual seeks to find the optimal fit between career preparation and goals and the reality of the world of work. Here the focus is on the individual or decision maker, although Ginzberg recognized the "reality" factor, including inequalities based on sex, race, income, and intelligence.[5] (Osipow, 1973, discusses these theories in more detail.) Vetter (1973), among others, has criticized these theories for their lack of fit to women's types of occupations entered, labor force participation patterns, and wages earned.

General stage theories of development (which may or may not focus on career choice) have received renewed attention within the past decade from research on adult development. Work by Levinson (1978) and Gould (1972) has been popularized (Sheehy, 1976), but also criticized for being based on samples of males. Levinson, for example, described the lives of 40 men and proposed that the life structure has a relatively orderly sequence during the adult years, with alternating stable and transitional periods. The childhood and adolescence stage lasts to approximately age 22; transition to the adult era ends around 22 when the man enters the adult world (ages 22-28); passes through the age 30 transition (28-33); and enters the settling down phase (33-40). The major tasks include forming a dream, a mentor relationship, an occupation, and love relationships. The adult identity is established. The midlife transition (40-45) links early adulthood and middle adulthood, and the transition to the late adult era occurs around 60 years of age.

Lowenthal, Thurnher, Chiriboga, and Associates (1975) studied both females and males at the time of normative life-course transitions (leaving home, having or planning for the first child, having the youngest child leave home, and retiring). They were concerned with the responses to these potentially stressful "marker" events in life, and found definite life stage and sex differences. Lowenthal and Weiss (1978) discussed the adaptive nature of interpersonal intimacy (one of Erikson's adult developmental tasks) at the time of stressful events. They emphasized that there is not a sequence of tasks for successive life stages, but several tasks or commitments that must be examined simultaneously for how they periodically wax and wane, and how these rhythms differ, and possibly conflict, between the sexes. They found, for example, of their eight groups, that women of middle and lower-middle class who were facing or in the early phases of the postparental stage were a risk group:

> Most of these women, who have mainly been family-centered, can anticipate another twenty-five or thirty years of reasonably healthy life. Many have not very clearly thought through the urge to find commitments, often related to a need for mastery or competence, beyond the family sphere. Yet they are caught in a bind, because they also yearn for a renewal of intimacy with their spouses. . . . Many of their husbands, increasingly dependent, are demanding more of their wives' time, . . . and such men are often jealous of any actual or potential outside interests on the part of their spouses. (p. 333)

These women also may have a social milieu that makes it difficult to return to school or to work. In a follow-up, it was also found that many of these women were reaching the age where there were increasingly dependent parents—their own and sometimes their spouses'—for whom they were responsible. Rubin (1979) has provided an extensive portrait of these women.

As yet there appears to be no comprehensive perspective on the life-span development of women in all areas, including career choice and development. Perhaps to some extent this is an unrealistic goal, if the work of Neugarten and Datan (1973) is taken seriously. They have proposed that not only the demographic changes in the timing of major life events are important but also that situational aspects change, dependent on the sequence of events for a particular individual and the historical events of the day or societal influences of the time. Huston-Stein and Higgins-Trenk (1978) have provided more attention to age and cohort differences in role choices, historical changes in role choices (work and family patterns, and attitudes and expectancies about women), sociocultural influences on women's life patterns (particularly barriers to changing roles and occupational structure), and individual differences in development among women. Especially important for women are the adolescent and early adulthood periods, because these are the times most women make decisions about the timing of marriage, childbearing, education, and work that are not easily reversed. Marriage and particularly the parenthood decisions have long-term consequences in terms of responsibilities traditionally given to women (see Hofferth & Moore, 1978). Career decisions are often delayed or postponed in commitment for many women until the other decisions are made or it becomes apparent that they may not occur. (See Tittle & Denker, 1980, Chapter 6 for further elaboration of this point.) It is the importance of these decisions and the awareness of options for women that led to the development of the marriage and parenthood values. To what extent are such values and decisions considered in the theories that explicitly define career decision-making?

CAREER DECISION-MAKING

The general theories of career development have not directly incorporated sex differences in occupations chosen and labor force participation patterns, nor do they include variables or developmental tasks likely to encompass the contingency planning (marriage and childbearing) and delayed commitment to careers that occur for many women. Krumboltz, Becker-Haven, and Burnett (1979) and Super and Hall (1978) have provided reviews of counseling psychology (including developing skills for career transitions) and career exploration and planning, respectively. Super and Hall agree that the concept of career development includes more than the worker role (as does Richardson, 1979), and Super places career decision-making with the career development process. Krumboltz et al. define decision-making skills as the ability to learn about oneself, learn about career opportunities, consider many alternatives, seek information, clarify values, make plans, see oneself in control, engage in exploratory processes with satisfaction, or overcome indecisiveness and its accompanying anxiety. In the list of skills, as in descriptions of vocational decision making models (Jepson & Dilley, 1974), there is an implicit understanding that the "content" to which the process is applied is limited to "career" and vocational information. "Content" should be redefined to include decisions examining the relative importance of occupation or career, work, marriage and parenthood.

To what extent have current descriptions of career decision-making expanded the "content" to include those values and decisions critical to women's career development? Variables to look for include, among others, factors influencing the career choice processes in women (Gutek & Nieva,

1978): attitudes about sex-role appropriateness of occupations; sex-stereo-typing by women in anticipated career choices; pioneer or innovators in sex-atypical occupations; home-making to career-orientation, and related attitudes about appropriate roles for women; and plans/explorations to anticipate the relative importance and integration of adult roles of worker, partner, and parent.

A symposium held at the American Personnel and Guidance Association meeting in Las Vegas, Nevada, April 1979 provided a forum to present the current status of approaches. The symposium was entitled, "Is Career Decision Making Career Maturity? The Models, the Measures, and the Data."

Super (1979) places career decision-making within career development theory and career maturity, but stated that neither can be conceived of without the other. That is, career development as the confrontation of a series of developmental tasks cannot be examined without attention to decision determinants, processes, and styles—decision-making theory. Super defines career maturity as the readiness to make decisions when required by the structure of schools, the working world, and by the sequences of biological and social development. Super's current model for research on career attitudes, knowledge, and skills includes the dimensions of Autonomy, Planfulness, Exploration, Career Decision-Making, Knowledge (self and work information), and Realism. There is no explicit discussion of women's career development.

Harren (1979) presented his work on career decision-making, defining his framework as, "a description of a psychological process wherein one seeks and organizes information, deliberates among alternatives, makes a commitment to a specific course of action, and takes steps to carry out that commitment" (p. 1). He described several major approaches to decision-making: The Gelatt model in which the emphasis is on helping the decision maker realistically assess the likelihood that a given decision can be implemented and will result in the achievement of the desired outcomes; and Katz's model which also considers probabilities, but where the focus is on clarifying the decision maker's values and value priorities. Both originated in mathematical decision theory, and are categorized as prescriptive models by Jepson and Dilley (1974), because their purpose is in prescribing *how* people ought to decide (but not *what* they ought to decide). Other approaches, for example, Tiedeman and O'Hara (1963), are descriptive, because they attempt to picture how decisions are made.

Harren's approach has aspects of both description and prescription: the approach assumes that progress through the stages of the decision-making process (description) depends on the characteristics of the decision maker (prescriptive of the effective decision maker), the type of decision involved (the developmental tasks are prescriptive), and the decision-making context. Harren's schema for career decision-making for typical-age undergraduates includes four main parts: the decision-making process, decision maker characteristics, developmental tasks, and the decision-making setting. Decision maker characteristics include the self-concept (identity and self-esteem) and decision-making style (rational, intuitive, and dependent). Of most interest in terms of the present research is Harren's description of the developmental tasks that confront his college-age decision makers.

Three student development tasks (areas) are proposed: Autonomy, Interpersonal Maturity, and Sense of Purpose. Sample career decision-making tasks within each area are:

Autonomy: To leave home; to go to college; to find a job.

Interpersonal Maturity: To choose a roommate; to find a life partner to marry; to choose a mentor, and to dissolve relationships that are deteriorating, restrictive, or destructive.

Sense of Purpose: To choose a major field of study in college; to find satisfying leisure activities; and to choose an occupation.

Whereas other aspects of the model may be examined for their relevance to women's experiences, these are particularly important in terms of the substantive examples of tasks proposed as relevant to career decision making. As one example, a task in developing skills to negotiate responsibilities/resolve conflicts within a marital (or two-person) relationship could be added to the interpersonal maturity tasks. For another example, Sense of Purpose for women (and men) should include fertility and marital expectations, as these are likely to influence the type of occupation chosen and extent of labor force participation of women (Psathas, 1968; Falk & Cosby, 1978). Katz (1979), in describing the central acquisition tasks for adult sex roles for females and males, distinguishes the emphasis on pursuing occupation (*to some* degree for females and *all* for males) and, for females (ages 15-35) resolving conflicts about combining vocation with marriage and primary responsibility for child care. Males in these ages have no (for most males) conflict in developing vocational interests and only secondary responsibility in child care.

The exact manner in which these and related sex-role variables are influential is not identified at present, although for the variable of anticipated labor force participation at age 35 Waite and Stolzenberg (1976) and Stolzenberg and Waite (1977) have provided nonrecursive models, showing apparently reciprocal causal effects for labor force participation plans and fertility expectations. Similar data are used by Mott (1978), with more extensive analyses of withdrawal and reentry to the labor force with children, and by Hofferth (1980) to show the influence of number of children on work experiences of noncollege girls.[6]

These sociological path models have implications for the research reported on Harren's model by Harren, Kass, Tinsley, and Moreland (1979). Path analyses reported by Harren et al. used several instruments (below) and the dependent variables of male dominance index for the college major (MDI-M) and male dominance index for occupational choice (MDI-O). The instruments used were:

Assessment of Career Decision-Making (ACDM), a measure of the degree a student has progressed through four stages toward choosing a college major.

Bem Sex-Role Inventory (BSRI), with 3 scales of the degree to which students endorse masculine qualities, feminine qualities or androgenous qualities.

Attitudes Toward Women Scale (AWS), a measure of the degree to which students endorse liberal or traditional views of sex-role appropriate behavior for women in general.

Attitudes Toward Masculine Transcendence Scale (AMTS), the degree of liberal or traditional views of sex-role appropriate behavior of men in general.

Cognitive Differentiation Grid (CDG), a measure of the degree of the career cognitive complexity (number of constructs the individual uses to differentiate among occupations). Separate grid scores were calculated for the number of constructs used to judge four male-dominant occupations (GRID-M) and four female dominated occupations (GRID-F).

The analyses were carried out for 161 males and 196 females who indicated they have made a satisfying choice of college major, and for 87 males and 148 females who made a satisfying choice of occupation. In the first path analysis, using the male dominance index for major, gender was directly linked to the dependent variable and was the most influential predictor of gender-dominant career choices. The three feminine-related scales (AWS, BSRI-F, and GRID-F) also had a direct, albeit smaller, influence. Both GRID-F and BSRI-F had negative coefficients, as did gender (coded M = 1, F = 2). The only positive path coefficient was for AWS. So females who were more liberal were more likely to choose male dominant occupations. Similar findings occurred for MDI-O, except that GRID-F showed no direct influence on the dependent variable. Gender was again the strongest predictor of the male dominance index. (R^2 for MDI-M was 32% and for MDI-O, 23%. The potentially modifiable variables, the sex-role measures, accounted for 21% and 11% of the variances, respectively.)

Other variables that might show direct influences on type of occupation may be labor force participation plans and fertility. Johnson and Jaccard's (1979) perceived consequences of marriage, career, and/or both options may also be relevant. Recalling the Norris, Katz, and Chapman use of occupational values to identify sex-typical and sex-atypical females and males, we can anticipate that future work may help to identify other modifiable variables (that is, in the sense that individuals can assess and examine their occupational values) to use in similar path analyses and may directly include the timing of child bearing plans. Within a traditionally female field, nursing, Feldbaum (1979) found that, among groups of nurse mothers, those who held the highest positions were those who had their children while very young. An alternative upwardly mobile group included mothers who deferred childbearing until they were older and had earned a graduate degree. The extent to which such patterns might occur in male-dominated occupations is unknown. These are, however, options of which women should be aware.

In conclusion, one other set of concepts drawn from the study of marriage and families that may add to the set of developmental tasks for career development is noted here. These concepts are found in the emerging study of marital conflict (Scanzoni, 1978) and studies of conflicts between work and family life (Pleck, Staines, & Long, 1980). Scanzoni's 10-state survey of married women (wife's age from 18 to 44 in 1971) had a number of pertinent findings:

> Women who preferred egalitarian marital arrangements defined work as a right; women whose sex-role preferences were traditional were more likely to regard employment as an option.
>
> Egalitarian women had a more significant impact on family lifestyle, social class position, and the sharing of household duties, including being coproviders with their husbands.
>
> Egalitarian women were also likely to be more effective negotiators and have greater bargaining power with their husbands.

Pleck et al. (1980) used data from the Quality of Employment Survey to examine conflicts reported by more than one-third of those workers (N = 1,084). Working women did *not* report work-family conflict significantly more often than working men. Of those workers reporting conflicts, women were more likely than men to report schedule incompatibilities (related to afternoon, evening, and irregular work shifts), fatigue, and

Sex Roles

Norms (expectations)
Behavior
Traditionally
Female — Marriage relationship
       — Parenthood (motherhood) & childrearing
       — Homemaking

Plans (anticipated behaviors)

Labor force participation and pattern
Marriage (timing)
Children (number & timing)
Homemaking responsibilities

Traditionally
Male — Education
     — Occupation

Stable norms despite entry of married women and women with children into the work force (Bernard, 1976). However, some shifts are occurring (Mason, Czajka, & Arber, 1976).

Values

Marriage	Parenthood	Occupational
Emotional Support	Joy	High Income
Children	Variety	Prestige
Financial Security	Sense of Pride	Helping Others

Now: How are these values and plans related to career decision making?

Long range: Can intervention based on exploration of these values and plans affect sex-equality in career decision making?

Career Decision Making (Now)

1. Educational plans
2. Type of occupations considered
3. Level of occupational aspiration
4. Number of years of full-time work planned before age 41

Criteria for Sex-Equality in Career Decision Making (Long range)

1. More occupations and more nontraditional occupations explored
2. Fertility/education plans related to preferred occupations and level of career/marriage/parenthood commitments
3. Articulation of occupational & homemaking responsibilities
4. Articulation of role cycles for husband and wife
5. "Negotiating" skills developed for egalitarian marriage (partnership)
6. Attainment of social competencies—both communal and agentic
7. Reduction of sex-stereotyped views of all adult roles

FIGURE 2.1 Sex Roles, Values, and Career Decision-Making

irritation (resulting from work) as impinging on their family life. Men were more likely to report excessive work time as a problem. These considerations of marital and work-family conflicts, as well as other research reported in this chapter, leads to Figure 2-1, which attempts to summarize some of the major concepts that relate sex roles, values, and career decision-making.

Sex roles traditional for men and women are identified in Figure 2.1: for men, education and occupation; for women, the marriage relationship, homemaking, and motherhood. Values appear as part of the career decision-making process, following Katz's (1973) use of values in SIGI. However, Figure 2.1 proposes the addition of marriage and parenthood values, to complement the occupational values and thus expand the individual's consideration of the spheres of adult life in which needs will be met and satisfactions found. None of the values in any way prescribes what should be important for individuals. They are intended to facilitate the individual's decision process. The plans or anticipated behaviors are the focus of the present study, along with the career decision-making variables listed in the top part of the right-hand column. For the long range, the question is whether intervention based on exploration of these values and plans can encourage sex equality in career decision-making. A number of criteria are also proposed for the long-range study of sex equality in career decision-making. These criteria extend from occupational, educational, and fertility plans, to plans for articulation of role cycles for husband and wife, and to development of negotiating skills for an egalitarian marriage. The ultimate criteria for the evaluation of any intervention based on theories of career choice, however, remain occupational desegregation and equality in earnings for sex and minority groups.[7]

NOTES

1. Females were omitted because preliminary results displayed less explanatory power, as well as for reasons of economy and compatibility with previous studies. It was suggested that a more general model would need to explicitly incorporate the marriage and child-bearing decisions (Nolfi et al., 1978, p. 93).

2. There may be some trend toward the integration of occupational majors of college students. Magarrell (1980) summarized data from the Cooperative Institutional Research Program showing that there was an increase between 1969 and 1979 for women entering business majors—from 12.5% to 23.1%; for engineering the increase was from .4% to 2.5%; and for education a decrease from 19.2% to 12.5%. Interest in probable professional majors went from 1.8% to 5.5% (i.e., for MD, DDS degrees). These changes, however, affect only a small proportion of women workers, and

would not affect the large numbers of women in clerical and sales occupations and the existing occupational segregation data.

3. The economic perspective on the family and economists' views of "choice" are considered in the next section on values.

4. Adapted from Mott (1978), p. 13.

5. Sociologists such as Blau et al. (1956) and Psathas (1968),and more recently Falk and Cosby (1978) have typically been more cognizant of the "realistic" factors in career choice.

6. These last four studies used the National Longitudinal Survey of Labor Market Experiences data base developed by the U.S. Bureau of the Census and the Ohio State University. The sample started in 1968 with about 5,000 women who were then representative of females aged 14 to 24 years.

7. Specific criteria for exploration and other career decision-making skills are given in Super and Hall (1978) and Krumboltz, Becker-Haven, and Burnett (1979).

Chapter 3

DEFINING THE MAJOR VARIABLES

Following from the review of the literature, there were a number of measures used in the study that required careful definition. The values for the occupational, marriage, and parenthood decisions were of first importance and received the greatest emphasis during a first-year pilot study that developed the interview schedule. The extension of concepts beyond those typically studied in the psychological literature led to the inclusion of a scale developed for use in studies of population fertility—the job-child preference scale developed by Lolagene Coombs—and the variable, "number of years of full-time work before age 41." The latter variable, or variants of it, have appeared in the sociological literature examining women's labor force participation (e.g., Waite & Stolzenberg, 1976). A number of questions relate to sex roles, for example, the job-child preference scale and number of years of full-time work before age 41 and ratings of a series of activities for families with children, because the ratings asked whether each activity was predominantly a man's or a woman's responsibility, or could be either person's responsibility.

The fragmentation in the previous research with respect to samples representing both sexes, several racial-ethnic groups, and more than one socioeconomic status group led to the efforts to carefully represent these status variables in the study. The definitions of SES and racial-ethnic groups are also described below.

The Value Sets

Three sets of values were used in the study: occupational, marriage, and parenthood. The occupational values from SIGI (Katz, 1973) are presented in Table 3.1. The values for marriage and parenthood used in the main study are given in Tables 3.2 and 3.3.

The definitions of the value terms given in Tables 3.1, 3.2, and 3.3 are simplified from the definitions used in SIGI and the pilot study. The SIGI definitions were shortened and adapted for Grade 11 students. The adaptations were satisfactory, with the possible exception of the occupational value, Interest Field, which had varying interpretations. Students often interpreted this value as having work that was interesting to them, rather than as meaning a developed basic interest area (art, science, and so on) to which they were career-committed.

The marriage and parenthood values were developed through a variety of sources: a literature search including the terms *values* and *sex roles;* readings in the areas of motherhood, marriage and family; trial of preliminary definitions with individual students and a sample of 40 eleventh graders; revisions and retryouts; and a use of Kelley's Role Construct Repertory Test (1955) to elicit constructs used to describe similarities and differences between individuals who were husbands and wives or mothers and fathers. (This latter technique worked with psychologists, but not with nonpsychologists.) Data from a pilot study of 98 eleventh-grade students resulted in further revisions, using the criteria that each value within a set should receive all possible ranks, and the distributions of ranks should be as rectangular as possible. These criteria reflect the view that there are "no correct responses" to a set of values, and that individuals will hold diverse values.

The procedures for presenting each set of values to students were the same. Each value term was presented to a student on a 3 X 5 card so that the cards could be sorted and values could be rank ordered within each set of values. The general directions were: "These cards describe values or satisfactions that people might consider important in choosing an occupation (deciding to get married, deciding to become a parent). Read through them and think about which ones are important to you. Tell me if you find anything that you don't understand." A comparison of values across the three sets was given in another question. The student was given a circle and asked to examine how important the areas of Work, Marriage, Children, and Other are when they are compared with each other. The task was to pretend that a circle represented the student's life, and the circle was to be divided like pieces of a pie, to show how important each area of Marriage, Work, Children, and Other would be in the student's life.

The Job-Child and Level of Involvement Scales

To examine the relative importance of two of these areas, Work and Children, two scales were included in the interview schedule. These scales were developed by Lolagene C. Coombs, of the Population Studies Center of the University of Michigan, to measure commitment to work in the job-family trade-off context (Coombs, 1979). She dealt with the problem of examining competing attitudes simultaneously by the method of conjoint measurement. Preference data for the components of desire for a job or career and desire for children were collected by asking a sample of students at the University of Michigan to rank order a set of 16 cards. Each card presented one combination (e.g., 0 children, full-time job) from the 16 possible combinations of 0, 1, 2, or 3 children and 0, 1/2, 3/4, or full time job. (Coombs felt these were reasonable ranges for the U.S. culture.)

Table 3.4 presents the four choices that make up the Involvement Level Scale and the four choices that make up the Job-Child Orientation Scale. The respondent's task, for each scale, was to select one of the four alternatives, under the situation described above where there are children under 10 years of age and the job is for pay outside the home. After the initial choice the interviewer presented an additional series of cards to obtain the respondent's complete preference order.

Number of Years of Full-Time Work

A series of questions were designed to elicit student plans for education, marriage, children, full-time work, and part-time work between the ages of 16 and 41. The questions and responses were placed on time lines. Students circled the ages at which they expected each event would occur. The expected ages for full-time and part-time work indicated a pattern whereby some students recognized they would be in the work force full-time and then would stop full-time work and would later resume it. Particularly for women, plans for marriage and children result in less continuous work patterns and exits and reentry into the labor force.

The variable of number of years of full-time work before age 41 takes both part-time work and years out of the labor force into account in this single index of plans for work. Waite and Stolzenberg (1976) examined the labor force participation plans of young women for age 35 in relation to their fertility plans. They found that the woman's plans to participate in the labor force when she is 35 have a substantial affect on the total of children the woman plans to bear in her lifetime. We expected that both the values and job-child scale of Coombs would show relationships with

(text continues on page 72)

TABLE 3.1   Occupational Values Revised for Use
with Eleventh-Grade Students[1]

High Income
An Occupational Value

Some money is important to everyone. But how important are the extras? People have different ideas about how much income is "high." So HIGH INCOME is not a specific amount. It means more than enough to live on. It means having extra money. You can buy things you don't need.

A

Prestige
An Occupational Value

If people respect you, look up to you, listen to your opinions, or ask for your help in community affairs, you are a person with PRESTIGE. Of course, PRESTIGE can be gained in several ways. But in presentday America, occupation is usually the key to PRESTIGE. Rightly or wrongly, we respect some occupations more than others.

B

Independence
An Occupational Value

Some occupations give you more freedom than others to make your own decisions. In some jobs you work without supervision or direction from others. Freelance artists or writers may work without supervision. Conversely, soldiers or people in big business organizations may not be able to make many decisions.

C

Helping Others
An Occupational Value

Most people are willing to help others; they like to do things for their friends and neighbors. But THIS DOES NOT COUNT HERE. The question here is, Do you want HELPING OTHERS to be a main part of your work? How much do you want to help people as part of your job?

D

Security
An Occupational Value

In the most SECURE occupations, you will not be afraid of losing your job. You do not have to worry about being fired or being replaced by a machine. You can count on your paycheck on Friday, and you know in advance how much it will be.

E

TABLE 3.1 (Continued)

Variety
An Occupational Value

Occupations with the greatest variety have many different kinds of activities and problems, many changes and new people to meet. VARIETY is the opposite of doing the same thing over and over. If you like VARIETY, you probably like new things and surprises, and like new problems, places, and people.

F

Leadership
An Occupational Value

Do you want to lead others, tell them what to do, be responsible for their work? People who want LEADERSHIP usually like to control things. If they are mature, they know that RESPONSIBILITY goes with LEADERSHIP. They are willing to accept the blame when things go wrong, even though it was not their fault.

G

Work in Your Main Field of Interest
An Occupational Value

Some people have only ONE MAIN FIELD OF INTEREST, for example, Science, Art, Verbal, Mechanics, Personal Contact, or Administration. Others are interested in more than one field. Most people want to have interesting work, BUT THIS DOES NOT COUNT HERE. Are there several fields in which you could find work that is satisfying to you? Or, how important is it to you that your work is in your one main field of interest?

H

Leisure
An Occupational Value

How important is the amount of time your occupation will allow you to spend away from work? LEISURE may include short hours, long vacations, or the chance to choose your own time off. To give a high weight to LEISURE is like saying, "The satisfactions I get off the job are so important to me that work must not interfere with them."

I

Early Entry
An Occupational Value

How important is it to you to start working right away? You can start some jobs with very little education or training. Others need years of education. If EARLY ENTRY is important to you, you do not want more education or training. If you are willing to spend time, effort and money for more education, EARLY ENTRY is *not* important to you.

J

---

[1] Katz (1973).

TABLE 3.2   Marriage Values Defined for Use with
Eleventh-Grade Students

Financial Security
A Marriage Value

Marriage can give you financial security.

If you marry someone who has a good income, you can have many things. A good income also lets you do many things that you couldn't manage on your own.

A

Emotional Support
A Marriage Value

Marriage can give you emotional support.

Married people can support each other emotionally during rough times. They can trust each other and share personal problems.

B

Helpmate
A Marriage Value

Marriage can give you a helpmate.

There are many chores in one's life, for example, cooking, paying bills, laundry, taking care of the car. With someone to help you, you can share these household responsibilities.

C

A Close Physical Relationship
A Marriage Value

Marriage can give you a close physical relationship.

When people are married, they can have a close physical relationship with someone they care for very much.

D

Prestige
A Marriage Value

Marriage can give you prestige.

When people get married, they can feel proud of their partners. And they can feel successful because of their partner's successes.

E

A Normal Life
A Marriage Value

Marriage can give you a normal life.

When you reach a certain age, family and friends expect you to get married. When all your friends are getting married, marriage seems like the natural thing to do.

F

TABLE 3.2   (Continued)

A Permanent Companion
A Marriage Value

Marriage can give you a permanent companion.

When you get married you can have a permanent friend and companion. You can go places and do things together.

G

Children
A Marriage Value

Marriage can give you children.

When people get married, they can begin a family. They can provide a home for children.

H

Your Own Home
A Marriage Value

Marriage can give you your own home.

When you get married you can set up your own place to live, and run it the way you like. You can be your own boss.

I

Someone to Rely On
A Marriage Value

Marriage can give you someone to rely on.

When you are married you can feel safe. There is someone who can protect and take care of you.

J

A Feeling of Leadership
A Marriage Value

Marriage can give you a feeling of leadership.

When you are married you can be responsible for your partner. You have the chance to guide someone else.

K

TABLE 3.3 Parenthood Values Defined for Use
with Eleventh-Grade Students

Accomplishment
A Parenthood Value

Being a parent can give you a sense of accomplishment.

In raising a child you take on responsibilities and meet many challenges. When you see that you have done a good job it gives you a sense of accomplishment.

A

A Sense of Pride
A Parenthood Value

Being a parent can give you a sense of pride.

You can feel pride through your children's achievement. Your children can be successful in life.

B

Variety
A Parenthood Value

Being a parent can give you variety.

You can watch your children grow and change. There is always something new and different in life with children.

C

Friendship
A Parenthood Value

Being a parent can give you friendship.

Children can be close friends to their parents. You will be able to talk to your daughter or son as a friend. You can go places and do things with your children.

D

Respect of Others
A Parenthood Value

Being a parent can give you the respect of others.

Your family and friends expect you to have children. Becoming a parent earns you their respect.

E

A Stable Marriage
A Parenthood Value

Being a parent can give you a stable marriage.

Children can make their parents feel closer. Marriages with children can be stronger and more permanent marriages.

F

TABLE 3.3   (Continued)

A Chance to Express Love.
A Parenthood Value

Being a parent can give you a chance to express love.

You can hug and cuddle young children. Caring for a child who needs you lets you show your feelings of love.

G

Confidence as a Man or Woman
A Parenthood Value

Being a parent can give you confidence as a man or woman.

Your own child can give you a feeling that you are a real woman or man. Having a child can be basic to your sense of womanhood or manhood.

H

Joy
A Parenthood Value

Being a parent can give you joy.

You can have laughter and joy in your home. A home with children can be sunny and happy.

I

Future Security
A Parenthood Value

Being a parent can give you future security.

When you get old, you can turn to your children for help. Children will love you and care what happens to you.

J

A Tie to the Future
A Parenthood Value

Being a parent can give you a tie to the future.

Parenthood means you can leave something of yourself to the future. Having something of yourself in your children and grandchildren is a kind of immortality.

K

A Sense of Importance
A Parenthood Value

Being a parent can give you a sense of importance.

When you have children you become an important person. What you say has more influence.

L

TABLE 3.4   Scales for Job and Children Trade-offs[1]

Involvement Level Scale	Job-Child Orientation Scale
(A) 0 children, no job	(A) No children, full-time job
(B) 1 child, 1/2 time job	(B) 1 child, 3/4 time job
(C) 2 children, 3/4 time job	(C) 2 children, 1/2 time job
(D) 3 children, full-time job	(D) 3 children, no job

[1]Coombs (1979).

this variable, as would number of children and the relative importance of work, children, and marriage. Views of sex roles in a more egalitarian or flexible manner should also relate to expectations of full-time work for women.

Sex-Role Activities

A variable that is likely to relate to plans for children and work expectations, as well as to the values, is the student's view of activities that have traditionally been sex-typed within families. As described earlier, career decisions made by women take into account their expectations for marriage and children (Falk & Cosby, 1978; Psathas, 1968). According to Bernard (1976) these expectations are influenced by social norms for the behaviors appropriate for females and males, that is, their sex roles. In the study sex roles were examined in two series of questions. The first was a series of activities for families with children, the second asked students to assign the percentage of responsibility the husband or wife should accept for three main responsibilities in a family: earning money, keeping house, and caring for children. Data for both series of questions are reported in Chapter 8.

The list of activities for families with children was drawn from the work of Eagly and Anderson (1974) and modified slightly for the present study. Students were asked to rate each of 22 activities on a scale from 1 to 5, where 1 meant that the activity was Only a Woman's Responsibility, 2—Mainly a Woman's Responsibility, 3—The activity could be Either Person's Responsibility, 4—Mainly the Man's Responsibility, and 5—Only a Man's Responsibility. The activities included in the list are those traditionally assigned to either a man or woman by virtue of their sex. For example, items included cleaning the house (dust, vacuum), mending clothes, repairing household appliances, and washing clothes. Eagly and Anderson used the series of activities to examine the question of whether in a sample of young adults (college students) there was a relationship between desired family size and preferences concerning adult sex roles. The set of activities used in their study was chosen after pretesting in another (earlier) study and indicated that students tended to consider them appropriate for only one sex.

In the Eagly and Anderson study very modest but significant correlations were found between sex-role nonequivalence (a total score derived from the activity items), opposition to Women's Liberation, low liberalism, high conservatism, strong religiousness, and desire to procreate a larger number of children. For both sexes, number of siblings, religion, rural-urban, and social class were, in general, not significantly correlated with the role and attitudinal variables.

In the present study the sex-role activities were used as individual items, because a factor analysis indicated between six to seven factors with small numbers of items on each (see Chapter 8).

Socioeconomic Status

Three occupational scales were employed in the classification of parent's socioeconomic background and student career aspirations. The occupations of the parents were coded on the Hamburger Revised Ocupational Scale for Rating Socioeconomic Status (Hamburger, 1958) and on the census measure of Socioeconomic Status (Bureau of the Census, 1963). The students' occupational goals were coded on the census measure and on the two-way classification scheme developed by Roe (1956).

The Hamburger Occupational Rating Scale was the basis for the categorization of subjects into the low or middle socioeconomic status (SES) groups. The occupation rated highest, either the mother's or father's, was used to determine the classification. The Hamburger Scale is comprised of six occupational categories: professional, semiprofessional, business, clerical, manual, and protective and service. Occupations that are classified within each of these groupings are placed on a seven point (ordinal) scale of socioeconomic status. The socioeconomic status level that is assigned to an occupation is determined by economic as well as social prestige factors. A manual is provided in which the criteria are given for category classification and SES-level ratings. The occupational title as well as the amount of educational training indicated is taken into consideration in the rating procedure. The dimensions of income, responsibility, behavior control, and particularly occupational prestige, differentiate between the occupations representative of each SES level within each of the six categories. For example, occupations within Category I (professional) range from doctor at level 1 to lab technician at level 3; in Category VI (protective and service), occupations range from police commissioner at level 1 to night watchman at level 7 (see Appendix 1).

For the purposes of the present investigation, students were classified as to socioeconomic status on the basis of the occupations that they reported for their parents or guardians. A student was designated as middle socioeconomic status when either parent or guardian was reported to be employed in an occupation classified at levels 1, 2, or 3 of the Hamburger Scale. When neither parent nor guardian met this criterion level, that is, their occupations were rated at levels 4, 5, 6, or 7 on the Hamburger Scale, a student was assigned to the low socioeconomic status category. Exceptions to these SES classification criteria occurred in a few rare cases in which parents, though employed in lower occupational level jobs, were college educated. In these instances students were classified as middle class on the basis of their parents' educational rather than present occupational level (e.g., Cuban families who moved to the U.S., were in professional occupations in Cuba, but in other occupations in the U.S.).

Difficulties occurred in SES classification on the basis of the Hamburger Rating Scale due to the fact that students seemed to know little about their parents' occupations. For the majority of occupations reported, the appropriate categories and SES levels were self-evident. There were some problems in which either the appropriate category and/or the appropriate SES level within a category was difficult to determine. This occurred when job descriptions overlapped two or more categories, for example, manual and service, professional and business, clerical and service, or when information relevant to the selection of SES level (income, job responsibility, and authority) was not always available.

The parental occupations were rated on the Hamburger Scale by coders familiar with the criteria outlined in the rating manual. Individual case problems and inconsistencies between occupational codings were reviewed and discussed throughout the rating procedure. When the socioeconomic status of a student was assessed as ambiguous, he or she was dropped from the sample. This occurred in a small number of cases.

Parental occupations and students' career aspirations were also coded on the socioeconomic status measures developed by the U.S. Bureau of the Census (Bureau of the Census, 1963). The Census measure of socioeconomic status is a multiple-item index incorporating occupational, educational, and income data derived from the Census records. The socioeconomic status score assigned to an occupation is determined by the combined average levels of education and income reported for the occupation. The score indicates the position of the average person in a particular occupation as based upon the education and income distributions for that occupation in 1950. The prestige of an occupation is not taken into consideration in the coding procedure.

Occupations are classified into seven general occupational categories: professional and technical workers; managers, officials, and proprietors; clerical and sales workers; craftsmen and foremen; operatives; service workers; and laborers. These groupings are further subdivided into 297 specific categories representing a total of 494 distinct occupational items.

A final check on the coding was carried out by listing all occupations for either or both parents for students within each of the 12 cells of the sample plan, along with the Hamburger and Bureau of Census codes. Two staff members checked each occupational title for consistency of coding and coding errors, both within and between the middle and low SES groups. Discrepancies in coding for any one occupation were resolved and the same codes used across cells.

Roe's (1956) two-way classification of occupations was the third technique used to code occupations. Students were asked to specify the occupation in which they were most interested, as well as the occupation they actually expected to do. Each of these responses was coded on the Roe scale. The scale is comprised of eight occupational groups, which were developed according to their primary focus of activity: service, business contact, organization, technology, outdoors, science, general cultural, and arts and entertainment. Each of these primary focus groups is subdivided into six levels on the basis of responsibility, capacity and skill dimensions. The number, range, and difficulty of the decisions required in an occupation determine the level at which it is coded. When responsibility is not commensurate with skill, responsibility is the determining factor for level classification. Roe (1956) provided a descriptive outline of the classification criteria for each occupational group at each responsibility level. (Occupations are given in Appendix 1.)

In summary, the SES of parents was coded by the Hamburger (1958) occupational scale, and the levels of the Hamburger scale were used to classify student SES as middle or low. Further information on parents' occupations was given by the Bureau of the Census categories and scores (1963). And, the scope of student occupational aspirations was indicated by using Roe's (1956) focus of activity groups and level of responsibility scale. As noted, a majority of occupations were readily coded. A sizeable number of students, however, knew very little about what their parents did at work. This applied to middle as well as low SES students and is symptomatic of the lack of concrete work and career information of these eleventh graders.

Assessing Ethnic Categories

The study design called for interviewing students in three ethnic groups: black, Hispanic, and white. In the interview a preliminary classification was made by skin color (white/nonwhite) and last name (Hispanic). Additional criteria used to determine Hispanic classification were: (1) if the student had been born in a Spanish-speaking location; (2) if the mother had been born in a Spanish-speaking location; and/or (3) if Spanish was spoken in the home. If the interviewer was unsure about any category, the student was asked the following question: "What ethnic group do you consider yourself a member of?"

Borderline cases involved primarily the Hispanic classifications, and included children of mixed marriages, especially where no Spanish was spoken at home. The Hispanic category includes students whose skin color may be white or black. The primary criterion was the cultural (ethnic) group to which the student belonged by virtue of language and/or self-identification.

The next chapter describes the procedures of the study and characteristics of the 600 students on such demographic variables as age, place of birth, and parental occupations.

Chapter 4

THE PROCEDURES

Study Procedures

The sample design represented a series of choices among several alternatives as indicated below. The choices resulted in the characteristics of the sample, in which both females and males, two SES groups and three sociocultural groups are represented equally. This chapter also examines the characteristics of these groups on such demographic variables as age, place of birth, and parental occupations. The reader will be aided in interpreting the study findings in later chapters by placing them within the social environment these variables describe.

DESIGNING THE SAMPLE

The study was designed as a survey of a representative sample of urban eleventh-grade students. The decision to use one grade level in high school was based on the knowledge that the majority of the 16- to 17-year-old population is still in the educational system, whereas at the college level about 50% of the age group is not in the main postsecondary educational system. Because the concern and focus of the study is the relationship among values and plans for education, work, marriage, and parenthood, the eleventh grade in high school was chosen as close to the implementation of choices, yet critical in terms of intervention programs. That is, the high school level was chosen to test the ideas that a set of values in each of the areas of occupations, marriage, and parenthood could be developed and that the relationships of these values to plans and expectations should provide data with direct implications for interventions and career education materials.

A major purpose of the study was to determine how one aspect of the choice process related to career decision-making would be similar or different in several sociocultural and economic groups. That is, what would be the relative importance of sex- and occupational-role-related values for young men and women in these groups? We assumed that there would be sets of sex-role-related terms (the values) that would meet two criteria when administered to a representative group of high school students: (1) high school students would vary in the relative weights assigned to the terms; and (2) high school students would discriminate among the terms. The first criterion emphasized the characteristic of variability in the judged importance of the values for each aspect of the sex role (e.g., marriage and parenthood). Terms or values needed to be ones that not all students endorsed. If all students rated the same few marriage values as first or second, the various needs or satisfactions individuals derive from marriage would not be well represented. The second criterion suggested that the terms must have different meanings and be capable of being differentiated by students. Discrimination was tested in several ways: Can the terms be rank ordered? What are the factors underlying the sets of occupational, marriage, and parenthood values? Do the factors differ for females and males?

The choice of the three factors in the sample design was dictated by both theoretical and practical concerns. It is important to know if groups of differing sex, SES, and sociocultural background have different plans and values since these differences would have implications for designing interventions. The differences would also have implications for theories of career development, as suggested in Chapter 2. Thus the sample represented three factors equally: sex (2) by economic level (2) by sociocultural group (3). A sample of 50 students per cell was collected, for a total sample size of 600. The decision to use two levels of SES was made on the basis of numbers—because these students are most likely to be in the public education system and are the largest groups numerically. Similar considerations applied to the sociocultural groups. Black, Hispanic, and white groups are the largest cultural subgroups and were included for this reason. All three factors are part of the "setting" imposed on choices related to career decision making of students in our culture. Concerns for generalizations of the findings across these different groups was an important consideration: Do plans and values differ for middle and low SES groups? Do plans and values differ for black, Hispanic, and white students? These groups also dictated the choice of the survey instrument—the individual, highly structured interview schedule.

THE INTERVIEW SCHEDULE[1]

Although the occupational, marriage, and parenthood values were the main focus of the interview, the interview was structured to include several main sections. The first section was concerned with demographic or background variables describing the student. This included questions on age, place of birth, mother's place of birth, where they have spent most of their lives, use of other languages, ethnic group, and religion. Several other questions also asked for information about whether they lived with their parents or apart, the type of program in which they were enrolled at school, and whether they had any prior work experience. Another set of questions was concerned with parents' occupational history. Questions were included on both father's and mother's occupation and education and the mother's work pattern, that is, in relation to marriage and children.

The next set of questions was concerned with the student's educational and occupational plans and expectations. Student achievement and level-of-education aspiration were included, as well as the type of work students had considered doing after their graduation. Plans for children and the effect of a family on plans for work were also ascertained. Another group of questions asked students to identify the persons they talked to about their educational, occupational, marriage, and parenthood plans.

These sections of the questionnaires were followed by the occupational, marriage, and parenthood values. Students were asked to rank order and to rate the importance of each term within the respective value sets. A summary question following the values asked students to indicate the relative importance of work, marriage, children, and other parts of their lives by dividing a circle into parts to show the importance of each general area. Scales examining the general level of involvement and a job-child orientation were also given, one before the ratings of the values, and one after the value ratings.

Another section of the questionnaire presented time lines, showing ages from high school to age 40, and asking the student to indicate the times at which major events would occur, for example, school, marriage, children, full-time and part-time work. The questionnaire concluded with a list of activities for families with children. Students were asked to rate who should be responsible for each activity as an indication of assignment of activities to females and males.

In summary, the interview was designed to tap a number of variables thought to be related to career decision-making. In addition to basic variables that described the characteristics of the sample and relevant information on parent and student occupational history, the plans, values, and relative importance of various adult roles were the subject of questions in the interview schedule.

THE SAMPLE

Although schools and students were selected to represent the 12 cells in the sample design, the 600 students in the study are a volunteer sample. Permission to contact schools in the urban New York City area was obtained from the administrative offices of the Board of Education for the public high schools and from the various Catholic diocesan offices for four of the boroughs in New York City. These offices also provided information on the schools most likely to have students representing the various categories in the sample design. When permission had been obtained from the administrative offices, principals were contacted at each individual school and, typically, the guidance counselor as well. Both administrators and principals were told of the general design of the study and the need for assistance in identifying students who might meet the sample requirements.

Four public high schools in the Bronx and Queens participated in the study. One private high school in Manhattan agreed to participate and 24 Catholic high schools in Manhattan, Bronx, Brooklyn, and Queens also participated. Table 4.1 presents the number of schools and students in each sample cell by type of school, Catholic or public. Only seven students were interviewed at the private school, six middle SES girls and one low SES girl.

For most of the cells more than 50 students were interviewed. In order to have a uniform 50 cases per cell, the cells were reduced using the following criteria:

1. Lack of ambiguity regarding SES classification;
2. Lack of ambiguity regarding ethnic classification;
3. Appropriate parent educational level (i.e., no low SES parents with college degrees);
4. Completeness of interview schedule;
5. Standard family living arrangement (i.e., at least one parent living at home);
6. Unmarried and/or not a mother (five students were eliminated on this basis).

These criteria were applied first. If more than 50 cases remained in a cell, random selection was used to reduce the cell size to 50.

TABLE 4.1   Number of Schools and Students by Type of School for
Each Sample Cell[1]

SES	*Type of School and Student Group*					
	White		*Black*		*Hispanic*	
Middle	Catholic	Public	Catholic	Public	Catholic	Public
Female	1(1)	4(50)	7(16)	4(35)	17(45)	3(7)
Male	2(8)	4(47)	8(26)	3(25)	8(37)	3(13)
Low						
Female	–	4(69)	1(8)	4(63)	5(23)	4(77)
Male	2(12)	4(52)	4(8)	4(54)	6(38)	4(37)

[1]( ) number of students: Number interviewed per cell > 50; sample reduced to 50
per cell for analysis.

As is evident from Table 4.1, the students who were most difficult to
locate were black and Hispanic middle SES students. Student SES cannot
be readily identified in public school records, nor is parental occupation or
level of education typically known by school staff in the large public high
schools. Thus, in order to complete the desired sample without conducting
many interviews that would not be used in the data analysis, a number of
sources were consulted to locate the schools most likely to have middle
SES black and Hispanic students. These sources included advisory boards
for the Center for Advanced Study in Education (which had representatives from these communities). Similarly, borough boards of education and
administrators in both the public and diocesan offices were recontacted.
As a result of the consultations, further effort to complete these cells of
the sample concentrated on identifying Catholic high schools. Because the
Catholic high schools are typically much smaller in size, local guidance
counselors knew students personally and could help identify students for
interviewing. Always, both student and parent signed a consent form to
participate in the study.

Whereas initially any student who volunteered for the project was
interviewed, the last stages of the data collection were focused on identifying students likely to meet the sample requirements. Because the student's
actual classification was not known until the interview was conducted, it
was necessary to follow these procedures of going to smaller schools where
counselors knew students.

DATA COLLECTION

The procedures within individual schools varied to some degree in method of contacting students. A typical procedure, however, for the public schools included an initial contact with the principal, a meeting with the principal, other administrators, and the guidance staff. One guidance counselor would be appointed to work with the project. Letters of permission for interviewing, scheduling arrangements, and procedures to pay students for interviewing, if in accord with the school regulations, were worked out with the guidance counselor. Students were paid a stipend of $3.00 as an incentive to participate and encouragement to view the interview in a responsible manner. The consent form was prepared in Spanish and English so that parents agreeing to student participation could read either version.

The beginning of the interview assured students of confidentiality of response and their privilege of not responding to any particular item. This latter option was rarely chosen, as the interview questions had been piloted with students, reviewed by school staff, as well as the project staff, and were concerned mainly with student perceptions and responses to questions about the values and sex-role variables. Length of interviews varied from 40 minutes to an hour and 10 minutes.

The interviewers for the project were either graduate students in doctoral programs in psychology or education, or graduates with an M.A. degree in education, with the exception of one interviewer who had a B.A. degree. Over the eight months of data collection, there were eight female interviewers and three male interviewers. There was no attempt to match or randomize sex of the interviewer and sex of the student. The limited number of male interviewers made such a procedure impractical. The interviewers had to be available on a variable time schedule according to when schools could be contacted, students located for participation, and consent forms obtained. The sample design imposed restrictions on the data collection, as noted above, with accompanying interruptions in scheduling for interviewers. There were, therefore, more female interviewers available who had the flexibility required in the amount and type of part-time work the interviewing constituted.

Training interviewers. Interviewers were trained by the following procedures. First, the interviewer was administered the interview by one of the three permanent project staff. Then the trainee administered the interview to the project staff. In addition, the interviewers had practice administrations with available students, not in the sample, and these interview protocols were reviewed by the project staff. Also, the trainee was observed administering at least one interview as part of the regular data collection procedure.

Characteristics of the Sample

The interview began with a series of questions about the student's status with respect to age, family religion, place of birth, and so on. The questions and response data are presented below. In addition to the data describing the total sample of 600 eleventh graders, typically the data were examined for differences among the main groups which constituted the sample design: sex, ethnic, and SES groups.

AGE, ORIGIN, LANGUAGE, AND RELIGION

1. How old are you?

A majority of students were 16 years of age (65%) or 17 (21%). A three-way ANOVA showed no significant differences in age for the sex or socioeconomic factors. There was a significant F for the ethnic factor ($F_{2,588}$ = 7.84, pr > F=.0004). Examination of the cell frequencies for that factor shows that fewer Hispanic than white students were less than 16 years old in this sample. That is, the Hispanic students tended to be older than the white students (mean ages for the three groups, where 1 = less than 16 years, 2 = 16, 3 = 17, 4 = 18, and 5 = 19+, were white = 1.990, black = 2.130, and Hispanic = 2.235, n = 200 each group). Scheffe's test shows the only significant difference is between the white and Hispanic groups.

3. Where were you born (state or country)?[2]

Eighty percent of all students in the sample were born in New York state. For whites, 93% were born in New York State. The second most frequent place of birth was Puerto Rico, Cuba, or another Spanish-speaking country (32% of the Hispanic students). About 12% of the black students were born in one of the southern states. Data for low and middle SES groups were very similar.

4. Where was your mother born?

The largest percentage of mothers was born in New York State (39%). The second largest percentage of mothers was born in Puerto Rico, Cuba, or another Spanish-speaking country (31%). A comparison of the data for students and their mothers shows that nearly three times as many mothers were born in Puerto Rico or the Spanish-speaking countries (179 mothers and 64 children). Similarly, more mothers of black students were born in southern states than were their children (87 mothers and 23 children). For mothers, 75% of the white mothers were born in New York State, 35% of black mothers (43% in southern states), and 8% of Hispanic mothers (and 90% in Puerto Rico/Spanish-speaking country).

TABLE 4.2   Family Religion as Reported by Students
in Each Sample Cell[1]

| SES | White[2] | | | Black[3] | | Hispanic[4] | |
	Cath-olic	Prot-estant	Jewish	Cath-olic	Prot-estant	Cath-olic	Prot-estant
Middle							
Female	8	8	30	14	22	49	1
Male	19	4	21	28	17	47	2
Low							
Female	35	4	9	8	34	45	5
Male	45	1	3	14	31	44	2
	107	17	63	64	104	185	10

[1] Total N each sample cell = 50, for example, white, middle SES, females, N = 50.
[2] Two white students reported no religion and 11 reported "other."
[3] Six black students reported no religion, 1 reported Jewish, and 25 reported "other."
[4] One Hispanic student reported no religion and 4 reported "other."

5. **Where have you spent most of your life?**

Of the 600 students participating in the study, 562 (94%) had spent most of their lives in New York State. This total is an increase of 13.5% over the number of students born in New York State. The increase is accounted for by 9 white students, 25 black students, and 47 Hispanic students. Examining the data by ethnic group showed that 97.5% of the white students, 93% of the black students, and 90.5% of the Hispanic students said they had spent most of their lives in New York State.

6. **Do you use another language at home?**

Almost 62% of the students (369) answered *no* to this question. The largest percentage of *yes* responses were from those students whose families used Spanish at home: 201 (33.5%) students. Of the 200 Hispanic students, 195 (97%) speak Spanish at home.

9. **What is your family's religion?**

The overall frequencies for family religion were 356 (59.3%) Catholic, 131 (21.8%) Protestant, 64 (10.7%) Jewish, and 49 (8.2%) reported as none or "other." The distribution by sample cell is shown in Table 4.2. All but 15 of the Hispanic students reported their family religion as Catholic. Slightly over half (53.5%) of the white students and 67 (32%) of the black students reported their family religion as Catholic. Referring to Table 4.1, it can be seen that the white students interviewed were primarily in the public schools and the large number of middle SES black students interviewed in the Catholic schools reflect a current reality of schools in New York City.[3]

10. Do you live with your parents?

Almost all students live either with one or both parents (97.5%). Only 15 students answered that they did not live with either one or both of their parents (by ethnic group, 9 Hispanic, 5 black, and 2 white students; by SES, 10 of the 19 were in the low SES subgroup).

19. How many children are there altogether in your family?

Responses to this question were coded from 1 to 9+ children. The mean and standard deviation for the total sample of 600 were 3.27 and 1.67, respectively. A three-way ANOVA showed two significant F values—for ethnic groups ($F_{2,584}$ = 6.41, pr $>$ F = .002), and for SES ($F_{1,584}$ = 39.98, pr $>$ F = .0001). Examining the ethnic group means by Scheffe's test shows that blacks had larger families than did either the white or Hispanic groups (means of 3.53, 2.96, and 3.22, respectively). The low-SES group had larger families than did the middle SES groups (means of 3.68 and 2.85, respectively).

EDUCATION AND OCCUPATION OF PARENTS

One group of questions was concerned with the level of education and type of occupation of both the mother and father. The series of questions probed for descriptions of the father's and mother's work activities to facilitate coding. Occupations were coded using two classification schemes described in Chapter 3—the Bureau of the Census (1963) and the SES classification using a combination of education and occupation as described by Hamburger (1958). A detailed series of questions also were included to describe the mother's work pattern in relation to marriage and children.

The questions are presented in the order in which they appeared in the interview. First, there are descriptions of the father's occupation, and level of education, then the mother's level of education, work history, and occupation. The majority of students had fathers who were employed full-time (477 or 79.5%). Another 6% had deceased fathers and smaller percentages reported that their fathers were retired, disabled, or it was not known whether he was working.

11. What is the main kind of work your father does?

This question was coded for a father, stepfather, or absent father, if the occupation was known. There were 42 students (7% of the sample) for whom data on the father's occupation either were not reported or could not be coded. All Professional and Semiprofessional occupations are coded at level 3 and above on the level of occupation scale of Hamburger (1958). In the total sample 13.6% of the fathers were employed in Professional occupations, 3.2% in Semi-professional occupations and 19.2% in Business (commercial) occupations. Almost half of the fathers were in Manual and

Protective & Service occupations (46.3%), and the remaining were in Clerical occupations (10.8%).

A three-way ANOVA on the level of occupation showed a significant main effect for SES, as expected ($F_{1,546}$ = 620.66, pr > F = .0001) and also a main effect for ethnic group ($F_{2,546}$ = 11.83, pr > F= .0001). One interaction was significant. SES by ethnic group had an $F_{2,546}$ = 2.96, with pr > F = .0526. The means for the groups were:

Means (N)

SES	White	Black	Hispanic
Middle	2.58 (92)	3.38 (92)	2.92 (99)
Low	4.97 (97)	5.30 (84)	5.30 (87)

The mean level of occupation for fathers of the middle-SES black students in the sample tended to be lower than those for white or Hispanic students, but the means were about the same for fathers of low-SES students in all groups.

Examination of the distributions and percentages of fathers in the Hamburger *type of work* categories for the major student groups shows that there are few differences in the percentages of females and males when the occupational category of their fathers is examined. There are differences for the SES categories (as expected due to the use of categories as part of the coding for SES). Whereas there are no differences in percentages of white, black, and Hispanic groups for the first two categories—professional and semiprofessional—there are some differences in the percentages of fathers in the remaining categories. More white and Hispanic students in this sample tended to have fathers in occupations classified as Business. There were fewer black and Hispanic fathers with clerical occupations, and fewer whites in the Protective and Service occupation category. All three groups had the same percentages of fathers in the Manual occupations. (The overall χ^2_{10} for ethnic groups was 25.53 (p = .0031).)

12/13. How much school did your father (mother) complete?

Students were asked how much education their parents (or stepparents or foster parents) had completed. Table 4.3 shows the frequency and percentage of education completed for eight codes and a ninth code, don't know, for both parents. The largest difference in percentages occurs for the category, Graduated from High School/High School Equivalency, where the percentage for mothers is 33.7% and for fathers is 26.7%. Only 8% of the fathers and 6.5% of the mothers had attended graduate or

TABLE 4.3   Frequency and Percentage of Level of Father's
Education and Level of Mother's Education

Level of Education	Father F	%	Mother F	%
None or some grade school	24	4.0	24	4.0
Completed grade school	30	5.0	29	4.8
Some H.S. but did not graduate	95	15.8	87	14.5
Graduated from High School/ High School equivalency	160	26.7	202	33.7
Technical or business school after High School	21	3.5	25	4.2
Some college, but less than 4 years	69	11.5	80	13.3
Graduated from a 4 year college	88	14.7	88	14.7
Attended graduate or professional school	43	7.2	37	6.2
Don't know	70	11.6	28	4.7

professional school. (Data were unknown for 70 of the fathers and 28 of the mothers.) Also, for this sample, mothers of black students had consistently higher average levels of education (across SES groups) than mothers in the other two groups.

14. **Does your mother work?**

For the total sample, slightly over half of the students (307, or 51.2%) responded yes, full-time work, and another 9.7% responded yes, part-time work (less than 20 hours per week). About 1% responded their mother was dead or living apart. If the student responded no, the student was asked, Has she worked in the past? Another 164 (27.3%) students responded yes to this second question and 40 (6.7%) responded no. All together, 88% of the sample students had mothers who had worked or were presently in the work force.

For the 51.2% of mothers currently working full-time, half were mothers of males and half of females in the sample (155 and 152, respectively). The distribution by ethnic group was 126 black mothers employed full-time, 94 Hispanic and 87 white mothers. The data by SES are also of interest: 190 mothers were middle SES and 117 low-SES mothers working full-time. For this urban sample, almost two of every three middle-SES mothers were working full-time and one in three low-SES mothers were working full-time. Of the 40 mothers who had never worked, 18 were middle SES, and 22 low-SES status; 9 were white, 9 were black, and 22 were Hispanic.

15. **What is the main kind of work your mother does?**

Students were asked to respond to this question either for their mother's present occupation or past occupation (if not presently working).

(Data are missing for 60 cases [10%] of the total sample of 600.) The mother's occupation was also coded using Hamburger's (1958) category of work and level of work. As with the classification of father's occupation, the Professional occupations are concentrated at levels 1, 2, and 3 of the Hamburger levels (a combination of occupation and education) and designated as middle SES for the present study. Almost a third of the mothers' occupations fell into the Clerical category, and another third were in the Manual and Protective & Service categories. Few mothers of students in this sample had occupations in the Semiprofessional and Business categories.

The distributions of type of work categories were examined for the main student groups. The expected differences by SES occurred, with fewer mothers of low-SES students holding Professional jobs. There are differences in the categories for ethnic groups, with more mothers of black students having worked in jobs in the Professional category, and more mothers of white students in the Clerical category (χ^2_{10} = 135.68, p = .0001).

A three-way ANOVA on the level of occupation showed significant main effects for ethnic ($F_{2,539}$ = 6.21, pr > F = .0022) and SES groups ($F_{1,539}$ = 229.24, pr > F = .0001). There was also a significant two-way interaction for ethnic group and SES ($F_{2,539}$ = 11.90, pr > F = .0001). The SES main effect is expected; the means for levels of SES are 2.99 for middle SES and 4.82 for low SES groups. The interaction effect is associated with the mothers of black students. They tend to have significantly higher level scores within the middle SES groups and to have lower scores within the low SES groups.

Of some interest is the comparison between the types of work categories most frequently found for fathers and mothers of students in this sample. These distributions tend to reflect traditional findings for occupations of females and males in the labor force, regardless of whether the Hamburger or Census categories are used. Fewer mothers are in the Business categories for both classification systems, and more mothers are in the Clerical and Sales categories. The somewhat higher frequency of mothers in the Professional category is due to the sample design, which permitted classification of student SES on either father's or mother's occupation.

16. Who is the main income earner in your home?

For the total sample, 379 (63.2%) stated that their father was the main income earner in the home, 141 (23.5%) said the mother was, and 80 (13.3%) indicated another source of income. Typically, the "other" was welfare or Social Security. The distributions of responses of father as main income earner and mother as main income earner were examined. The distributions *within* either the father or mother categories as main income carner tend to be similar. That is, there are no major differences by sex, SES, or ethnic group. The difference is *between* the parents, where there are more black mothers who are the main income earner for the student sample in this study. (For the three ethnic groups, and mother, father, other codes, χ^2_4 is 35.65, p = .000.) Twice as many black students, compared to the white and Hispanic students, report their mothers as the main source of income (Ns of 73 vs. 33 and 35, respectively).

17. **Has your mother always worked?**

When students replied that their mothers were working or had worked, questions 17 and 18 were asked to examine the work patterns. For the total sample, 208 students (34.7%) replied that their mother had worked continuously and full-time; another 77 (12.8%) that their mothers had worked mostly continuously, with short interruptions; 128 (21.3%) that their mothers had worked off and on, stopping work for periods of a year or more; and 80 (13.3%) that they had worked only briefly, less than four years altogether. About 5% said their mothers had never worked and 1% that they were uncertain or did not know. (The remaining 12% reported another pattern that did not fit the four main work patterns listed.)

18. **Timing of mother's work**

The work pattern was checked in more detail in a series of questions: Did your mother work—before marriage? Before children?, and others, to which students responded yes, no, or uncertain. Of those women who worked, the responses indicate that about two-thirds of the women worked before marriage. Only about one-third were working when their youngest child was 1 to 3 years old. As the children reached elementary school and older, the mothers reentered the labor force and the percentage of mothers working while the youngest was 12 years old was about the same as the number working before marriage.

HIGH SCHOOL PROGRAM AND WORK EXPERIENCE

The last set of variables that provide a context for understanding the study findings are concerned with the student's type of program in high school and the student's work experiences as of the eleventh grade.

23. **What program are you enrolled in at school?**

Somewhat over half of the students (56.8%) were enrolled in the college preparatory/academic high school program. Another 25% (150 students) reported that they were in the general program in their school, and the next largest percentage of students were in the commercial or business program (6.3%). The main differences in the percentages among groups are that more middle- than low-SES students are in the college preparatory program (70% and 44%, respectively) and that somewhat more of the white students reported being in college preparatory programs

(65% compared to 53.3% for black students and 52% for Hispanic students). There was a small difference in the frequencies of females and males enrolled in the college preparatory program—175 females (58.3%) and 166 males (55.3%).

24. Have you ever worked—for pay (not chores in your home)?

This question asked whether students had the experience of paid work outside their home. Seventy percent of the 600 eleventh-grade students had worked for pay. The categories for this question included full-time work (.5%), part-time work (17.8%), only summer full-time (21.5%), only summer part-time (14.8%), and summer and part-time (15%). Almost a third of the sample (30.2%) had never worked. When the full-time categories were combined, 132 or 22% were or had been employed full-time, and 286 or 48% part-time.

Examination of the data for the groups indicated (combining the full-time and part-time work categories) more low- than middle-SES group students had work experience and more males than females. The work experience varied by ethnic group also: 70% of the white group had work experience, 77% of the black group, and 56.5% of the Hispanic group. The data can be stated another way by looking at the group of students who have no work experience. A larger number of Hispanic students, middle-SES students, and female students had never worked when compared with the other subgroups.

25. What type of full-time/part-time work?

Students' responses to the question of what type of work they had done were coded into the Roe (1956) categories. Each of the types of work experience, full-time or part-time, was coded separately. For those 201 students reporting full-time work experience, the majority (68.2%) were in jobs classified in the Service category; 1.5% were Business; 14% in Organization; 10% in Technology; 2% in Outdoor; .5% in Science; 1% in General Culture; and 2.5% in Arts and Entertainment. The distribution for the 286 students with part-time work experience showed a similar distribution, although a somewhat lower percentage was in the Service category (51%) and a larger percentage in the Organization category (37%). There were some differences among groups: more boys than girls had work experience classified as Technology (14% vs. 4%); and a larger percentage of black students had work experience in the Service category.

Summary

The characteristics of the young men and women in this sample provide a context within which to place the findings in the next chapters. About two-thirds of these youth are 16 years of age; over three-fourths, regardless of ethnic group, were born in New York State. However, one-third of the Hispanic youth were born in Puerto Rico, Cuba, or another Spanish-speaking country. The place of birth differed for the mothers of these students. About 40% of all the mothers were born in New York State, but almost 90% of the mothers of Hispanic students were born in a Spanish-speaking country. More mothers of black students were born in southern states than were their children. These data on place of birth reflect general migratory and immigrant trends for New York City. The result, however, is that almost all of the youth (94%) have spent most of their lives in New York State. The Hispanic students also reflect their recent immigrant status because almost all of these students speak Spanish at home.

One important characteristic of the sample is the reported religious affiliation. These affiliations also reflect the predominantly Catholic religion of the Hispanic students, as well as the low-SES white students in the public schools. Also, many middle-class black parents have children enrolled in the Catholic school system. Almost all of the students live with one or both parents and are, on the average, in families with three or more children. These data reflect the balance among low and middle SES, because the low-SES student groups were in larger families than the middle-SES groups. Black students also tended to be in larger families than white students.

Data on the father's and mother's occupation and education showed that the highest educational attainment for over half of the parents was a high school or high school equivalency degree. Less than 10% of parents were reported to have attended graduate or professional school. The reported occupations for fathers showed expected differences for SES groups, but also differences in the distribution by occupational type among ethnic groups. There were no differences among parents of students in the different ethnic groups for the Professional and Semiprofessional categories, but there were for Business, Clerical, and Protective and Service categories.

About half of the mothers of these students were currently working, and, when combined with mothers who had worked in the past, a total of 88% of these students had mothers who had been or were presently in the work force. More mothers of black youth and middle-SES youth were presently in the work force full-time. For this urban sample, almost two of every three middle-SES mothers were working full-time and one in three low-SES mothers was working full-time. These data are in accord with national data that show the more education a woman has the more likely she is to be in the labor force.

Occupational distributions of mothers' work categories reflected traditional findings for occupations of females and males in the labor force.

Fewer mothers were in the Business categories and more were in the Clerical and Sales categories. The work patterns of the mothers showed that about one-third had worked continuously and full-time since completing their education. Of all the mothers with work experience, about two-thirds had worked before marriage but only a third of all the women were working when their youngest child was one to three years old. As children reached elementary school and older, the mothers reentered the labor force and the percentage of mothers working while the youngest child was 12 years old was about the same as the number working before marriage. These data show the traditional entry-exit-reentry patterns of many working mothers. As our data on the students show, both the females and males expect themselves (for males, expectations for their future wives) to follow these patterns in their plans for work, marriage, and children (see Chapter 8).

These students also confirm college enrollment data: over half (57%) were in high school college preparatory or academic programs. Another 25% were in general programs. Group differences were most marked by SES groups: 70% of middle-SES students are in college preparatory programs and 44% of low-SES students. A majority of students (70%) had some paid work experience outside their home. More low-SES students had work experience (75% vs. 65% for middle SES), more males than females had work experience (78% vs. 62%), and more black and white students had work experience than did the Hispanic students (77%, 70%, and 56%, respectively). These work experiences are not distributed in the same proportions into occupational categories as those for adult workers. More students report work experiences in the Service categories than in any other, and very few have any experiences in Science or Business. As we might predict, students have had little opportunity to experience the majority of occupations of adult workers, or even to work in the organizations that employ the majority of adult workers.

These youth have already given us some important information within which to examine their own plans for education and work. Are their expectations for education congruent with their high school programs and higher than the educational status attained by their parents? And, particularly for the young women in this sample, do their plans for working in relation to their family plans reflect the reality of their mothers' lives or the stereotypes of traditional sex roles? For the young men, are their plans for their wives in agreement with what these women plan and the experiences of their own parents? Some of these questions are answered in the next chapter, which examines their plans and expectations for education and work.

NOTES

1. A copy of the interview schedule is available upon request from the author.

2. Question numbers are the same as in the interview schedule. This means some question numbers are omitted and may be out of sequence.

3. Dena Kleiman reported on John Jay High School in New York (*New York Times,* Wednesday, May 9, 1979) that although the neighborhood has many middle-class black families, most of them send their children to parochial and other private schools. Students in the city schools are predominantly poor or lower middle class. The ethnic enrollment of the city schools is 21.5% black, 45% Hispanic, and 33.5% "other."

Chapter 5

ADOLESCENT PLANS AND EXPECTATIONS:
Education and Work

Eleventh-grade students are at least a year away from implementing their plans for further education and beginning work. Some decisions have been made for their courses as preparatory to education or work, but they have had limited experience with the diverse set of occupations they can "choose" among. During the interview students were asked to evaluate themselves as students, to self-report their average school grades, and to describe their educational aspirations. Further questions asked about their occupational aspirations—to list any occupations they had considered, which occupation they were most interested in doing, and which one they thought they would actually do. The extent to which students report that teachers or counselors talk to them about work was also included. There were also a series of questions about work decisions that students expect to make for themselves and similar questions about the decisions they expect their future spouse to make.

Additional questions about whether students planned to marry, if having a family makes a difference in work plans, and how students intended to combine work and family give insight into their values for different adult roles and life styles (which are examined more fully in Chapter 8). Another perspective on student views of these roles is given by the responses to open-ended questions about the most admired adult whom the student knows personally. The persons to whom students talk about their educational, occupational, and marriage and parenthood plans also provide an understanding of the manner in which these adult roles are examined by students.

Educational Expectations

STUDENT ACHIEVEMENT

Students were asked, How good a student would you say you are? About half of the 600 students (295) stated they were in the middle of the class, 193 (32%) said they were above the middle of the class, 65 (11%) said they were one of the best students in the class, and 45 (7.5%) said they were just good enough to get by. A three-way ANOVA showed no significant difference by sex, but did show significant main effects for ethnic group and SES ($F_{2,586}$ = 2.83, pr $>$ F = .0598; $F_{1,586}$ = 20.22, pr $>$ F = .0001). Low-SES students rated themselves lower in their class than did the middle-SES students; means were 2.68 and 2.39, respectively (the higher the score, the lower the standing). Using Scheffe's test, the comparison of means for ethnic groups showed a significant difference between white and Hispanic students. White students tended to rate themselves higher than did the Hispanic students (means for white, black, and Hispanic students were 2.46, 2.51, and 2.64, respectively).

The question on actual grades asked, What is your school average? This question asked students to provide a quantitative estimate of their class standing. A 3-way ANOVA for the 588 cases with data on this variable showed significant main effects for sex, ethnic group, and SES, but no interactions. (The Fs were 15.50, 5.80, and 47.51, respectively, all with $p < .01$.) The scale for this variable was coded 1 = D (average of 69 or below), 2 = C- (average of 70-72), 3 = C (73-76), 4 = C+ (77-79), 5 = B- (80-82), 6 = B (83-86), 7 = B+ (87-89), 8 = A- (90-92) and 9 = A (average of 93-100). The mean for the total group of students was 5.33 and the means for the levels of the three factors were:

		$\overline{X}$	SD
Sex	female	5.63	1.9
	male	5.04	1.9
Ethnic	white	5.56	2.0
	black	4.98	1.8
	Hispanic	5.45	2.0

| SES | middle | 5.84 | 1.8 |
| | low | 4.80 | 1.9 |

Females, middle-SES students and white students self-reported higher school averages. These data differ from the self-ratings that were presented in the more qualitative form of statements, where females and males showed no difference in the average self-rating given. The correlation between the two self-report questions on class standing and school average differed slightly for females and males: $r = -.61$ for males and $r = -.69$ for females.[1]

EDUCATIONAL ASPIRATIONS

Educational aspirations were elicited by the question, How much education do you think you will have? Half of the sample thought that they would graduate from a four-year college. Another 26% thought that they would have as much education as professional or graduate school. Only 7% (41 students) thought they would finish high school and have no further education. The remaining 15% thought they would attend a technical, nursing, or business school after high school, graduate from a two-year college, or have some college but less than four years.

The small percentage (7%) of students who stated they would finish high school only is a marked contrast to the level of education of parents for this sample of students, because 27% of the fathers and 34% of the mothers had completed high school only. The pattern overall for the students was almost a reversal of their parent's education. Seventy-five percent of the students thought they would have at least a four-year college education; less than 25% of their parents had graduated from at least a four-year college. Part of the reversal may be accounted for by the tradition of education in New York City, and in particular the experiment of open admissions that was evident in the early 1970s, as well as the general increase in college attendance. The New York State Education Department reported that 46% of the NYC public high school graduates of 1977-1978 enrolled in four-year colleges. Another 36% were enrolled in two-year colleges or other postsecondary institutions (*New York Times*, August 27, 1979). As discussed in Chapter 2, however, there is a difference between expectations and reality, and many of these students will not attain their aspirations for college degrees.

SES differences in educational aspirations are consistently found in past research, as are some ethnic group differences. However, sex differences in first-year college enrollments have largely disappeared. To what extent are the findings here consistent with these trends? A three-way ANOVA showed significant SES and ethnic group main effects only (Ethnic: $F_{2,577}$ = 5.15, pr > F = .0061; SES: $F_{1,577}$ = 72.28, pr > F = .0001). The scale for educational aspiration was: 2, finish high school only; 3, technical, nursing, or business school after high school; 4, graduate from a 2-year college; 5, some college but less than 4 years; 6, graduate from a 4-year college; and 7, professional or graduate school. The means for the two SES groups are 6.12 for middle and 5.18 for low-SES students. The ethnic group means are: 5.40 for white students, 5.78 for black students, and 5.78 for Hispanic students. As the means indicate, somewhat more black and Hispanic students than white students expected to graduate from a four-year college and attend a professional or graduate school. The similar aspirations of boys and girls reflect both college attendance data and current research on educational aspirations of high school students. Also, data from the National Longitudinal Survey of the High School Class of 1972 shows that 34% of the males and 40% of the females who entered college had obtained a bachelor's degree by October 1976, although 45% of the females and 40% of the males had no higher education at all (Golladay & Noell, 1978). The higher educational aspirations of blacks is well documented in other studies (Allen, 1979).

Further indication of the likely change from aspirations to attainment is indicated by the discrepancy between type of high school program and educational goal. Only 57% of the students categorized their high school program as college preparatory/academic, compared to the 76% who thought they would at least graduate from a four-year college.

As sex differences in educational aspiration have disappeared, the question arises whether students' perceptions of the other sex are in accord with these findings. One question was included so that the self level of education desired could be compared to the level of education each student thought their spouse would have. These data are compared for female and male self decisions and future spouse decisions in Table 5.1. The responses of females and males for their respective spouses (male and female) show a slight trend for females to think their spouses will have a higher level of education than they themselves will, and, conversely, for males to predict that their spouses will have a lower level of education than they will. For example, females who plan to graduate from a four-year college tend to predict that their spouse will also (83%), but males predict a slightly lower rate (74%).

Occupational Planning

In contrast to the findings for educational aspirations for high school boys and girls, earlier research has shown that data for occupational

TABLE 5.1   Frequencies and Percentages of Self (Female or Male) Educational
Plan and Spouse's Expected Education

Self Decision on Education	Finish High School		Non-College Further Education		Graduate From College		Total	
	N	%	N	%	N	%	N	%
Finish high school								
Females	7	(44)	1	(6)	8	(50)	16	(100)
Males	12	(50)	6	(25)	6	(25)	24	(100)
Technical, nursing, or business school after high school								
Females	5	(28)	5	(28)	8	(44)	18	(100)
Males	7	(54)	0	(0)	6	(46)	13	(100)
Graduate from a two-year college								
Females	7	(27)	5	(19)	14	(54)	26	(100)
Males	8	(53)	1	(7)	6	(40)	15	(100)
Some college—less than four years								
Females	3	(30)	1	(10)	6	(60)	10	(100)
Males	6	(67)	1	(11)	2	(22)	9	(100)
Graduate from a four-year college								
Females	19	(13)	5	(3)	121	(83)	145	(100)
Males	27	(18)	12	(8)	112	(74)	151	(100)
Professional or graduate school								
Females	3	(4)	1	(1)	72	(95)	76	(100)
Males	7	(9)	1	(1)	72	(90)	80	(100)
Total Females	44	(15)	18	(6)	229	(79)	291	(100)
Males	67	(23)	21	(7)	204	(70)	292	(100)

aspirations differ in types of occupations, earnings after high school, and
labor force participation patterns. Thus, a series of questions were concerned with occupational planning and another series of questions (see
Chapter 8) asked about the timing of work and relative importance of
work, marriage, and family.

OCCUPATIONAL ASPIRATIONS

The first question asked, What jobs have you considered doing after
graduation? The responses to this item were coded in terms of the number
of jobs or occupations students listed, and the two questions identified the

occupations students were *most interested in doing* and the occupation they stated they *would actually do.* Responses to the latter two questions are coded for the Roe (1956) categories and for the Census (1963) categories also. Students were asked both questions, because there are often shifts in responses between the two questions.

The students were asked the question, the interviewer recorded the occupations, and, if the student responded with fewer than five jobs, the student was asked: Are there jobs you once considered but don't want any longer? Despite the probing, the majority of students responded with less than five jobs. The range was from zero to eight; the mean for all 600 students was 3.1 jobs considered, with a standard deviation of 1.2. A three-way ANOVA tested for main effects. There were no differences in the responses for sex, ethnic, or SES groups. The results are consistent with those reported for the National Assessment of Educational Progress (Tiedeman, Katz, Miller-Tiedeman & Osipow, 1978). The NAEP surveyed 17-year-olds (including a sample of out-of-school youths) in career and occupational development. Youth were asked to name up to five jobs they considered for the future. Over 86% named at least one job; and in the present sample all but 7% named at least one job. For the NAEP 56% named at least three jobs, and this urban sample showed 72% naming at least three. But only 12% named five or more (and 15% of the NAEP sample did so). Eleventh-grade students, judging from these responses, have not considered many jobs, and this finding is invariant across both sexes, the three ethnic groups and two SES categories.

Both questions on the occupation (job) students might do were coded on Roe's (1956) classification of occupations by group (type or primary focus of occupation) and level (degrees of responsibility, capacity, and skill). Table 5.2 presents the frequencies and percentages in each group and level of the Roe scheme for: (1) Job most interested in doing; and (2) job most likely to actually do. As shown in the table, the groups of occupations students are most interested in doing were: Science, Organization, and Arts & Entertainment. (See Appendix 1 for jobs in each category.) The levels with the greatest frequencies are at the top of the scale, in terms of levels of responsibility required—Levels 1, 2, and 3. There are some changes in these percentages when the jobs students state they are most likely *to do* are examined. There is an increase in the percentage likely to have a job in the Organization category and a decrease in the Arts and Entertainment percentages (from 19% to 13.4%). The levels of responsibility show a slight decrease in the percentages for the two highest levels, and an increase for Levels 3 and 4 (an increase of 1% in Level 3 and an increase of 3% in Level 4).

Table 5.3 presents the number and percentage of females and males for the Roe classification scheme for the job students stated they were most

TABLE 5.2 Frequency and Percentage of Responses of Total Sample[1] in Each Roe Classification for: (A) Job Most Interested in Doing and (B) Job Most Likely to Actually do

		Service		Business		Organization		Technology		Outdoor		Science		General Culture		Arts & Entertainment		Total	
Level		N	%	N	%	N	%	N	%	N	%	N	%	N	%	N	%	N	%
1	A[1]	29	5.0	-	-	5	.9	19	3.3	-	-	61	10.5	3	.5	2	.3	119	20.4
	B	23	4.0	-	-	2	.4	16	2.8	-	-	53	9.3	1	.2	-	-	95	16.7
2	A	18	3.1	3	.5	35	6.0	20	3.4	1	.2	43	7.4	61	10.5	72	12.4	253	43.3
	B	19	3.4	2	.4	46	8.1	17	3.0	1	.2	41	7.2	68	12.0	44	7.8	238	41.9
3	A	8	1.4	1	.2	43	7.4	19	3.3	3	.5	9	1.5	15	2.6	29	5.0	127	21.8
	B	7	1.2	3	.5	54	9.5	16	2.8	2	.4	11	1.9	14	2.5	23	4.1	130	22.9
4	A	18	3.1	2	.3	26	4.5	15	2.6	-	-	2	.3	5	.9	8	1.4	76	13.0
	B	22	3.9	2	.4	35	6.2	19	3.3	-	-	1	.2	4	.7	8	1.4	91	16.0
5	A	1	.2	-	-	2	.3	3	.5	1	.2	-	-	-	-	-	-	7	1.2
	B	2	.4	-	-	2	.4	4	.7	3	.5	1	.2	-	-	1	.2	13	2.3
6	A	-	-	-	-	-	-	-	-	-	-	1	.2	-	-	-	-	1	.2
	B	-	-	-	-	-	-	-	-	-	-	1	.2	-	-	-	-	1	.2
Totals	A	74	12.7	6	1.0	111	19.0	76	13.0	5	.9	116	19.9	84	14.4	111	19.0	583	99.9
	B	73	12.9	7	1.2	139	24.5	72	12.6	6	1.1	108	19.0	87	15.3	76	13.4	568	100

[1](A) Missing N = 17 2.8% of 600; (B) Missing N = 32 5.3% of 600.

TABLE 5.3 Number and Percentage of Females and Males in Major Groups and Levels of the Roe Classification for "Job Most Likely to Actually Do"[1]

		Service	Business Contact	Organization	Technology	Outdoor	Science	General Culture	Arts & Entertainment	Total
									Groups	
Females	N	46	3	72	7	1	63[2]	51	40	283
	%	16.3	1.1	25.4	2.5	.3	22.3	18.0	14.1	100
Males	N	27	4	67	65	5	45	36	36	285
	%	9.5	1.4	23.5	22.8	1.8	15.8	12.6	12.6	100

		1	2	3	4	5	6	Total	M	SD
					Levels					
Females	N	45	129	51	56	2	-	283	2.44	1.00
	%	15.9	45.6	18.0	19.8	.7	-	100		
Males	N	50	109	79	35	11	1	285	2.48	1.06
	%	17.5	38.2	27.7	12.3	3.9	.4	100		

[1] Missing N by main factors: middle SES N = 18, Low SES N = 18; ethnic group, white N = 14, black N = 9, Hispanic N = 9.
[2] Includes nurses, pharmacists, veterinarians.

likely to actually do. The main differences for the type of occupation given for the Roe groups were in the Service, Technology, and Science groups. Females were more likely to identify jobs they were likely to do that were classified in the Service (16.3% to 9.5% for males) and Science (22.3% to 15.8%) categories. The Science category, however, in the Roe scheme includes nurses, pharmacists, and veterinarians, and including nurses inflated what is traditionally a male-dominated interest area, especially in the top levels of responsibility (scientists, university and college faculties, medical specialists). Males were more likely to name a Technology occupation than females (22.8% to 2.5%).

The levels of occupations are also shown in Table 5.3. Levels were compared for the main groups in the sample design. The three-way ANOVA showed no significant main effect for sex ($pr > F = .63$). The effects for ethnic and SES groups were significant: Ethnic–$F_{2,556} = 10.30$, $pr > F = .001$; and SES–$F_{1,556} = 45.35$, $pr > F = .0001$. The means and standard deviations for the ethnic and SES groups were:

	White	Black	Hispanic	Middle	Low
M	2.72	2.35	2.31	2.18	2.73
SD	1.11	.97	.97	.92	1.06

Table 5.4 gives the frequency and percentage of responses for the total sample using the Bureau of the Census codes (1963). The distribution was highly skewed toward the Professional category, with 411 students stating they would actually do an occupation classified in this category. The Census scores were also highly skewed. The three-way ANOVA for the two-digit Census scores showed only one significant main effect, for SES, and one interaction for sex by ethnic group. The main effect was $F_{1,555} = 30.72$, $pr > F = .0001$; the interaction was $F_{2,555} = 7.77$, $pr > F = .0005$.

The means for Middle SES and Low SES were 87.81 and 81.63, respectively. The means for the interaction showed that for females, the highest Census score means are for the white and black groups; for males the highest Census score means are for the Hispanic and black groups. (Female means were: W = 85, B = 85, H = 82; male means were: W = 81; B = 85; H = 89.)

Because the educational attainments of parents and aspirations of children varied so greatly, the census occupations of parents and children were compared. These data are shown in Table 5.5.

Students are much more likely to aspire to professional/technical occupations when compared to their parents' occupations. These proportions are also greater than those for 17-year-old students' aspirations found in the NAEP (Tiedeman et al., 1978). NAEP results showed 49% of the

TABLE 5.4 Student Occupation, "Most Likely To Do": Frequency and Percentage of Responses in Each Category and for Score Groupings on the Census Codes

Census Categories	Census Score												
	00 – 29		30 – 59		60 – 69		70 – 79		80 – 89		90 – 99		Total	
	F	%	F	%	F	%	F	%	F	%	F	%	F	%
Professional	-	-	2	0.3	9	1.5	58	9.6	125	20.4	217	36.1	411	67.9
Business	-	-	1	0.2	1	0.2	8	1.5	26	4.3	12	2.0	48	8.2
Clerical & Sales	-	-	-	-	1	0.2	5	0.8	36	6.0	7	1.2	49	8.2
Craftsmen/Foreman	-	-	6	1.0	10	1.8	6	1.1	-	-	-	-	22	3.9
Operatives	-	-	4	0.6	4	0.7	-	-	-	-	-	-	8	1.3
Service Workers	1	0.2	13	2.2	1	0.2	10	1.6	-	-	-	-	25	4.2
Laborers	-	-	-	-	4	0.7	-	-	-	-	-	-	4	0.7
Total[1]	1	0.2	26	4.3	30	5.3	87	14.6	187	30.7	236	39.3	567	94.4

[1] Missing data N = 33 (5.5%).

TABLE 5.5   Percentage of Parental Occupations: Census Categories

| | | Occupation of | | |
Census Category	Father %'	Boys %	Mother %	Girls %
Professional/Technical	18.5	70.1	24.3	74.9
Business	22.4	10.9	6.3	6.0
Clerical & Sales	9.8	3.9	32.4	13.4
Crafts/Foreman	14.9	7.4	1.3	.4
Operatives	15.8	2.8	16.5	–
Service Workers	15.6	3.5	18.9	5.3
Laborers	3.0	1.4	.4	–

17-year-olds most interested in professional and technical occupations, a lower rate than the 75% for girls and 70% for boys in the eleventh grade. Whereas the girls' aspirations do not appear as stereotyped as their mothers' actual occupations, the girls again show less diversity in occupations (32 census categories used vs. 54 categories for boys), and within the professional category there are higher frequencies for traditionally female occupations such as nurse, medical/dental technician, and teacher.

The other occupational categories follow more closely data reported by the NAEP. Nine percent of the 17-year-olds mentioned clerical; these were almost all females, as were service workers. No females were interested in crafts, and the present study had less than one percent for that category. We can expect that the percent of students interested in the professional/ technical categories will decrease over the next two years, and that a majority of students will choose occupations traditionally ascribed by gender.

INFLUENCES ON OCCUPATIONAL CHOICE

In an effort to understand the why of career choice, students were asked exactly that question: Why did you choose that career? Student responses were coded into six categories (Block et al., in press): (1) *Ability*—the talents, capacities or personality characteristics mentioned as relevant to career choice. Skills were coded only when they implied a special capacity of the person (I'm good at math). Trained skills (I can type) were not coded here. (2) *Enjoyment/Interest*—Preference for a particular type of work when the implication is that this kind of work is more enjoyable to the student than another kind of work (I like children, I'm interested in mechanics, I'm excited by flying). (3) *Helping Others/*

Personal Achievement—specific mention of accomplishment, achievement, or satisfaction at attaining a personal or social goal (I want to help others solve their problems; I want to help children; I want to build better bridges). (4) *Practical Considerations*—mentions of job availability, educational prerequisites, job opportunities, and security are all coded within this category. If the student rejected a first career choice because of practical problems, such a reason was coded here (the student wants to be an accountant because acting careers are unreliable). (5) *Status/Prestige*—this category includes both the status of a particular job and indications that future goals of advancement (rising in the hierarchy) are considered in choice of a career. (6) *Financial Aspects*—responses were coded here when money is a part of the choice process (the job pays well, I have a cousin who is an accountant and my cousin makes a lot of money).

For the 543 students responding, Enjoyment was mentioned most frequently by students (57%) as a reason for career choice, then Practical Considerations (26%), Helping Others (17%), and Ability (17%). Financial Aspects were mentioned by 8% and Status/Prestige by 4%. Sex differences were found for four categories. Females mentioned Helping Others/Personal Achievement almost twice as often as did males (22% vs. 12%). Males mentioned three categories significantly more often than did females: Practical Considerations (33% vs. 18%); Status/Prestige (6% vs. 2%) and Financial Aspects (13% vs. 4%). Three of these four differences were consistent across lower- and middle-SES groups. Only the Status/Prestige category was mentioned more often by middle-SES students than low-SES students (6% vs. 2%). Ability was the only category cited less frequently by Hispanic students as a factor in career selection than for black or white students.

Students were also asked whether an individual or an event had been a particular influence in the choice of a specific career. Eight content categories were identified: (1) Family member in the occupation of choice; (2) nonfamily member functioning in the occupation; (3) family member not in occupation but from whom student has received encouragement or suggestions; (4) Friends or others not in occupation but from whom the student has received encouragement or advice; (5) Teacher or other academician who has influenced the student; (6) Personal experiences of work or hobbies that have led to an interest (e.g., the student fractured an ankle, which led to contact with a physical therapist which led to the student's interest in physical therapy); (7) Academic experience that influenced student (I took a science course and got interested in botany); (8) Media influence through reading material or TV.

The influential individual or event for career choices was perceived similarly by students in all groups. There were 479 responses and no category was mentioned more than about 20% of the time. The primary influential variables appear to be a direct personal experience (21%), a family member in the occupation (18%), and an experience occurring within the academic environment (16%). Influence by a family member (both in the occupation and not) tended to be mentioned more often than nonfamily influencers (31% vs. 18%). Media/books were mentioned by 9% and teachers by 6%.

Examples of the influences students cite are:

Occupation Stewardess: I know a stewardess and she told me about it.

Occupation Court Lawyer: We did occupational briefs, the courses are what I love, and I want to do something I enjoy and will do well in it.

Occupation Lawyer: My uncle is a lawyer and I've spoken to him a lot about it.

Occupation Doctor: My brother was hurt when I was young and I helped him till the ambulance came. Since then I wanted to be a doctor.

Occupation Secretary: Because that's what they offer in this school; because they gave me typing and I liked it.

The variety of reasons students give for choosing an occupation show the almost random process that exists. The predominant influence of persons known to the student but outside the educational system (mentioned in 49% of the responses) and direct experience outside the school (21%) show that only 30% of the responses reflect influences currently modifiable by intervention systems, for example, teachers and other school staff, school materials, and other media. A concern with the influence of individuals and school staff led to the inclusion of additional questions on these two aspects of the influence process.

To examine the extent to which students chose occupations that were known to them directly, the question was asked, Do you know anyone who is a _____?

This question asked whether the student knew anyone actually working in the occupation/job which the student gave in response to the question on the job they will actually do. Slightly over half (55.2%) of the students (N = 580 responding) knew someone in the occupation, either a parent (6.4%), a close friend or relative (31.4%), or someone else (17.4%). The remainder, 45%, said they did not know anyone in the occupation.

There was also a concern with the extent to which teachers and counselors assist students in formulating occupational plans. Two questions were asked about frequency of contact, Has a teacher ever talked to you about any kinds of work for you? and, Has a counselor ever talked to you about any kinds of work for you?

For the total sample, 210 students (35%) stated that a teacher had talked to them about work possibilities. The remaining 65% said that no teacher had talked to them. An even smaller percentage reported that a counselor had talked to them about any kinds of work they might do (164 students, 27%).

Examining the main sample groups, there were no significant differences among the sex, ethnic, or SES groups for yes responses to the question of whether a teacher had talked to them about their work possibilities. Within the 27% of the sample who had talked to a counselor about possible work, there were no significant sex or SES group differences. There was a significant χ^2 for ethnic groups. More black students reported they had talked to counselors about work than did the white and Hispanic students (42% vs. 26%, and 33%, respectively).

The findings for a national sample of 17-year-olds show both a similarity and a difference. Counselors were identified by 36% of the NAEP students as a person with whom occupational plans had been discussed at least once, with somewhat more females than males (41% vs. 31%) having talked with counselors and somewhat more whites than blacks (37% vs. 32%). Overall, however, neither the NAEP or the present study indicate school personnel are reaching a majority of students. Although we did not ask about computer assisted guidance systems, they were not available in the schools we visited. (*Who* students do talk to is discussed later in this chapter.)

There is a disparity between influences spontaneously cited by students on occupational choice and the frequency of contact with counselors and teachers in work-connected discussions. There is agreement, however, between the percentages indicating they knew someone in the occupation and the open-response percents (about 50% or half the students). The influences, however, on occupational choice are not limited to the ones we have examined so far. An influence of major importance is the effect of having a family. That is, to what extent will having a family influence student perceptions of their work future? The examples given earlier of the influences that students cited were all for women students. Their responses to the question, Will having a family make a difference in your plans for work? evoked these responses:

Occupation Stewardness: Yes, when you work as a stewardess they only allow time off to have one child. (I) will leave about 30 to have a family.

Occupation Court Lawyer: Yes, that's why I want to wait till 26, because when the children are small I definitely want to stay home. When I'm 35 I want to go back to work.

Occupation Doctor: Yes, I would have to stop work, raise family, and then go into private practice.

Occupation Lawyer: Yes, I feel a parent should devote most of her time to her children.

Occupation Secretary: Yes. If I don't have a decent job in terms of money, I won't be able to keep working. I'll have to be with them.

Other students gave responses such as, Yes, career and children will be pulling at each other; sometimes I'll have to stay home because of the children. Yes, You'd have to quit job. Yes, only when they're small. Yes, I would probably stop working. Yes, (my) place is at home with children. Yes, if husband objects to job. I'm scared it will. Once you have kids I might have to stop; I was brought up fine with both parents working, but I don't know if I can do that. Yes, I'll stay home after I have kids, till they're about 10 because I want to have them grow up with me, not someone else. Yes, when they're young I wouldn't want to work full-time or then, of course, my husband could take care of them.

We can anticipate sex differences in student responses to work plans, and these are examined next.

Work Decisions

Because the work decisions of women are influenced by family plans, the first questions were about marriage, children, and a career versus job, or level of commitment, pattern. Another series of questions examined specific work decisions, such as working hours, work continuity, combining work and family, and decisions that students would expect their spouses to make on these same questions. Throughout these work decisions, responses were examined for any group differences.

MARRIAGE, FAMILY, AND WORK PATTERNS

The responses of young women students to the influence of family on their work plans indicates the importance of marriage and family plans. To what extent do these urban students plan to marry and have children? Students were asked these questions directly.

Almost all students responded they would like to get married. A second question asking, Will you marry? was included toward the end of the interview, and 563 students (94%) responded yes. Only 32 (5%) said no.

TABLE 5.6   Number and Percentage for Children Desired
             and Children in Students' Own Families

No. of Children	No. of Children Would Like[1]		No. of Children in family	
	F	%	F	%
1	16	2.8	51	8.6
2	257	46.4	175	29.4
3	157	28.3	166	27.9
4	89	16.1	93	15.6
5	20	3.6	47	7.9
6	10	1.8	31	5.2
7	–	–	17	2.9
8	1	0.2	8	1.3
9+	4	0.7	8	1.3
	N=554		N=594	

[1] Seven students stated 0 children.

About 92% (551) said they planned to have children. Only 45 (7.5%) said they did not plan to have children.

The responses to the question on the number of children desired ranged from 0 to 9+. Table 5.6 presents the number and percents for children desired and the number of children in the students' families. The mean number of children desired was 2.8 (SD of 1.2) and the mean for their own families was 3.3 (SD of 1.7). The correlations for these two variables are not significantly different from zero (r total sample = .071; r females only = .067; r males only = .080).

A three-way ANOVA for the number of children desired shows only the sex main effect is significant, $F_{1,549} = 9.77$, pr $> F = 0019$. The mean number of children desired by females in this sample was 2.94 (SD = 1.3, N = 271) and for males the mean number of children desired was 2.63 (SD = 1.1, N = 283). There were no significant interactions, indicating that the only reliable group difference on the variable of number of children was that female students desired, on the average, more children than did male students.

The effect of having a family upon plans for work has been illustrated earlier. The responses to the question, Will having a family make a difference in your plans for work? were classified as Yes, No, or Uncertain. For the total sample 229 students (38.2%) said having a family will make a difference in their plans for work. Slightly over half, 316 students (53%),

TABLE 5.7   Number and Percentage Responding *Yes*, Family
Will Make a Difference in Work Plans

SES	White		Black		Hispanic		Total	
	N	%	N	%	N	%	N	%
Middle								
Female	29	30.2	14	29.2	27	31.8	70	30.6
Male	15	15.6	6	12.5	13	15.3	34	14.8
Low								
Female	33	34.4	15	31.2	24	28.2	72	31.4
Male	19	19.8	13	27.1	21	24.7	53	23.1
Total	96	100	48	100	85	100	229	100

said no, it would not make a difference, and 31 (5%) were uncertain (24,
4%, did not respond). Of the 287 female students responding to this
question, about half (50%) stated yes, a family would make a difference;
123 (43%) said no, and 7% said they were uncertain. This figure can be
compared with data from the Herzog et al. (1980) sample of high school
seniors. In a question on the "traditional" arrangement (husband employed full-time and wife not employed), fully 40% of the females felt
they could not accept this arrangement (but only 15% of males could not).
Examples of the "no" responses by the females in our sample give some of
the reasons why the traditional arrangement is not perceived as acceptable
(see below). For the 289 male students responding, 87 or 30% said yes, a
family would make a difference, 192 (66%) said no, and 10 (3%) were
uncertain. ($\chi^2_2 = 35.59$, p = .000 for sex and responses to this question.)
Table 5.7 gives the data for the 12 groups on the yes, family will make a
difference in work plans, response.

Although more females than males said the family would make a
difference, the difference is not as large as might have been expected. Part
of the paradox is in the reason given for the yes response. By far the
majority of males stated that having a family would make a difference
because they would have to work harder, become a steady provider for the
family, or similar reasons. Examples of the responses for males who said
Yes, or No to this question include:

Yes, I would have to take care of kids and not have as much time to
study for career.
Yes, if I'm away from home it would spoil family relation. I wouldn't
want to be away.
Yes, you have to spend time with family.

Yes. Have to share money with family, increased responsibility.
Yes. Have to work harder.
Slightly, I would try to devote more time to my family.
No, because I am out making a living to support my family.
No. Plan to be in upper income bracket, will be able to support them.
No. Have to get a job anyway, my hope is it will support the family.
No. Be working anyhow.

Examples of the reasons females gave for saying no show varying degrees of awareness of the options and realities for women who try to combine work and family and of the satisfactions of work:

No. Occupation is for yourself.
No. Have a babysitter and won't have children till 25.
No. (I) should have a career in case (my) husband wants to leave I can support myself, be independent.
No. I don't want it to make a difference; I want to have as much freedom as my husband.
No. I figure today the way the money situation is both parents have to work if you want to live well. You're very lucky to stay home if husband earns enough.
No. Children will stay with relatives.
No. I would still like to work—wouldn't want to stay home all the time.
No. I think I can manage both together.
No. (I) was able to take care of myself as a child; my children could do the same.
No. Because my husband and I will split the responsibility.
No. Not much conflict; can just stop for short time when pregnant.

The females who responded *yes* gave as the reasons why that they might have to stay out of the work force until their children could go to school or attend an organized child care group, and that they might have to work part-time. Taken in these contexts, the *yes* responses mean very different effects for female and male students.

Table 5.7 also shows that fewer blacks said having a family would make a difference in their plans for work. (χ^2_4 = 25.71, p = .000 for ethnic group and question responses.) These ethnic differences agree with other research literature, particularly the commitment of black women to education, work, and family. Student responses did not differ significantly for the two SES groups.

The next question was concerned with the work patterns students anticipated for themselves as part of establishing the level of work commitment for students. This question consisted of a rank order and rating task using five cards. The five cards described combinations of career versus

TABLE 5.8   Descriptions on Work Pattern Cards

A. *Full-time career*—Some people get a great deal of satisfaction out of their work. They enjoy working and would work even if they didn't have to. They work full time through most of their lives. They may take a few years off while their children are young, but then they return to their career.

B. *Part-time career*—Some people enjoy working and get personal satisfaction from their work, but they don't like to work full time. These people have careers like substitute teacher, artist or writer or the kind of work they can do at home. This type of work gives them a lot of extra time which they may spend with their children or on hobbies.

C. *Full-time job*—Some people work mostly so they can earn money. These people work full time most of their lives to support themselves and their families. They may take a few years off when their children are young, but then they return to their full-time job.

D. *Part-time job*—Some people work most of their lives at part-time jobs. This way they can earn some money but still have a lot of time left for other things—like hobbies or raising their children.

E. *Not working*—Some people choose not to work. They prefer to do other things with their time. They may spend time with friends, take care of their families, or follow a special interest. These people feel that other things are more important to them than working.

job, full-time versus part-time, and not working as the last pattern. Table 5.8 presents the descriptions on the cards. The rankings were coded from 1 (high) to 5 (low). The ratings were given on a scale from 0, I would dislike this very much, to 8, I would like this very much. These ratings were transformed to a mean of 50 and a SD of 10 *within* each rater in order to adjust for different raters using different parts of the rating scale.

The highest ranks were given to full-time career, part-time career, and full-time job, in that order. Not working was the least-preferred pattern. The orders of the mean ranks are very similar across groups, with the exception of the mean ranking given the pattern, part-time job. The female and white groups tended to rank part-time job as more desirable than full-time job, in contrast to the other main groups. The standardized ratings offer more information on the change in the average ranks.

Three-way ANOVAs were computed for each of the five work patterns using the standardized ratings (M = 50, SD = 10 within rater). The sex main effect was significant (p = .05 or less) for four of the five patterns (all except part-time job, where the two-way interaction of ethnic and SES groups was significant). The ethnic main effect was significant for the full-time career and not working patterns, and all three main effects plus one interaction were significant for the full-time job pattern.

The means for full-time career pattern show that the male students rated this pattern higher than did the women (61.7 and 60.3, respectively, with SD's of 7.9 and 8.9). The means for the ethnic groups show that the Hispanic and black students rated this pattern higher than the white students (means of 61.9, 61.7, and 59.4, respectively, with SDs of 7.5, 7.2, and 10.1).

The pattern of part-time career received higher mean ratings from female students (mean = 56.7, SD = 6.9) than from male students (mean = 54.7, SD = 7.6). The full-time job pattern showed all main effects and one interaction were significant. Males rated a full-time job higher than females (50.8 and 48.3); black and Hispanic students rated this pattern higher than white students (means of 51.5, 49.6, and 47.5); and low-SES students rated this pattern higher than middle-SES students (50.6 and 48.4, respectively). The interaction of sex and ethnic groups for full-time job can be seen in the means below:

		Ethnic	
Sex	White	Black	Hispanic
Female	44.8	50.4	49.7
Male	50.2	52.6	49.5

Although white females gave a lower rating to full-time job than did black and Hispanic females, Hispanic and white males gave the lower ratings to this work pattern.

The significant interaction for part-time job was for SES and ethnic groups. The means were:

		Ethnic	
SES	White	Black	Hispanic
Middle	47.9	46.9	49.1
Low	49.4	48.5	47.0

For middle-SES students, part-time job was rated highest by Hispanic students and lowest by black students. For low-SES students, white and black students gave higher ratings than the Hispanic students.

For the pattern not working the significant sex and ethnic main effects were due to female students rating this pattern higher or as more desirable than male students (means of 36.3 and 35.0, respectively) and to white students rating this pattern higher than Hispanic and black students (means of 38.0, 35.2, and 33.6, respectively). But it was the least preferred of all the patterns for all groups.

Overall, the mean ratings show that the fairly consistent sex differences occur because the female students are likely to rate part-time career or not working higher than male students. Both the black and Hispanic students rate full-time work higher and not working lower than white students.

The questions on marriage, family, and work patterns show some differences among the groups in the study. Sex differences in number of children desired showed that women wanted a slightly greater number of children than men (2.94 to 2.63) and women anticipated a greater effect on their work plans from having children than did men. What is most noticeable, however, is that about 40% of the female students said that having a family would *not* influence their plans for work. The reasons given for this response show that at least some proportion of those responding *no* are aware of divorce statistics, the economy, and the intrinsic satisfaction that can come from work. Rankings of work patterns tend to be similar across groups but a comparison of ratings shows that the traditional pattern of sex differences in preferences—females preferred part-time work or lower work commitment—can still be found looking at the sample as a whole. These differences also reflect the views of the 50% of the girls who stated that Yes, having a family would affect their plans for work.

SELF AND FUTURE SPOUSE WORK DECISIONS

Beginning with a lead-in question, Will you work? students responded to a series of seven questions about their work decisions after school. In all but two cases, students stated they would work for pay after completing school.[2]

What will your working hours be? Half of the students, 304 or 51%, stated they expected to work full-time. The other 50% was divided between those expecting to work "Mostly full time" (31%), those expecting to work "Sometimes full time, sometimes part time" (14%), and 4% expecting to work "Mostly part time (less than 20 hours per week)."

The responses for full-time work hours show little difference among the ethnic or SES groups. The major differences are between females and males, with females giving consistently fewer expectations for full-time working hours, regardless of ethnic group or SES status. ($\chi^2_3 = 45.71$, p = .000 for sex and categories 1-4; χ^2 for ethnic and SES groups are not significant.) For females, 73% expected to do mostly or all full-time work; for males the corresponding figure was 90%.

What will your work continuity (pattern) be? A large majority said they would expect to work either "continuously" (256 or 43.1%) or "mostly continuously (short interruptions)" (273 or 46.0%). Another 54 (9.1%) students stated they expect to work "off and on, stopping for periods of one year or more." Only 11 students (1.9%) expected to work "Briefly, less than four years altogether."

A three-way ANOVA showed significant F values for sex ($F_{1,582}$ = 79.98, pr $> F$ = .0001) and for ethnic group ($F_{2,582}$ = 4.81, pr $> F$ = .0085). More males than females expected to work continuously, as shown by means of 1.46 and 1.94, respectively (where continuously was coded "1" and mostly continuously as "2," and Off and on was coded "3" and Briefly as "4"). Consistent with other data on this sample, black students had means indicating they expected to work more continuously than Hispanic or white students (means of 1.6, 1.7, and 1.8, respectively).

Will you change your work often? This question asked whether students would work in one field through their working lives, or vary this pattern. A majority of students (60%) felt they would start in one field, and remain in this field through their working lives. The second largest category was the 30% of students who stated they were likely to start in one field, and change to a new field at some time. The remaining 10% planned to try a variety of different jobs, not all in one field. The chi-squares for sex, ethnic, and SES groups were not significant.

How will you combine work and family? The question had two parts: The first part had three categories that asked for a general pattern about work and marriage/children. Slightly over half the students (343 or 57.2%) said they expected to "work continuously regardless of marriage/children." Another 11 students (2%) stated they intended to work before marriage only, and 232 (39%) intended to work before children. Of those intending to work continuously, 63 (18%) were females, and the remainder were males (χ_2^2 = 327.66, p = .000). There were no differences in this continuous work category between middle- and low-SES students, and only slight differences for ethnic groups: 127 black students as compared to 112 Hispanic and 104 white students expected to work continuously (χ^2 for ethnic groups and three response categories had p = .0721).

The second part of the question examined when students would work in relation to the ages of their children. The percentages for this question are based only on responses for those 232 girls who said they intended to work after having children. Table 5.9 shows the frequencies for work in relation to age of children. Of the 232 female students, only 15 (6.5%)

TABLE 5.9   Frequency of 232 Female Responses to
Combinations of Work and family

Work when children are:	White N	%	Black N	%	Hispanic N	%	All Female Responses N	%
1 1-3 years	2	2	10	14	3	4	15	6.5
2 3-5 years	24	29	32	45	30	38	86	37.1
3 5-12 years	40	49	22	31	36	45	98	42.2
4 12+ years	16	20	7	10	10	13	33	14.2
Total	82	100%	71	100%	79	100%	232	100%

expect to work when their children are 1-3 years old. However, 79% expect to work when the children are between 3 and 12 years old. A chi square for the female students in the three ethnic groups was significant (χ_8^2 = 18.37, p = .0186). More black females indicated an intention to return to work when children are younger.

The χ^2 for SES groups had a p = .0569, and the trend was for more middle-SES students to plan a return to work when children were 3-5 years old (43% vs. 30%).

After students answered the set of work decisions for themselves, they were asked to answer the same set of questions for their future spouses—to say what decisions their spouses would make for work and school.

What level of education will your spouse have? Overall, 73.2% of the students thought their spouse would have a college education and 6.5% (39) students predicted they would have noncollege further education. The remainder (19.3%) stated their spouse would have a high school education only.

Table 5.10 shows the number and percentage in each type of education decision for the main sample groups. More females than males thought their spouse would have a college education (78% vs. 70%). Or, stated for the male students, male students did not expect as many of their future wives to have a college education as did female students for future husbands (χ^2_2 = 5.83, p = .0543). In this sample more of the black students expected their spouses to have a college education. (χ^2_4 = 10.68, p = .0304, for ethnic group and response categories.) And, more of the middle-SES students expected their spouses to have a college education (χ^2_2 = 28.82, p = .0000).

Will he/she work? A majority of students stated their spouses would work, 563 or 94%. Only 10 (1.7%) said their spouses would not work and 22 (4%) stated their spouses would be a homemaker.

What will the working hours be? The distribution of responses was more variable for this question than for the earlier question asking for the

TABLE 5.10   Number and Percentage of Expected
Education Decisions for Spouses

Group	High School		Non College Further Education		College Education		Total	
	N	%	N	%	N	%	N	%
Sex								
Female	47	16	18	6	232	78	297	100
Male	69	23	21	7	207	70	297	100
Ethnic								
White	51	26	13	6	136	68	200	100
Black	27	14	10	5	159	81	196	100
Hispanic	38	19	16	8	144	73	198	100
SES								
Middle	34	12	15	5	247	83	296	100
Low	82	28	24	8	192	64	298	100

student's own working hours. More students selected categories other than "full time" or "mostly full time" for their spouses working hours. For example, in Table 5.11 39% (of those responding to one of the four patterns) predicted that their spouses would work mostly part-time (less than 20 hours per week). All were male students estimating what their spouses' work hours will be.

Of the 248 (44%) students who thought their spouses would work full-time, 224 were female responses. Only a small number of male students (24 or 9%) estimated that their wives would work full-time. These predictions by boys are very discrepant from the girls' predictions of their own working hours.

What will the work pattern be? The work patterns predicted for spouses varied according to the sex of the respondent. A three-way ANOVA for the four main work patterns showed the main effects for sex, ethnic, and SES groups were significant: Sex—$F_{1,562}$ = 497.04, pr > F = .0001; Ethnic—$F_{2,562}$ = 3.11, pr > F = .0452; and SES—$F_{1,562}$ = 3.64, pr > F = .0571. The means for the sex, ethnic, and SES groups were (the lower the value, the more continuous the predicted work pattern):

	$\overline{X}$		$\overline{X}$		$\overline{X}$
Female	1.37	White	2.01	Middle	1.90
Male	1.55	Black	1.88	Low	1.98
		Hispanic	1.92		

TABLE 5.11   Spouse Working Hours Predicted by
            Female and Male Students

Code		Female		Male	
		N	%	N	%
1	Full time	224	74.9	24	9.0
2	Mostly Full Time	60	20.1	54	20.2
3	Mostly Part Time	–	–	105	39.3
4	Sometimes Full Time Sometimes Part Time	15	5.0	84	31.5
	Total	299	100	267	100

The means for the SES groups show, for example, that low-SES students predicted a less continuous work pattern for their spouses than did the middle-SES group.

Following the trends of the other questions in these work decisions for spouses, 94% of the males thought their wives would work *less* than continuously, whereas 98% of the females stated their husbands would work either continuously or mostly continuously. About 41% of the males did predict, however, that their wives would work "Mostly continuously (short interruptions)." Forty-three percent of the males predicted their wives would work "off and on, stopping work for periods of one year or more," and only 9% predicted "Briefly, less than four years altogether."

Will there be work changes? Table 5.12 shows both the predicted responses for self and for spouse in terms of occupational stability. Chi-square for the responses for spouses' decisions was 24.40 (p = .0000). Fewer females than males thought their spouses would try a variety of jobs, not all in one field. Males predicted less job stability or more changes for their spouses than they did for themselves, whereas the female students predicted about the same amounts (category 3).

The responses for ethnic groups did not differ significantly, but those for SES groups did (χ^2_2 = 7.49, p = .024). Fewer low-SES students predicted highly stable work patterns for their spouses than did middle SES students (44% vs. 57% for category 3).

How will work and family be combined? The responses to this question are coded in two sections. Chi-squares for the main factors showed only the sex groups differed significantly (χ^2_1 = 361.01, p = .0000) when responses, continuous work and work before children and before marriage, are compared. Of more interest, however, is the comparison between the female responses for themselves and the male responses for their spouses.

TABLE 5.12 Number and Percentage of Responses by Sex to Alternative Work Changes for Spouses

| | Females | | | | Males | | | | Total | | | |
	Spouse N	%	Self N	%	Spouse N	%	Self N	%	Spouse N	%	Self N	%
1 Try a variety of different jobs, not all in one field	41	14.2	28	9.7	83	31.5	30	10.2	124	22.5	58	10.0
2 Start in one field, change to a new field sometime	85	29.4	93	32.3	68	25.9	80	27.2	153	27.7	173	29.7
3 Start in one field, remain in this throughout working life	163	56.4	167	58.0	112	42.6	184	62.6	275	49.8	351	60.3
Total	298	100	288	100	263	100	294	100	552	100	582	100

TABLE 5.13   Predicted Combinations of Work and Family for Female
Students (Self) and for Male Students (for Spouses)

Code	Response	Females-Self F	%	Males for Spouses F	%
1	work continuously regardless of marriage/children	63	21.6	32	12
2	work before marriage only	11	3.8	16	6
3	woik before children	218	74.7	218	82
	Total	292	100	266	100
1	work when children are 1-3 yrs. old	15	6.5	15	6.8
2	work when children are 3-5 yrs. old (and not before)	86	37.1	69	31.1
3	work when children are 5-12 yrs. old (and not before)	98	42.2	88	39.6
4	work when children are over 12 yrs. old (and not before)	33	14.2	50	22.5
	Total	232	100	222	100

Table 5.13 presents the responses of females to these questions for
themselves (question 52.5) and for males giving responses for their spouses
(question 53.6). There is a tendency for fewer males to expect their wives
to work continuously than do females (12% vs. 22%).

The second half of Table 5.13 presents the responses on timing of work
and age of children. Few females and males expect women to work when
the children are ages 1 to 3 (about 7% in each group), and the general
trend is for the males to predict a more delayed return to work for their
spouses than the females predicted for themselves.

Student plans can be compared also to the responses of all students to
the same questions about when their mothers worked. Thirty-five percent
of the students reported that their mothers worked while the youngest
child (in their family) was 1-3 years old. The percentage rose to 42%, while
the youngest child was in day care/nursery school, and to 62% while the
youngest was in elementary school. Thus, the realities of the mother's
work patterns are not reflected in the expectations of these eleventh
graders, both females and males.

The questions on work decisions continue to show differences between
boys and girls in their work continuity, hours of work, and combining

work and family. The other major finding arising from this series of questions is the disparity between the expectations males have for their future wives' decisions and the decisions the females expect to make for themselves. The males do not expect as continuous a work pattern as females generally predict, nor as much full-time work as the girls predict. Males also predict that their spouses will have more different jobs, about three times the proportion that girls predict for themselves. There is also a general trend for males to predict a longer time at home with children for females than females predict for themselves. In these series of questions, the girls are in greater agreement with current trends in labor force participation than are the boys' expectations for their future wives. Because there are these differences, many of them contingent on the bearing of children, it is of concern to examine the extent to which students talk to others about their plans in the marriage and family areas, as well as in the occupational area.

Who Do Students Talk to About Their Plans?

The last series of questions reported in this chapter are concerned with the persons students talk to about their educational, occupational, marriage and parenthood plans for the future and adult role models (admired or liked adults). Students were asked, Who do you talk to about your occupational plans? educational plans? and marriage and family plans?

The open-ended responses to these questions were coded into 10 categories, as shown in Table 5.14. For the total sample of 600 students the largest percentage of responses for both occupational and educational plans was for the "other/combination" of persons. This typically meant students talked to parents, other family members, and friends about their occupational and educational plans. There were few students who said they did not talk to anybody about these plans. The response, however, to the question of marriage and family plans was different: fully one-third of the students said they did not talk to anybody about marriage or family plans. The person to whom a student talked most frequently was a friend their own age or, again, a combination of persons in their lives.

There are some differences in persons talked to according to the main sample groups. Appendix 2 presents the data for frequency and percentages for occupational, educational, and marriage and family plans.

For discussions about occupational plans more daughters reported talking to their mothers than did sons, and for SES groups, more low-SES students (11%) report they do not talk to anybody about their occupational plans. For educational plans there are no significant sex differences and again 10% of the low-SES students reported talking to "nobody"

TABLE 5.14   Frequency and Percentages for Persons to Whom Students
            Talk About Their Plans

Category	Occupational Plans		Educational Plans		Marriage and Family Plans	
	F	%	F	%	F	%
Father (& foster)	30	5.0	33	5.5	8	1.3
Mother (& foster)	86	14.3	118	19.7	92	15.3
Parents, family	92	15.3	153	25.5	64	10.7
Sibling	21	3.5	19	3.2	17	2.8
Other relative	15	2.5	10	1.7	9	1.5
Friend own age	35	5.8	22	3.7	105	17.5
Myself	-	-	-	0.2	6	1.0
Professional	29	4.8	27	4.5	-	-
Other/Combination	240	40.0	174	29.0	102	17.0
Nobody	52	8.7	43	7.2	197	32.8

about educational plans. (χ^2 for SES groups is not significant at $p < .05$.)
For marriage and family plans, however, from 22% to 44% of each of the
major sample groups report they do not talk to anyone. Twice as many
boys (44%) report they don't talk to anyone as girls (22%).

The scope of the student's perspectives on planning for further education and major adult roles seems narrow when the 10 categories are
examined. Immediate family, relatives, and peers cannot represent to
students all the occupations and ways of combining work and family. Few
professionals or other, nonrelated adults are available for talking about
plans. This conclusion was reinforced by the response of students to the
study interview. Many would have welcomed the opportunity for further
talk. Career education interventions cannot be narrowly focused on only
one adult role.

Who Are Students' Role Models?

A series of questions were asked about an adult the student admired:
What adult do you know personally who is living a life you would like to
have? What do you like or admire most about (name of this person)? How
would you like to be like them?

These questions were intended to examine whether the student had a
role model, whether the role model was the same sex or opposite sex, what

aspect of the person the student wanted to emulate, and the relationship of the role model to the student. In the pilot study this question had been asked generally, What adult is living a life you would like to have? But this question elicited responses of popular singers or prominent sport figures, about whom students had little information, or elicited the response, *no one*. Earlier studies by Oberle (1974) and Oberle, Stowers, and Falk (1978) had examined role-model preferences of black students, based on the concept of a role model as a more limited identification with an individual (as opposed to a reference individual) in only one or a selected few of the individuals' roles. We were particularly concerned with *what* about the individual was liked or admired in terms of the possible adult roles of worker, parent, and marriage partner.

The question was modified to ask about an adult the student *knew personally* whom they liked or admired. This modification improved the amount of information students knew about the adult model and reduced, but did not eliminate, the *no one* response. The *no one* response was often accompanied by the explanation that the student was different from any adult the student knew and was independent of the adults the student knew. Almost a third of the sample (32%) did not identify an adult whom they admired.[3] The analyses that follow are based on the 410 students who did name an adult role model, someone whom the student admired or liked with respect to at least some aspect of their lives as adults.

The sex of the adult was coded according to whether it was the same as the student or the opposite sex to the student. Of the 396 students who clearly identified the adult, 84% liked or admired an adult of the same sex; only 65 students (16%) named an adult of the opposite sex. There were slightly more females who identified adult models of the opposite sex (22% of female models were adult males and 11% of male models were adult females).

The aspect of the adult life the student wanted to emulate was coded for whether the student mentioned the work or family pattern of the adult, or aspects of the person's personality (e.g., the person was thoughtful of others, well-liked, confident, handled life easily, or had a good sense of humor). Another set of categories was used if the student mentioned more than one aspect of adult life.

The percentages of students mentioning only one aspect of the adult's life were: personality (104 or 25%); work pattern (65 or 16%); and family pattern (16 or 4%). Combining each aspect of the adult life with at least one other resulted in the following percents: Work pattern, 49%; Family pattern, 24%; and Personality, 54%. Somewhat more females than males identified an aspect of the family pattern (21% vs. 9%). The main aspects of adult life cited alone or in combination with another part were the adult's personality and work pattern (i.e., some part of the person's working life). Aspects of family life were not cited as often by eleventh-grade students. A major part of the satisfactions many persons experience as adults through marriage and family are not mentioned as frequently as work or personality characteristics.

The relationship of the adult model to the student was also coded. Of the 410 who responded, 271 (66%) identified someone related to them. The highest frequency was the 150 students (36.6%) who identified a relative other than father, mother, grandparent, or sibling. The adult identified was the father for 9.8% of the students, the mother for 7.6%, a grandparent for 2.4%, and a sibling for 9.8%. An older friend was identified as the most admired adult for 16.3% of the students and a professional (typically a teacher or doctor known to the family) for 5.6%. Twelve percent of the boys stated their fathers and 9% of the females stated their mothers were the most admired adult. (Some of these percents are similar to those found by Oberle et al., 1978, but the difference in our study of eliminating glamour figures precludes direct comparisons.)

As indicated above, students varied in the aspect of adult life they focused on in describing an admired adult. Samples of these categories are given below, first for girls and then for boys.

Aunt, aged 57. The girl admires her family life; her husband works and she takes care of kids; she takes them back and forth to school and takes care of them. Admires the way she takes care of her kids and manages with her husband and housework.

Brother's girlfriend, aged 26. She is getting a Master's in art education.

Aunt. She went to Germany with job, is social worker. Admires her warmth, patience, tolerance of others. This girl would like to have her (Aunt's) qualities.

Mother. She knows how to comfort and listen to problems. She helps me in that way.

Father (45-50). (He) treats us all fair; has eight kids, and takes time and money for his kids. I hope to be able to cope with a family the way he does.

Father. (He's) smart, he knows how to handle situations. (Admires) his personality, leadership, ability.

Uncle. He has a job teaching, speaks Spanish; (I) would like to teach what he knows.

Employer. He owns nine stores, doesn't work hard, makes a lot of money and he travels a lot.

In summary, these eleventh-grade students typically named an adult role model of the same sex, named a relative in the immediate or close family, and focused on the personality or work aspects of the adult. Almost a third, however, of the students did not identify an admired or liked adult role model in the interview setting. The focus on personality and work patterns may reflect the immediacy of these aspects of adolescent development. The lack of focus on family patterns again may reflect the lack of discussion and examination of alternative choices for these parts of adult life that will particularly affect women's career and employment planning. In the next chapter the occupational, marriage, and parenthood values are presented. The characteristics of student responses to the values and their relationships to education and occupational decisions are examined.

NOTES

1. The correlation is negative because the scale of class standing used a lower value for higher standing.

2. "School" could be either high school or college.

3. The *no* responses were distributed approximately equally between males and females, the three ethnic groups, and the two SES groups.

Chapter 6

ADOLESCENT VALUES:
Job and Family

An important part of psychological theories of occupational choice has been the concept of *values*. The idea of values is not as explicitly considered in sociological and economic theory of occupational choice or labor market participation, but enters implicitly through such concepts as "significant others" in the Wisconsin model of status attainment and the vocabulary of "tastes" and "preferences" in economic theory. By contrast, the explicit consideration of values in psychological theory offers the advantage of presenting descriptions of these values to those in the process of making life choices so that it may be possible for the individual to become aware of values. As Katz (1966) has described the function and importance of defining individual values, the individual needs to ask, in addition to *What are my values?* such questions as *Where have my values come from?* and then the individual is better prepared to ask, *Where are they taking me?*

Because occupational values had been developed for use in the career choice process by college students (e.g., Katz, 1973), and because career theories had been criticized for their lack of attention to women's sex-role socialization and work patterns, the development of the marriage and parenthood values as described in Chapter 3 was undertaken. Past research on the needs or satisfactions that individuals experience in marriage and parenthood has been very limited, as was reviewed in Chapter 2. Yet informal articles attest to the need for defining and clarifying these values. For example, a survey by a magazine called *Medical/Mrs.* had more than 1,000 replies to a questionnaire entitled, "A doctor's wife: The myth vs. the reality" (Bennetts, 1979). According to Bennetts,

> For many it was the American dream, female version: marry a nice young doctor and live happily and prosperously ever after, while he does noble work and she devotes herself to him, his career and his children. . . .
>
> What the doctors' wives expected, they said, was prestige, secuity, happiness, pride and the satisfaction of performing as loyal helpmate to a man of service. What many of them got instead was disappointment. (p. B10)

In the expectations of these wives are values in the occupational, marriage, and parenthood domains. The expectation that all these values would be satisfied through one domain, marriage, is unrealistic. Thus there is a need for defining and separating the values into their respective domains, and examining the extent to which they are perceived as separate or overlapping.

The marriage and parenthood values in the present research are a first effort at defining and examining the characteristics of responses to these values. In the first part of this chapter the distributions of rankings and ratings given the values are examined, because the rationale for the values is that there is no single value or value description that will be ranked as most important by every person. This rationale was the basis of the development of the occupational values (Katz, 1966, 1973), and was fundamental to the development of the values in the pilot studies for the present study. Unless a heterogeneous group of individuals endorses different values as most important to them in their decision making for occupations, marriage, or parenthood, the values will not represent the diversity of human needs and satisfactions that are proposed by most psychological theories (e.g., Maslow, 1954; Rokeach, 1973). The values also would be less useful in applications such as the computerized interactive guidance system SIGI and would hold less potential for counseling students to clarify and understand their own values.

Katz (1966) has discussed the influence of parents, church, peers, socioeconomic status, and other variables as influencing the development of occupational values. These same sources influence the norms and behaviors of sex roles. For this reason, the analyses in this chapter also examine the relationship of the values to student status on the three main factors of the study design, sex, ethnic, or sociocultural group membership, and socioeconomic status (SES). To the extent possible, the relationship found for the present sample can be compared to those found in other studies (e.g., Norris, Katz, & Chapman, 1978), at least for the occupational values.

The first sections of the analyses of the values are therefore concerned with the distributions of rankings and ratings for the total sample of 600 eleventh graders, and with the similarity or difference in responses of students when classified as members of sex, ethnic, and SES groups. These analyses are presented first for the occupational values and then for the marriage and parenthood values developed in this study. The next section examines the interrelationship of the three value sets by means of factor analyses for the total sample, females and males.

After examining the values and their interrelationships, the relationship of the values to educational and occupational decisions (aspirations) is studied by means of discriminant function analyses. That is, to what extent are groups formed by level of educational or occupational aspiration predicted or identified by their occupational, marriage, or parenthood values?

Individual and Group Responses to the Values

OCCUPATIONAL VALUES

The 10 occupational values that were rank ordered and rated by students were: High Income, Prestige, Independence, Helping Others, Security, Variety, Leadership, Interest Field, Leisure, and Early Entry (Katz, 1973). As mentioned earlier, an important criterion for the values is their ability to evoke different rankings and ratings of importance from respondents. That is, not all respondents should place the same value term as most or least important. Although this criterion is already well demonstrated for the occupational values, it is useful to examine the distributions of rank orders and ratings for them again here, particularly because they have served as a model for the development of the marriage and parenthood values.

The number and percentage of students assigning ranks from 1 (high) to 10 (low) to each value in order of their importance to the student's choice of an occupation are presented in Appendix 3.1. An examination of the second column for each value, the percentage column, shows fairly rectangular distributions across the rank order numbers. For example, the distribution for the value High Income, ranges from a low of 6.5% to

12.5%, with seven of the ranks having a percentage of 9.5-12.5. This distribution is consistent for the values, with the exceptions of Field of Interest and Early Entry. Field of Interest was given high ranks (1 or 2) by about half of the sample. And, consistent with the high level of educational aspirations for this sample, Early Entry received the lowest rank of 10 from half of the sample. It should be noted, however, that even for Early Entry each rank order was used: Eight students ranked Early Entry as most important to them in choosing an occupation.

Similar data are found for the ratings in Appendix 3.2. Ratings could range from 0, not important at all, to 8 greatly important. The distributions of ratings tend to have smaller standard deviations than the ranks (which forced students to spread out the numbers given to values).

The occupational values ranked and rated highest or most important and least important are the same, when the means are used to identify these values. There is only a change in order in the ranks and ratings:

Ranks Most Important	Ratings Most Important	Ranks Least Important	Ratings Least Important
Field of Interest	Field of Interest	Early Entry	Early Entry
Helping Others	Security	Leisure	Leadership
Security	Helping Others	Leadership	Leisure

For the eleventh-grade students, the most important value to think about in choosing an occupation was that it was in their field of interest (e.g., science, art, verbal, and so on). The least important was Early Entry, defined as starting work right away, rather than spending time, effort and money for more education. These most and least important values are for all 600 students. The data were also examined for differences among the main groups in the sample.

A multivariate analysis of variance using the main factors of sex, ethnic group, and SES and the 10 occupational values as dependent variables was run on the ratings that students assigned to the 10 values. Significant main effects were found for sex, ethnic, and SES groups (Wilks Criterion):

Sex: $F_{10,579} = 7.36$ pr $> F = .0001$
Ethnic: $F_{20,1158} = 2.18$ pr $> F = .0020$
SES: $F_{10,579} = 3.06$ pr $> F = .0008$

No significant two-way (or three-way) interactions were found. Further analyses examined the univariate ANOVA for each occupational value and were computed using transformed (standardized) ratings. The ratings for each individual were transformed to standard scores, with a mean of 50 and a standard deviation of 10 (a mean and standard deviation were computed for each individual using the ten ratings, and used for the linear standard score transformation).

Six main effects were significant for six values: High Income, Helping Others, Variety, Leadership, Field of Interest, and Leisure.

Value	F Value (1,588)	Probability of Larger F
High Income	22.91	.0001
Helping Others	33.51	.0001
Variety	13.53	.0003
Leadership	21.69	.0001
Field of Interest	6.11	.0137
Leisure	6.16	.0133

The frequency distribution for ranks, and the mean and standard deviations for the ranks and the transformed ratings are presented for females and males in Appendix 3.3. Males gave higher ratings to High Income (mean of 52.8 vs. 49.1), Leadership (mean of 47.5 to 43.5), and Leisure (48.2 vs. 46.5). Female students gave higher ratings to Helping Others (55.8 vs. 51.1), Variety (mean of 51.4 vs. 48.5), and Field of Interest (60.7 vs. 59.0).

These sex differences can be compared with the sex differences in ratings found by Norris, Katz, and Chapman (1978) for a sample of 433 System of Interactive Guidance and Information (SIGI) users in six college settings. For purposes of comparison here, the untransformed ratings are compared with their unrestricted or initial ratings for the youngest of the three age groups they had in their sample. (The youngest age group was 18 and under and had 94 females and 46 males.) These data are given in Table 6.1.

For the Norris, Katz, and Chapman total sample, sex differences were found for six occupational values. Males gave higher mean ratings than females to High Income, Independence, and Leadership. Females gave higher ratings to Helping Others, Field of Interest, and Early Entry.

TABLE 6.1   Means and Standard Deviations of Occupational Ratings
Compared to Norris, Katz, and Chapman Sample

Occupational Value	Norris et al. Sample (18 and under)[1]				11th-grade Students (16-17 years old)[2]			
	F		M		F		M	
	M	SD	M	SD	M	SD	M	SD
High Income	5.42	1.50	6.17	1.26	4.60	2.16	5.48	2.03
Prestige	4.88	1.79	5.11	1.66	4.79	2.03	5.01	1.96
Independence	5.50	1.67	5.48	1.54	5.11	1.99	5.34	1.83
Helping Others	5.59	2.00	4.26	1.81	5.97	1.78	5.27	1.91
Security	6.13	1.63	6.52	1.54	5.72	1.81	5.94	1.92
Variety	5.80	1.61	5.43	1.84	5.06	2.04	4.79	1.90
Leadership	4.45	1.92	5.37	1.49	3.58	2.22	4.53	2.27
Field of Interest	6.32	1.60	5.98	1.54	6.88	1.53	6.65	1.62
Leisure	4.27	1.70	4.54	1.48	4.12	1.93	4.67	1.86
Early Entry	3.67	2.01	3.09	2.12	2.38	2.30	2.45	2.28

[1] Ns are 46 males and 94 females.
[2] Ns are 300 males and 300 females.

Examining the means for the 18 and under group, the difference between the sexes for Independence is not significant. The other means are all in the same direction as for the total group of males and females.

There is a similarity between the sex differences found in the Norris, Katz, and Chapman study and the present study of eleventh-grade students. In both sets of data males give higher ratings to the occupational values of High Income and Leadership, and females give higher ratings to the value of Helping Others. The differences occur in one value for which males gave significantly higher ratings in the present study (Leisure) and one to which females gave higher ratings (Variety). The eleventh-grade students also did not differ by sex on the ratings given to Early Entry, which did occur in the Norris, Katz, and Chapman data. The present sample, however, does differ from their study in several respects that may explain the data on Early Entry (e.g., many eleventh-grade students have not thought realistically about education and work after high school and the earlier tradition of open admissions in the City University of New York may influence the expectation of entering college and delaying entry into the labor force). Also, early entry may have a different meaning for those already enrolled in college.

For the present study, SES groups were compared also. SES main effects were significant for three values:

High Income: $F_{1,588} = 3.82$ pr $> F = .0510$

Helping Others: $F_{1,588} = 3.81$ pr $> F = .0515$

Early Entry: $F_{1,588} = 21.20$ pr $> F = .0001$

Low-SES group students gave higher ratings to the occupational values of Helping Others (mean of 54.2 vs. 52.7) and Early Entry (mean of 38.7 vs. 34.9); middle-SES students gave higher ratings to the value of High Income (mean of 51.8 vs. 50.2).

Ethnic group as a main effect was significant for only one occupational value, Leisure ($F_{2,588} = 8.56$ pr $> F = .0002$). Students in the black group gave the lowest ratings to this value (45.8) and students in the white group gave it a higher rating than the other two groups (49.5; Hispanic mean was 47.1).

In summary, the occupational values met the criterion described for values: there was a distribution of rankings and ratings assigned to the values. The group differences found were most pronounced for females and males (six values showed significant differences in ratings), somewhat in evidence for SES groups (three values had significant differences in ratings), and barely in evidence for ethnic groups. Only one value showed significant differences among the three ethnic groups represented in this study.

MARRIAGE VALUES

As described in Chapter 3, the marriage values were developed for the present study. The 11 marriage values that students rank ordered and rated were: Financial Security; Emotional Support; A Helpmate; A Close Physical Relationship; Prestige; A Normal Life; A Permanent Companion; Children; Your Own Home; Someone to Rely on; and A Feeling of Leadership. As with the occupational values, an important criterion for the marriage values was the ability to evoke different rankings and ratings of importance from students. Appendices 3.4 and 3.5 give the number and percentage of students assigning ranks from 1 (high) to 11 (low) to each value in order of their importance to the student's decision to marry, and ratings from 0 (least) to 8 (most) important.

Both tables show that each marriage value received all of the possible ranks and ratings but that the distributions are not as rectangular as they are for the occupational values. For example, the percentages assigned ranks in Appendix 3.4 range as low as .7 (four students gave a rank of 11 to Emotional Support). Emotional Support was also very highly ranked with 45.3% of the sample giving it a rank of 1. In Appendix 3.5 the ratings for Emotional Support were similarly skewed, with one student giving it a rating of 1 and three students a rating of 0 (least important to their decision about marriage). Again the distribution of ratings have smaller standard deviations than the distributions of ranks.

The marriage values ranked and rated highest or most important and low or least important are the same, with one exception, when the means are used to identify the values:

Ranks Most Important	Ratings Most Important	Ranks Least Important	Ratings Least Important
Emotional Support	Emotional Support	A Normal Life	A Normal Life
A Permanent Companion	A Permanent Companion	A Feeling of Leadership	A Feeling of Leadership
A Close Physical Relationship	A Close Physical Relationship	Your Own Home	Prestige
		Children	

The most important values in deciding to get married, as given in this set of values, for eleventh-grade students were: Emotional Support; A Permanent Companion; and A Close Physical Relationship. The least important values were: A Normal Life and A Feeling of Leadership. The data were examined for differences among the main groups in the study.

A multivariate analysis of variance (MANOVA) was carried out using the main factors of sex, ethnic, and SES groups and the 11 marriage values as dependent variables. The MANOVA used the ratings from 0-8, untransformed.

Significant main effects were found for all three factors:

Sex: $F_{11,577} = 5.48$ pr $> F = .0001$

Ethnic: $F_{22,1154} = 1.61$ pr $> F = .0365$

SES: $F_{11,577} = 2.38$ pr $> F = .0070$

There were no significant two-way or three-way interactions.

Univariate ANOVAs were computed using the transformed ratings as separate dependent variables. Sex differences were found for the marriage values of Financial Security, Emotional Support, Prestige, A Normal Life, Your Own Home, and A Feeling of Leadership.

Value	F Value (1,587)	Probability of Larger F
Financial Security	8.27	.0042
Emotional Support	4.73	.0301
Prestige	19.76	.0001
A Normal Life	8.71	.0033
Your Own Home	6.61	.0104
A Feeling of Leadership	4.64	.0317

Appendix 3.6 presents the frequency distributions by sex for ranks and the means and standard deviations for the transformed ratings (mean = 50, SD = 10). Female students gave higher ratings to the marriage values of Financial Security (48.2 vs. 45.5), Emotional Support (59.8 vs. 58.4), and Prestige (47.8 vs. 44.3). Male students gave higher ratings to A Normal Life (42.1 vs. 39.3), Your Own Home (49.0 vs. 47.1), and A Feeling of Leadership (42.3 vs. 40.6).

SES main effects were significant for the marriage values of Emotional Support, A Close Physical Relationship, A Normal Life, and Your Own Home. Middle-SES students gave higher ratings to the marriage values of Emotional Support (mean of 60.3 vs. 57.9) and A Close Physical Relationship (mean of 56.6 vs. 55.2). Students in the low-SES group gave higher ratings to the values Your Own Home (mean of 42.1 vs. 39.3) and A Normal Life (mean of 48.8 vs. 47.3).

Ethnic group, as a main effect, was significant for two marriage values: Financial Security and Children. Students in the black group gave higher ratings to Financial Security than did the other two groups. (48.9 vs. 46.2 for whites and 45.4 for Hispanics). Hispanic students gave higher ratings to the marriage value of Children than did the other two groups (54.3 vs. 53.0 for whites and 51.4 for blacks).

In summary, the marriage values met the criterion described for the values, but not as satisfactorily as did the occupational values. Whereas there was a full distribution of rankings and ratings for all possible numbers for each marriage value, the distributions were not as rectangular as they were generally for the occupational values. Nevertheless, students did rank and rate the values and some systematic group differences were found. Again, the group differences were most evident for females and males and six values showed significant differences in ratings. Four values were rated differently by the low- and middle-SES groups, and two values were also rated differently by the three ethnic groups.

PARENTHOOD VALUES

Students rank ordered and rated 12 parenthood values: A Sense of Accomplishment; A Sense of Pride; Variety; Friendship; The Respect of Others; A Stable Marriage; A Chance to Express Love; Confidence as a Man or Woman; Joy; Future Security; A Tie to the Future; and A Sense of Importance. As with the directions for the occupational and marriage values, students were told, "These cards describe values or satisfactions that people might consider important in deciding to have children. Read through them and think about which ones are important to you." They were then asked to rank order, from 1 high to 12 low, the values and then to rate them on the scale from 0 least important to 8 greatly important.

The distributions of ranks assigned and ratings given to each value are presented in Appendices 3.7 and 3.8 for the total sample. Each parenthood value, with one exception, also received a complete set of possible ranks. The exception was A Chance to Express Love, which did not receive any ranks of 12, the lowest possible rank. The value did, however, receive all possible ratings, from 8 through 0. The distributions of ranks and ratings for the parenthood values varied in their approximation to a rectangular distribution more so than the other two sets of values. For example, the ratings for several of the parenthood values were very skewed: The values of Friendship, A Chance to Express Love, and Joy had high percentages of students giving them a rating of 8.

The parenthood values ranked and rated highest or most important, and low or least important, are the same when the means are used to identify the values:

Most Important	Least Important
A Chance to Express Love	The Respect of Others
Joy	Confidence as a Man or Woman
Friendship	A Tie to the Future

The most important values in deciding to have children, within the present set of values, for eleventh-grade students were A Chance to Express Love and Joy. The least important values were The Respect of Others and Confidence as a Man or Woman, as a need or satisfaction in deciding to become a parent. Although these values were least important, it should be remembered that small groups of students gave them the highest possible ranks and the definitions apparently have meaning for some students.

The rating data were examined for group differences. A MANOVA showed significant sex, ethnic, and SES main effects:

Sex: $F_{12,576} = 7.41$ pr $> F = .0001$

Ethnic: $F_{24,1152} = 1.78$ pr $> F = .0117$

SES: $F_{12,576} = 2.50$ pr $> F = .0034$

There were no significant two-way or three-way interactions in the MANOVA.

Univariate ANOVAs were calculated using the transformed ratings of the parenthood values as separate dependent variables. Sex differences were found for the parenthood values of Variety, Friendship, Respect of Others, A Stable Marriage, A Chance to Express Love, and A Tie to the Future.

Appendix 3.9 presents the frequency distributions by sex for ranks and the means and standard deviations for the transformed ratings (mean -50 and SD = 10). Female students gave higher ratings to the parenthood values of Variety (51.7 vs. 47.9), Friendship (58.5 vs. 56.3), and A Chance to Express Love (61.0 vs. 59.2). Male students gave higher ratings to the values of Respect of Others (41.6 vs. 39.6), A Stable Marriage (49.8 vs. 44.5), and A Tie to the Future (47.6 vs. 46.1). Respect of Others received low ratings from both females and males.

SES main effects were significant for the parenthood values of Variety, Friendship, Confidence as a Man or Woman, Joy, and A Sense of Importance. Middle-SES students gave higher ratings to Variety (50.6 vs. 49.0), Friendship (58.3 vs. 56.5), and Joy (60.9 vs. 58.5). Students in the Low-SES group gave higher ratings to the parenthood values of Confidence as a Man or Woman (43.9 vs. 42.0) and A Sense of Importance (48.3 vs. 46.5).

Examination of the significant main effects for the ethnic factor showed significant differences between the group means for two values, A Sense of Pride and A Chance to Express Love. Students in the black group gave higher ratings to A Sense of Pride (53.2 vs. 52.0 for white students and 51.5 for Hispanic students), and students in the Hispanic and white groups had higher mean ratings for A Chance to Express Love (60.6 and 60.5 vs. 59.2).

For the parenthood values, as for the occupational and marriage values, the majority of differences were found for females and males. Six values showed differences for females and males. Five values had differences for SES groups, and 2 of the 12 values had different mean ratings for the 3 ethnic groups.

Factor Analyses of the Values:
The Question of Independence

From the analyses of the ranking and rating of the values, it was found that students were able to rank and rate each of the three value sets, and that meaningful interpretations were possible for the group differences found within each set. A further question remains, however. Do the different value sets tap the same dimensions or factors? If the occupational, marriage, and parenthood values were found to be accounted for by an underlying structure with only a few dimensions, then the addition of the marriage and parenthood values to research studies or guidance activities on career awareness and career decision-making would not be useful or parsimonious. If, conversely, the values have an underlying factor structure that indicates a more diverse set of values or attitudes are being tapped, then both researchers and others interested in sex roles and career decision-making may find more than one of the value sets to be meaningful. In this section the question of the number of factors or dimensions that appear to underlie all the values is examined—for the 10 occupational values, the 11 marriage values, and the 12 parenthood values. The intercorrelations in the matrices for these analyses range from −.40 to +.30, and typically are modest in size.

Earlier studies report sex differences in values and interests. Because the analyses of group differences found sex differences in ratings of 18 of the 33 values, the factor analyses were carried out for the total sample and separately for each sex. Appendix 4 reports the 14 significant factors (using a criterion of an eigen value of 1.00 or higher) for each of the three factor analyses, and gives the values with loadings of .3 or better for the rotated factors (loadings between .2 and .3 are reported also). A few selected factors are presented here to illustrate the number of dimensions that underlie the occupational, marriage, and parenthood values. There are some factors which load primarily with occupational or marriage or parenthood values, but there are other factors that indicate an overlap in the values being rated in the three sets.

Tables 6.2 and 6.3 present loadings of selected values on factors from the three factor analyses—female, male, total group. These values and factors were selected to illustrate the similarities and differences between the female and male analyses in terms of alternative patterns of loadings (.3 or higher) for values. Table 6.2 shows values with similar factor loadings in the three factor analyses. Table 6.3 shows sex differences in the factor loadings for selected values in the three factor analyses.

TABLE 6.2 Selected Values with Similar Factor Loadings
in Female, Male, and Total Samples

Value Area[2]	Female[1] Value	Loading	Value Area	Male[1] Value	Loading	Value Area	Total[1] Value	Loading
	(Factor 4)			(Factor 12)			(Factor 2)	
O	Prestige	.88	O	Prestige	-.50	O	Prestige	-.79
M	Prestige	.55	M	Prestige	-.80	M	Prestige	-.56
O	Variety	-.30	M	Children	.33	O	Variety	.44
	(Factor 5)			(Factor 5)			(Factor 7)	
	A Sense of			A Sense of			A Sense of	
P	Accomplishment	-.74	P	Accomplishment	.77	P	Accomplishment	.76
P	A Sense of Pride	-.74	P	A Sense of Pride	.75	P	A Sense of Pride	.75
P	Variety	-.34	P	A Stable Marriage	-.34			
P	A Chance to Express Love	.41						
P	A Stable Marriage	.31						

[1] $N_F = 299$; $N_M = 299$; $N_T = 598$.
[2] O = Occupational, M = Marriage, P = Parenthood

139

TABLE 6.3   Sex Differences in Factor Loadings of Selected Values in Female, Male, and Total Samples

	Female			Male			Total	
Value Area	Value	Load-ing	Value Area	Value	Load-ing	Value Area	Value	Load-ing
	(Factor 3)			(Factor 4)			(Factor 3)	
O	High Income	-.74	O	High Income	.78	O	High Income	-.71
O	Helping Others	.31	O	Helping Others	-.76	O	Helping Others	.71
O	Variety	.33				O	Security	-.33
M	Financial Security	-.72						
M	Children	.38						
M	Permanent Companion	.35						
	(Factor 12)			(Factor 8)			(Factor 12)	
O	Leisure	-.71	O	Independence	.70	O	Independence	.87
P	A Sense of Importance	.54	O	Leisure	-.70	O	Leisure	-.31
O	Helping Others	.38						
O	Field of Interest	.34						
	(Factor 13)						(Factor 8)	
O	Independence	-.74				O	Leisure	-.52
O	Helping Others	.45				M	A Close Physical Relationship	-.52
M	Prestige	-.45				P	A Sense of Importance	.67
M	Children	.33				P	Variety	-.36

Table 6.2 gives the factors and loadings for the occupational value of Prestige and the marriage value of Prestige. The definitions of these values are:

Prestige: An Occupational Value

If people respect you, look up to you, listen to your opinions, or ask for your help with community affairs, you are a person with PRESTIGE. Of course, PRESTIGE can be gained in several ways. But in present-day America, occupation is usually the key to PRESTIGE. Rightly or wrongly, we respect some occupations more than others.

Prestige: A Marriage Value

Marriage can give you prestige. When people get married, they can feel proud of their partners. And they can feel successful because of their partner's successes.

These two values are consistently part of a bipolar factor for the females, males, and total sample, defining one end of a factor. In the second half of Table 6.2 the two parenthood values of A Sense of Accomplishment and A Sense of Pride function similarly. The two definitions are:

A Sense of Accomplishment: A Parenthood Value

Being a parent can give you a sense of accomplishment. In raising a child you take on responsibilities and meet many challenges. When you see that you have done a good job it gives you a sense of accomplishment.

A Sense of Pride: A Parenthood Value

Being a parent can give you a sense of pride. You can feel pride through your children's achievement. Your children can be successful in life.

The two parenthood values cluster together and for the female and male samples again define one end of a bipolar factor. There are, however, two additional parenthood values that load .3 or higher on the factor for the female sample (Variety and A Chance to Express Love).

The "dissimilar" factors shown in Table 6.3 are examples of factors where the factor interpretation is very direct for the males, and less clear-cut or, rather, involving apparently different interpretations on the part of the female students. The occupational values of High Income and Helping Others have high loadings on one bipolar factor for the eleventh-grade males (and in the total sample). A preference for a high income as a characteristic of a desired occupation is accompanied by a low rating for an occupation that involves helping others. For the female students, however, there is an overlap with several of the marriage values in defining the bipolar factor. The marriage value of Financial Security accompanies the weighting of High Income, and the occupational value of Helping Others is accompanied by the marriage values of Children and A Permanent Companion. A similar phenomenon occurs for the factors in the second half of Table 6.3, perhaps emphasizing again in the factor structure of these values the conditional nature of women's career decision making and the difficulty of separating these values that accompany traditionally different sex roles for men and women.

The second half of Table 6.3 shows the loading of two occupational values, Independence and Leisure, on one factor for the male students. For females, the highest loadings of these two occupational values occur on separate factors (factors 12 and 13).

For males Independence and Leisure define opposite ends of a single factor. A high preference for Independence as part of the characteristic of an occupation is accompanied by a low preference for an occupation that would give the student free time for important satisfactions that are not part of a job. For females, a low preference for the Leisure value is accompanied by a preference for one of the parenthood Values—A Sense of Importance as a satisfaction in deciding to become a parent—and some preferences for Helping Others and Work in Your Main Field of Interest. A low preference for the occupational value of Independence (factor 13) is accompanied by a low preference for Prestige (through marriage) and preferences for Helping Others as part of an occupation and Children, as a satisfaction in or part of the decision to become married.

In summary, the factor analyses examined the underlying dimensions or factors for all 33 values—occupational, marriage, and parenthood values. There are common meanings between the value sets and also unique meanings, where a factor may consist of values from only one of the three sets. There are also differences in the associations among values for females and males that are reflected in the factor structure when examined separately for the two groups. These differences suggest that any research studies using the three value sets should analyze data separately by sex before combining females and males in one total sample for analyses.

One particularly interesting finding is that several of the occupational values formed bipolar factors for males, but did not cluster as uniquely for females. For females, the occupational values were always combined with marriage or parenthood values. One interpretation of this finding is that it reflects the traditional separation of sex roles in our culture: Males are identified with occupational roles, and females are identified with home-making and motherhood. The traditional separation of roles for adults by sex may mean that males more readily separate the values satisfied by occupations from these satisfied in marriage and parenthood. Females have more difficulty in this separation, as seen, for example, in the loading of the occupational value, Helping Others, on several factors. This interpretation is purely speculation, at this stage, and in need of further study. The interpretation of the values and their potential relationship to career decision-making are examined further in the remainder of this chapter and in Chapters 7 and 8.

The Relation of the Values to Educational and Occupational Decisions

Along with knowing that the values in the areas of occupations, marriage, and parenthood have intrinsic interest, particularly because they are not highly overlapping, it is also important to understand their relationship to career decision-making variables. For the students in the eleventh grade, the career decision-making variables of concern are their plans or expectations for education and work. These plans and expectations have been assessed in the present study by questions about the student's level of education, How much education do you think you will have? and about the occupation which the student is most likely to do. These two variables, level of education and level of occupation, are examined in relationship to the three sets of values in this section.

LEVEL OF EDUCATIONAL ASPIRATION

As described earlier, there were no sex differences in educational aspirations. Discriminant analysis is used here to examine whether groups formed by level of educational aspiration are differentiated by the values. That is, do students with different levels of educational aspirations also respond differently to the three sets of values?

Because these analyses with the values are largely exploratory, the discriminant analyses were carried out for the total sample, then for females and males separately. Only the sex groups are analyzed separately; many of the values in each set showed sex differences. The analyses were not conducted separately for SES and ethnic groups because fewer values showed differences for these groups. As will be seen below, the analyses also defined the educational groups differently in order to see the maximum discrimination between groups that might be attained in these exploratory analyses.

Total sample. The groups formed for the discriminant analysis of the total sample were:

	N
Group 1 - Graduate from two-year college (or less)	134
Group 2 - Graduate from a four-year college	297
Group 3 - Professional or graduate school	157
Total	588

The results are given separately for each of the three value sets.

For the *occupational values,* the two discriminant functions were significant (Wilks's Lambdas of .76 and .96, χ^2 p = .000 and .002), and 50% of the "grouped" cases were correctly classified. The three main values for the discriminant functions were:

Function 1	Function 2
-1.03 Helping Others	-.48 Variety
- .97 Leadership	-.75 Field of Interest
- .93 Independence	-.36 Leadership

The centroids (mean discriminant scores) for each of the groups on the discriminant functions were:

	Function 1	Function 2
Group 1	.72	-.13
Group 2	-.11	.19
Group 3	-.40	-.26

Group 1 students with the lower (for this sample) educational aspirations, were likely to rate Helping Others, Leadership and Independence and Variety *lower* than the other two groups. Students in Group 3, with the highest aspirations, were likely to rate Helping Others, Leadership, and Independence somewhat higher, and less likely to rank Variety as high as Group 2 students.

For the *marriage values,* the two discriminant functions were significant (Wilks's Lambdas of .87 and .95, χ^2 p = .000 for both), but only 38% of the "grouped" cases were correctly classified. The findings must again be considered as exploratory. The main values for the discriminant functions were:

Function 1	Function 2	Function 2 (con'd.)
.77 A Normal Life	-1.1 Prestige	-.96 Children
.63 Financial Security	-1.0 Financial Security	-.96 Someone to Rely on
.62 Your Own Home	-.96 A Helpmate	

The centroids of the groups on the discriminant functions were:

	Function 1	Function 2
Group 1	.44	.09
Group 2	-.03	-.01
Group 3	-.32	-.06

Group 1 students with lower educational aspirations were more likely to give higher ratings to the marriage values of A Normal Life, Financial Security, and Your Own Home. Group 3, with the highest educational aspirations, were likely to give lower ratings to these values.

For the *parenthood values,* the two discriminant functions were significant (Wilks's Lambdas of .84 and .94, χ^2 p = .000 for both), but only 38% of the "grouped" cases were correctly classified. The findings must again be considered as exploratory. The main parenthood values for the discriminant functions were:

Function 1	Function 2
.94 A Sense of Pride	1.18 A Stable Marriage
.93 A Tie to the Future	1.04 Future Security
.89 Joy	1.00 Confidence as a Man or Woman
.80 Friendship	.81 Respect of Others

The centroids of the groups on the discriminant functions were:

	Function 1	Function 2
Group 1	-.39	.22
Group 2	.00	.02
Group 3	.33	-.23

Group 1 students, with the lower educational aspirations, were likely to give the highest ratings to A Stable Marriage, Future Security, Confidence as a Man or Woman, and Respect of Others. Group 3, with graduate and professional school goals, were more likely to give higher ratings to A Sense of Pride, A Tie to the Future, Joy, and Friendship, than were Group 1 students.

In summary, there are occupational, marriage, and parenthood values that appear to discriminate among groups with different levels of educational aspirations. Group 2 was not well classified in any of the discriminant analyses, perhaps as a function of the level of educational aspiration measure or the optimism of some students in putting themselves in the category of "graduate from a four-year college." As might be expected, the occupational values provided the "best" discrimination because 50% of the groups were correctly classified with the values, and lower percentages with the marriage and parenthood values (38% in each set).

Analyses by sex. Discriminant analyses were computed for educational groups separately for the female and male eleventh-grade students. Instead of using three educational groups, two more extreme groups were formed to examine the values that might discriminate groups that were more clearly differentiated at the beginning. The two groups were:

		Number of	
		females	males
Group 1:	Codes 2-5, finish high school + technical school after high school + graduate from a two-year college + some college but less than four years	71	63
Group 2:	Code 7, professional or graduate school	78	80
	Total	149	143

TABLE 6.4   Weights and Group Means for the Discriminant Function for
             Occupational Values: Education Groups

Female		Male	
	Standardized Discriminant Function		Standardized Discriminant Function
Value	Coefficients	Value	Coefficients
Early Entry	.86	Early Entry	.79
Variety	.37	Helping Others	.23
High Income	.22	Security	.22
Security	.22	Variety	-.16
Independence	-.19	Field of Interest	-.11
Leadership	-.21		
	Centroids of Groups In Reduced Space		
Group 1	.5472	Group 1	.6268
Group 2	-.4978	Group 2	-.4935

As discussed below, the percentage of the actual groups correctly classified
increased by this procedure and in an exploratory analyses can add to an
understanding of the values and these career-related plans. All the analyses
had Wilks's Lambda values for which χ^2 were significant ($p < .05$).

The *occupational values* that provide the best discrimination between
the educational groups (that is, are weighted most heavily on the discriminant function) differ somewhat for females and males. The major values
on the discriminant functions and the group means on the discriminant
function are shown in Table 6.4. For females the group with the highest
educational aspirations, for professional or graduate school, will be more
likely to give a low rating to the values Early Entry, Variety, High Income,
and Security. They are more likely to give higher ratings to the values of
Independence and Leadership than are female students who do not plan to
graduate from a four-year college. The percent of "grouped" cases correctly classified was 75.2%.

For males the group with the highest educational aspirations is also
likely to give a low rating to Early Entry, but will also give lower ratings to
the values of Helping Others and Security than will males with lower
educational goals. The male students with higher educational goals will
also tend to give higher ratings to the values of Variety and Field of

TABLE 6.5   Weights and Group Means for the Discriminant Function for
Marriage Values: Education Groups

Value	Female Standardized Discriminant Function Coefficients	Value	Male Standardized Discriminant Function Coefficients
Your Own Home	-1.31	A Normal Life	.41
A Normal Life	-1.23	Emotional Support	-.49
Children	-1.10	A Permanent Companion	-.41
Security	−1.00	Children	-.34
A Helpmate	- .97	A Helpmate	-.25
	Centroids of Groups in Reduced Space		
Group 1	-.2582	Group 1	.5257
Group 2	.2334	Group 2	-.4141

Interest. For males the percent of "grouped" cases correctly classified was
75.5%.

Although there is some overlap in the occupational values which separate groups with two different educational goals (Early Entry and Security), there are also several values that are discriminating for only one sex
(High Income, Helping Others, Independence, Leadership, and Field of
Interest) and one value that is different in sign (Variety), apparently
having a different implication for the sexes in respect to amount of
education planned.

The marriage values were also examined for their ability to discriminate
between groups with different educational goals, although there is no a
priori reason to expect the marriage values to provide high discrimination.
The major values and the group means on the discriminant function are
shown in Table 6.5. The percent of "grouped" cases correctly classified
differed for females and males. For females, 62.4% were correctly classified; for males, 74.1% were correctly classified. These results are also
reflected in the group means or centroids, where the closer means for
females indicates that the groups with different educational goals are not
as well discriminated as are the males.

For females with lower educational goals there was a tendency to give
somewhat higher ratings to the values of Your Own Home and A Normal

Life. Female students with higher educational goals were likely to give higher ratings to the marriage values of A Helpmate, Security, and Children. The male students with professional education goals were likely to give lower ratings to the values of A Normal Life, and higher ratings to Emotional Support, A Permanent Companion, Children, and A Helpmate as values in the decision to get married than were male students with lower educational goals. It is interesting to note again that the female students with different educational goals were not well differentiated by the marriage values, perhaps reflecting a more common perception of marriage for women, regardless of level of educational goals, than the perceptions that men have.

The *parenthood values* were also examined for their ability to discriminate between the groups with different educational aspirations. The parenthood values and the occupational values provided similar discrimination between groups. The percentage of "grouped" cases correctly classified was 71.8% for the female students and 74.8% for the male students. The weights for values and the group means are presented in Table 6.6. The values that the women with higher educational goals tended to rate higher were those of Joy, A Sense of Accomplishment, and Friendship as needs or satisfactions to consider in deciding to become a parent. Women with lower educational goals tended to rate the values of A Stable Marriage and Future Security more highly.

The values that men with lower educational goals tended to rate more highly (than men with goals of professional education) were A Stable Marriage, A Sense of Importance, Confidence as a Man or Woman, Future Security, and Respect of Others as values to be considered in making the decision to become a parent. Two values, Future Security and A Stable Marriage, overlapped both analyses and tended to be rated higher by students of both sexes with the lower educational goals of the two groups.

Both the occupational and parenthood values provided better discrimination between the two educational groups than did the marriage values. Whether this is because marriage tends to have more common meanings for all women or because the marriage values are not well specified cannot be answered with the data at hand.

LEVEL OF OCCUPATIONAL ASPIRATION

Roe (1956), described earlier, developed a two-way classification of occupations. One dimension defines the type of occupational *group* (Service, Business Contact, Organization, and so on) and the second dimension is the *Level* of occupation (e.g., in Service, Level 1 is therapist, counselor; Level 2 is social worker; Level 3 is Detective, City Inspector; Level 4 is barber, practical nurse; Level 5 is waiter, taxi driver; and Level 6 is elevator

TABLE 6.6   Weights and Group Means for the Discriminant Function for
Parenthood Values: Education Groups

Female		Male	
Value	Standardized Discriminant Function Coefficients	Value	Standardized Discriminant Function Coefficients
Joy	-.64	A Chance to Express Love	-.10
A Sense of Accomplishment	-.38	A Stable Marriage	.77
Friendship	-.24	A Sense of Importance	.66
Future Security	.34	Confidence as a Man or Woman	.59
A Stable Marriage	.31	Future Security	.47
		Respect of Others	.43
	Centroids of Groups in Reduced Space		
Group 1	.4927	Group 1	.5552
Group 2	-.4486	Group 2	-.4366

operator). Using the Roe classification, two groups were formed based on
the level of occupation given by students in response to the question, What
occupation (job) do you think you will actually do? Discriminant analysis
was again used to examine the relationship between each of the value sets
and the higher (Levels 1 and 2) and lower (Levels 3-6) groups on occupational level. These results are described here for the total sample, females
only, and males only, for all of the values.

Total sample. The discriminant function for the *occupational* values
was significant (Wilks's Lambda = .89, χ^2 p = .000). The percentage of
grouped cases correctly classified was 63%. The major values on the
discriminant function were: -1.2 Helping Others, -.85 Field of Interest,
-.83 Leisure and -.80 Variety. The group means on the function were:

Group 1   -.25   N = 333   (Levels 1 and 2)

Group 2   .36   N = 235   (Levels 3-6)

The group (1) with higher levels of occupational aspirations tended to rate
the values of Helping Others and Work in Your Field of Interest higher
than did Group 2.

The discriminant function was significant for the *marriage values* also (Wilks's Lambda = .96, χ^2 p = .006). The percentage of grouped cases correctly classified was 60%. The major marriage values on the discriminant function were -.64 Emotional Support, -.36 A Permanent Companion, and -.31 Children. The group means on the function were:

Group 1	-.17	N = 333
Group 2	.25	N = 234

There is a tendency for students with higher levels of occupational aspiration to rate these values higher in thinking about deciding to get married than do students with lower levels of occupational aspirations.

The discriminant function for the *parenthood values* was significant (Wilks's Lambda = .96, χ^2 p = .01). The percentage of grouped cases correctly classified was 52%. The groups are not well separated as shown by the centroids on the discriminant function:

Group 1	.05	N = 332
Group 2	-.07	N = 235

The major values on the discriminant function are:

A Stable Marriage	1.13
Future Security	1.09
Confidence as a Man or Woman	1.08
A Sense of Pride	1.07

There is a tendency for students with higher occupational aspirations to rate these values higher than the group with lower occupational aspirations. But these findings, although stable, are only suggestive, because the groups are not well discriminated.

Analyses by sex. The separate analyses by sex did not show much improvement over the discriminant analyses for the total sample for level of occupational aspiration, and the data are not reported here. The data showed more overlap and fewer differences between females and males in terms of the values in each set that provided what differentiation there was between groups formed on the basis of level of occupational aspiration. The lack of discrimination between the groups may be due to several factors. The factors include the ages of the students and perhaps an accompanying lack of serious consideration of careers because they are not perceived as immediate decisions. Alternatively, the measure of level of occupational aspiration may not be well-suited for this age group or may not provide sufficient differentiation between the levels of aspiration because of the high percentage of the sample aspiring to professional/ technical occupations. Further research may clarify the relative importance of these possible explanations, because the values do indeed permit reasonable classification of students with widely disparate educational goals.

Summary

The occupational, marriage, and parenthood values have been examined from several perspectives. The main focus has been on three questions: (1) Can eleventh grade students rank order and rate the values or do all values receive high ratings? (2) are there differences among sex, ethnic, and SES groups in their ratings of the values, on the average? and, (3) how independent or overlapping are the three value sets? Major criteria for the values were that high school students would discriminate among the value terms and would vary in the relative weights assigned to them. These characteristics were demonstrated again for the occupational values, and with some degree of success for the marriage and parenthood values.

All distributions between the groups in the sample design are highly overlapping. To answer the second question, however, a multivariate analysis of variance was computed using the main factors of sex, ethnic group, and SES and each of the value sets as dependent variables. For all three sets significant main effects were found for each factor, with no interactions. Further analyses showed that there were sex differences in mean ratings for the occupational values of High Income, Helping Others, Variety, Leadership, Field of Interest, and Leisure. Female students gave higher ratings to Helping Others, Variety, and Field of Interest. Males gave higher ratings to the remaining three values. SES group differences were found for three occupational values: High Income, Helping Others, and Early Entry. One ethnic group main effect was significant, for the occupational value of Leisure.

Among the 11 marriage values that were developed there were sex differences on six values. Female students gave higher ratings to Financial Security, Emotional Support, and Prestige, as values or satisfactions in making the decision to marry. Male students gave higher ratings to A Normal Life, Your Own Home, and A Feeling of Leadership. Differences between SES groups were found for four marriage values and two values had significant differences for the ethnic groups. The marriage values did not have as ideal distributions for values as did the occupational values.

For example, Emotional Support was given the highest rank by 45% of the sample, resulting in a highly skewed distribution of ranks. Whereas the distributions were not as rectangular as they were generally for the occupational values, the rankings and ratings covered the entire range of all possible numbers for each marriage value. Systematic but typically small group differences, mentioned above, were found.

The 12 parenthood values were also defined for this study. Each parenthood value, with one exception, received a complete set of possible ranks; several of the parenthood values had very skewed distributions (Friendship, A Chance to Express Love, and Joy). The values rated highest as important in deciding to have children were A Chance to Express Love, Joy, and Friendship. Least important were the values of The Respect of Others, Confidence as a Man or Woman, and A Tie to the Future. Six parenthood values were significantly different in mean ratings given by girls and boys: Variety, Friendship, Respect of Others, A Stable Marriage, A Chance to Express Love, and A Tie to the Future. SES differences were significant for five values and two values had significant differences for the ethnic groups.

Over all the values, it was found that high school students varied in the importance ratings or relative weights assigned to the values. The groups in the sample did differ in the importance assigned to the values, although differences are typically small. The largest number of group differences was between females and males, then SES groups, and there were very few differences between ethnic groups. There were no significant interactions, indicating that the few differences among group responses for white, black, and Hispanic students were consistent within sex and SES groups. Thus the values can be responded to by a wide variety of students and should be useful in further work.

The factor analyses of the three value sets indicate that they tap different dimensions and are not highly overlapping. Although not reported here, factor analyses of each value set separately resulted in five factors for each set for a majority of groups, whereas the factor analyses for the three value sets resulted in 14 factors. The intercorrelations for the values generally are low to modest, apparently reflecting the different needs or satisfactions among students.

Of particular interest is the finding that several of the occupational values formed bipolar factors for males but did not cluster as uniquely for females. For females, the occupational values were always combined with marriage or parenthood values. One interpretation of this finding is that it reflects the traditional separation of sex roles in our culture: males are identified with occupational roles and clearly separate these roles from other adult roles. Females are associated with homemaking and mother-hood responsibilities and they may not clearly distinguish values that are primarily satisfied in the occupational domain. The finding may also reflect a difficulty in separating these roles, as illustrated in the loading of the occupational value, Helping Others, on several factors for the girls. The traditional separation of roles for adults by gender may mean that males more readily separate the values satisfied by occupations from those satisfied in marriage and parenthood.

Of course, the extent to which these domains of occupations, marriage, and parenthood should be distinct in satisfying needs and hence values is debatable. In examining the individual values, however, it is apparent that the two definitions of prestige, for example, mean different satisfactions or needs met in an occupation as contrasted with marriage. Occupational Prestige is defined as having the respect of others, and persons seeking your opinions and asking for your help with community affairs. Marriage Prestige is defined as feeling proud of your partner and feeling successful because of your partner's successes. The latter definition is similar to Lipman-Blumen's vicarious achievement: women who fulfill their own achievement needs through the achievement of their husbands or another. Discussion of these values by students should help to clarify the dynamics of satisfying needs through others versus through your own activities.

The following transcript illustrates a female student, Dolores, discussing the order in which she ranked the occupational, marriage and parenthood values, and could serve as the starting point to examine values:

I: Now what I'd like to ask you to do, is just tell me briefly why you put the occupational values in this order.

S: I put helping others first because I want to help people; and then independence because I don't want someone to tell me how to help them, because everyone is different and there can't be one set way, where this person did it, do it the same way; and my main field of interest would be personal contact because I want to deal with people on one-to-one. And prestige—I want people to look up to me, I don't want them to say, she's just doing it because it's her job. I want them to feel I'm doing it because I want to help them. I don't want to be doing the same thing everyday, I'd get tired after a while. Leadership—I don't really want to lead others, but I want them to understand that if I tell them to go this way, I'm not telling them to do it because I like the idea of being able to tell someone what to do but because maybe that's what's right for them. Security—everyone wants security. I want to be sure to keep my job—always have it there. I want to work, but then I want to know that if I need time off to spend doing other things, I can do that sometimes. Money is important, I can't say it's not. I want to have money; I don't want to have just enough, but more than just enough.

I: But this is not a high value compared to the others for you?

S: No, but I would like to have it. And the early entry—that part—'cause you might have a job now that you didn't have to go to school for, but you might not want to go all your life, and then it might be too late for you to go to school, right?

I: Would you like to tell me a little bit about what you were thinking as you put them [the marriage values] in order, starting with the one that's most important to you, emotional support.

S: It's more important because, well, you marry someone because of the feelings you have toward them, that's important, and that you have not just a mental relationship, but a physical one too. You have to be able to know that if you're hurting you can go to them and have them hold you, that makes you feel good sometimes. And a helpmate, because people feel because you're the woman, you clean and do this, but I don't look at it this way—we do it together. The house belongs to both of us. And I want to know that if I really need a person, that he will be there (someone to rely on), a permanent companion, because with boyfriends, he's here now, he's gone later—your husband is supposed to be there always; it doesn't always work out but he's supposed to be a permanent companion means he's there. Prestige—because you do feel kind of good about being married, and you're proud of your partner. You see, he did all of this, I'm living here, and look what I have. And he did it—sometimes he does it out of love for you. Children—I want children after all of that, 'cause I don't want to have children and have no way to raise them and no love at all, their own home. I want to have a home. But running it—I should run it, and my husband should run it, but all that should be planned ahead of time.

I: But that's not as important as all the others?

S: No.

I: A feeling of leadership? That's not important? I mean, that's kind of down on your list there. . . .

S: Yes, because leadership, well, I don't know; perhaps it's that word. It makes me feel like a ruler, and I don't really want to rule anybody. And financial security, I don't think it's right, well, some people have to, I guess, want to get married for money, but nothing's there, cause what happens when the money runs out? And a normal life—people do get married, 'cause well, my friend's married and now I'm here all by myself—that's not a good reason to get married.

I: Do you want to tell me again what you think about the cards on parenthood values?

S: Sense of pride—that's important because I'm going by what I've seen in other people—makes you so proud to see your children doing something, and children do it sometimes for their parents, because parents make them feel, I want to make them proud of me. So, that's pride. Friendship—some of the pride is friendship, because if you can't talk to your children, that's bad. If you can't talk to them, and you know something is bothering them, and they need somebody to talk to, parents are the best person, close to friends. To express love, because everybody, even though nobody admits it, everybody likes to have somebody love them, and to show love towards them. Joy is part of love—I don't want false happiness; don't want anybody to make me believe they're happy in my house but I want them to really be for real, and if you have all the other things, you should have that. And watching my children grow, I'd be proud of them (sense of accomplishment) and seeing that they're making it, that would make me happy to see my children grow.

I: So now we're down to the sixth value.

S: That's a tie to the future, 'cause after my children have all grown up and I could be gone or something, they'll say, yeah, that's the daughter or son of so-and-so; look at her—her parent, she'd be proud to see her now, and I want it to be that way. Variety—I guess it would be nice watching your children grow, and seeing different problems you watch them go through, and it would be nice.

I: That's not as important as some of the others. . . .

S: No. A sense of importance—I would want to be important enough, not only because I'm their parent, but because I'm their friend. I want them to think of me as a human being, a friend, and their parent, but not just their parent. A stable marriage—I guess that would bring you back together if you separated and had children, but children can also make you break up.

I: So that's not as good a reason to decide to become a parent?

S: No. And confidence as a man or woman. How does that really prove your manhood or womanhood? I really don't get that. And I have always cared about the respect of others, but I'm not going to have children just to make it look good; I'm going to have them because I want them—that's important. And future security—that's not right to think when I get old let my children take care of me, I took care of them all these years. People have that feeling, but it's not right—let them have their own life, don't let them worry about parents. So it's not important.

As the transcript illustrates, the three sets of values provide the basis for students to begin to examine their values in relation to plans for these areas. The occupation Dolores has identified for herself is that of lawyer. Earlier in the interview she mentioned the occupation of teacher, but reported that she had not been encouraged in that by a guidance counselor because of her shyness.

The values were also examined for their relationship to level of educational and occupational aspirations. In those analyses, extreme groups were identified (for this sample, professional or graduate school aspirations vs. less than four years of college, for education). The values that distinguished high aspiration females were Independence and Leadership and parenthood values of Joy, A Sense of Accomplishment, and Friendship. In Dolores's ranking of the values, Independence was highly rated (although Leadership was not), and Friendship, Joy, and Accomplishment were rated more highly than A Stable Marriage and Future Security. In these ratings Dolores tended to rank higher many of the same values as the females in the sample with higher educational aspirations.

Level of career aspiration was not well discriminated by the values. Among other reasons, it may be that both the level index and the distance of the goal played a part in the lack of discrimination, particularly for the occupational values that might be most expected to relate to these choices. There is less reason to expect the marriage and parenthood values to assist in discriminating among levels of occupational choice. There were, however, a number of other variables to which the occupational, marriage, and parenthood values might be logically related, and these are examined in the next chapter on family planning and labor force participation plans.

Chapter 7

ADOLESCENT VALUES AND FAMILY PLANNING

There have been a number of factors proposed as influential on women's career decisions and labor force participation. Among them are the level of work commitment of individual women and the number of children desired. Although the exact direction of causality for adult workers is subject to research (e.g., Waite & Stolzenberg, 1976), for the eleventh-grade students in this study no attempt is made to describe causality. Instead, several measures have been used as dependent variables in regression analyses that examine the strength of relationships and the variables most important in predicting the dependent variable. These dependent variables are first, two scales to examine the preferences students have for level of commitment to a job and raising children; second, the number of children desired; and third, the number of years of full-time work planned to age 41. The values as well as other variables have been used in these regression analyses. The last section of the chapter examines the values and other preferences or plans that distinguish sex-typical and sex-atypical groups formed on the basis of each value set. This analysis follows a method used by Norris, Katz, and Chapman (1978) and seeks to provide further understanding of the values, in part for their use in working with students.

Children and Work Preferences

Two scales were used to examine the preference students have about their level of commitment to the areas of having a job and raising children and their orientation or emphasis toward one or the other of these activities. Females respond with their own preferences and males with the preferences "just what you think you would like for your wife." As described in Chapter 3, the two scales yield scores from one to seven (Coombs, 1979). One is the Involvement Level (IL) Scale, where a one indicates a low preference for involvement in the total job and child domain (1 = no children and no job) and seven is high involvement (3 children and a full-time job). The J-C Scale ranges from one, greatest preference for a job (no children and a full-time job), to seven, greatest preference for children (3 children and no job).

SEX DIFFERENCES IN PREFERENCES AND
LEVEL OF INVOLVEMENT

The responses to the IL and J-C Scales are examined for all eleventh graders, as well as for the main sample groups. The distribution of responses to the IL scale for the students approximated a normal distribution with the exception of the top category. The percentages for each scale value for 599 students were: 1, lowest IL, 4.3%; 2, 10.3%; 3, 16.3%; 4, 24.7%; 5, 18.3%; 6, 9.2%; and 7, 16.7%. As shown in Table 7.1 and Figure

TABLE 7.1   Group Means and Standard Deviations for the IL Scale

Group	Mean IL Scale Value[1]	SD	Group	Mean IL Scale Value	SD
Sex			Sex x Ethnic		
Female	4.72	1.64	Female		
Male	4.01	1.69	White	4.09	1.54
Ethnic			Black	5.33	1.52
White	3.96	1.60	Hispanic	4.75	1.64
Black	4.87	1.72	Male		
Hispanic	4.27	1.66	White	3.83	1.65
			Black	4.41	1.79
			Hispanic	3.79	1.55

[1] Range 1-7.

7.1, the highest category had very different frequencies for the female and male students. The ANOVA for the IL scale showed significant main effects for sex and ethnic groups, and one interaction, sex by ethnic group (Sex: $F_{1,587}$ = 29.1 pr > F = .0001; Ethnic: $F_{2,587}$ = 16.4 pr > F = .0001; and Ethnic by Sex: $F_{2,587}$ = 2.93 pr > F = .0543). The means for the groups with significant F values are shown in Table 7.1.

Females were asked to respond to the IL and J-C Scales in terms of what they would prefer for themselves, if they could have just what they wanted, assuming the children were under 10 years of age and the job was for pay outside the home. Males were asked which combinations they would most like for their wives to have, if they (the males) could have just what they wanted. As shown by the means for the sex and ethnic groups, females preferred a greater degree of total involvement in the entire job and child domain than males stated they wanted for their wives. Among the ethnic groups, the black students preferred the greatest degree of overall involvement and the white students a lower degree of involvement. For the sex and ethnic groups, the interaction term appears due to the shift in order of the means between males and females: for females the order (from highest to lowest degree of IL preference) was black, Hispanic, and white; for males the order was black, white, and Hispanic. SES group means on the IL scale were: middle, 4.35, SD = 1.67; low, 4.39, SD = 1.73.

Similar directions were given for the Job-Child Orientation Scale: females stated the preference for themselves and males the preference for their wives. Both groups assumed children under 10 years of age and the job for pay outside the home. For the total sample of 600, the percents of students having each scale value were: 1 (lower J-C, no children and full-time job) 13.2%; 2, 7%; 3, 5.2%; 4, 21%; 5, 18.2%; 6, 18.5%; and 7 (strongly children oriented), 17%. The ANOVA shows significant main effects for sex and ethnic groups, and an ethnic by SES group interaction (Sex: $F_{1,588}$ = 21.44 pr > F = .0001; Ethnic: $F_{2,588}$ = 9.09 pr > F = .0001; and Ethnic x SES: $F_{2,588}$ = 2.90 pr > F = .0559). The means for the groups with significant F values are shown in Table 7.2.

As the data for the means show, the males preferred a higher degree of child orientation for their wives than females preferred for themselves. Within the ethnic groups, the white students preferred a higher level of child orientation than the black students, consistent with other studies. The interaction between the SES and ethnic groups is reflected in the different order of means within the middle- and low-SES groups. Middle-SES Hispanic students had the highest degree of preference for children (compared to a job) and low-SES white students had the highest degree of preference for children.

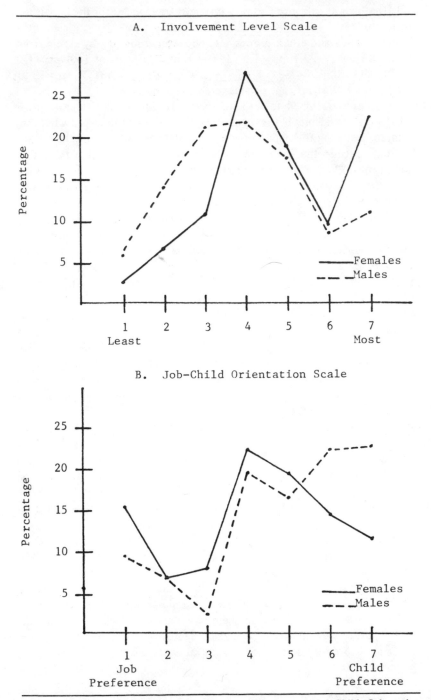

Figure 7.1: Distribution on Involvement Level Scale and Job-Child Orientation Scale: Females and Males.

TABLE 7.2   Group Means and Standard Deviations for the J-C Scale

Group	Mean J-C Scale Value[1]	SD	Group	Mean J-C Scale Value	SD
Sex			Ethnic x SES		
Female	4.12	1.92	Middle		
Male	4.83	1.89	White	4.67	1.97
Ethnic			Black	4.24	1.85
White	4.86	1.95	Hispanic	4.71	1.81
Black	4.06	1.93	Low		
Hispanic	4.50	1.86	White	5.06	1.91
			Black	3.89	2.00
			Hispanic	4.28	1.89

[1] Range 1-7.

Figure 7.1 depicts the frequency distributions for the IL and J-C scales for females and males. In addition to the difference in the distributions identified by the means, the figure shows, for example, that the percentages at the top of each scale differ considerably for females and males. As noted earlier, on the IL scale about twice as many females state a preference for the highest degree of involvement with work and children (full-time job and three children) as males state they would prefer their wives to have. Similarly, the ratio of 2:1 occurs for the males' preference for their wives to have children as compared to females preference to have children versus a job. These data provide further confirmation of the differences in the manner in which females and males view adult roles for the two sexes and could well be used in career education and career planning for both sexes.

Also of considerable interest is the independence of the scales. Coombs reported two scales for the sample of adults on which the scales were developed. The use of the scales with another sample and age group can provide further substantiation of the scaling process. In the present sample the independence is shown by the cross tabulation of the frequencies for the IL and J-C scales. These frequencies are shown for the total sample, and females and males separately in Appendix 5. The data are represented also by the correlations between the two variables. The correlation between IL and J-C for the total sample was $-.123$ (p = .0025, N = 599), a statistically significant but very low correlation. Neither of the correlations for the female and male samples was statistically significant (different from zero): for females r = .080, p = .169, N = 300; and for males r = .097, p = .0928, N = 299. The scales were essentially uncorrelated within the female and male samples, a very desirable characteristic. Further evidence of the difference in the constructs measured by the two scales is gained from examining their relationship to other variables.

PREDICTORS OF INVOLVEMENT LEVEL AND WORK PREFERENCES

The two Coombs's scales were examined in relation to other variables in the present study. Because the scales show sex differences, these analyses were conducted separately by sex. The analysis considered each scale as a dependent variable, and asked what other variables in the study contributed to the prediction of female or male scores on the IL or J-C scale. The tables of intercorrelations for major variables in the study (demographic variables, the three value sets, family activities, the circle for work, marriage and children, and the time lines) were reviewed for identification of the variables with the highest correlations with the dependent variables. (And for the number of children desired, as will be described below.) Other than the values, the variables showing the highest correlations with each dependent variable were entered into a stepwise multiple regression analysis.

Table 7.3 presents a summary of the stepwise regression analysis for the IL scale. Data are presented separately for females and males. The data show that the variables that predict the IL scale differ for the sexes. For the women students, the variables that are related to a higher preference for involvement in the total domain of work and children are: higher ratings for a full-time career (as opposed to part-time work or a job or no work); the number of years they expect to work full-time before age 41; a higher age for completion of education; an expectation for full-time work (this variable has 1—full-time work, to 4—sometimes full-time, sometimes part-time work); and a lower rating for the occupational value of High Income. The multiple correlation for all five variables with the IL scale is .447 (R^2 = .20).

For males, prediction of the IL scale involves their preference for the involvement of their wives in the total domain defined by both work and children. The IL scale for males has a lower multiple correlation than for females, R = .392 (R^2 = .154). Those males who tend to prefer a higher total involvement level for their wives give higher ratings to: expectations that their spouses will work continuously (this variable is coded 1 = work pattern of continuous work, 2 = mostly continuous, 3 = off and on, and 4 = briefly); Full-time Job; Circle: Number of children; Family activities: Earning salary that supports the family (higher rating to wife has responsi-

TABLE 7.3   Summary of Step-wise Regression-Involvement Level Scale

| Variable | Females (N = 244) | | | | |
	B	Beta	Standard Error B	F	R Each Step
Career Pattern: Full-time Career	.03486	.1732	.0124	7.85	.292
No. years full-time work before age 41	.06019	.2021	.0182	10.88	.361
Age completing education	.10926	.1689	.0386	8.00	.404
(Self) working hours	-.23912	-.1638	.0873	7.50	.430
0-High Income	-.02054	-.1223	.0099	4.30	.447
(Constant) 1.19253					
	Males (N = 265)				
Spouse-Work pattern continuous	-.40753	-.1785	.1341	9.23	.226
Career pattern: full-time job	.03095	.1643	.0108	8.19	.278
Circle: No. segments for children	.16211	.1638	.0577	7.88	.319
Family activity: earning salary that supports family	-.36887	-.1523	.1418	6.77	.348
M-Security	.02025	.1494	.0078	6.46	.374
P-A Sense of Pride	.02151	.1172	.0106	4.15	.392
(Constant) 1.98789					

bility); the marriage value of Security; and the parenthood value of A Sense of Pride.

The combination of variables that predict the high IL score for females centers on work and occupational variables. The combination of variables differs for males who are expressing a preference for wives with a high IL score. These variables involve both work patterns for their spouses *and* their own ratings for children. Also, they include both Financial Security (as a marriage value) and A Sense of Pride. It is also important to note that these males agreed that "Earning Salary that Supports the Family" is not mainly a man's responsibility to the same degree as it is for males with a lower IL preference score (and also, presumably other traditional sex-role views).

It is interesting to speculate on the difference in the combinations of variables predicting the IL scale. For males, the combinations make sense when examined at their face value. For females, the lack of any variables relating to children may seem unrealistic. These variables, however, may not appear because *all* the women in this sample are similar in their expectations or acceptance of the socially predominant expectation of

TABLE 7.4   Summary of Stepwise Regression-Job-Child Orientation Scale

Variable	B	Beta	Standard Error B	F	R Each Step
Females (N = 299)					
Circle: No. Segments for Children	.29440	.2570	.0589	24.94	.424
Years Full Time Work by Age 41	−.05733	−.1635	.0175	10.74	.501
Wife responsibility to earn money	−.02594	−.2034	.0063	17.16	.547
M-Children	.03559	.1848	.0098	13.17	.571
Career Pattern: Not Working	.03474	.1646	.0104	11.26	.593
M-Permanent Companion	.03193	.1389	.0108	8.83	.609
(Constant)−.77546					
Males (N = 297)					
M-Security	−.03394	−.2213	.0068	15.54	.243
M-Children	.04145	.1989	.0115	13.08	.304
O-Security	.03236	.1611	.0111	8.51	.347
Family Activity: Earning Salary that Supports Family	.33422	.1257	.1446	5.34	.368
P-Friendship	.02501	.1233	.0111	5.10	.388
(Constant) -.33314					

marriage and parenthood at this stage in their lives. That is, because almost all these young women expect to marry and bear children, the question is that of adding in the level of work commitment. The higher beta weight for number of years of full-time work also suggests an "additive" view. The analysis for full-time work (later in this chapter) examines ethnic group differences and the IL scale. Another explanation, of course, is that the task is difficult for eleventh graders and the construct is not as appropriate for this sample as for college students and older adults.

The sharpest contrast between job and child tradeoffs is provided by the J-C scale. Table 7.4 summarizes the regressions for the Job-Child Orientation Scale. Again data are reported separately for females and males. The multiple correlation for females was noticeably higher than the R for males: R for females = .609 (R^2 = .37); R for males = .388 (R^2 = .15). The variables that predicted the J-C scale differ for the boys and girls in this sample, as they did for the IL scale.

For female students, the variables that predicted a *child* orientation (high end of the J-C scale) as opposed to a *job* orientation were: Circle—a higher number of segments (weights) for children; fewer number of years of full-time work by age 41; a lower percentage of responsibility for the wife to earn money in a family with children; a higher rating to the marriage value of children; a higher rating to the work pattern, "Not Working"; and a higher rating to the marriage value of A Permanent Companion.

For males, the variables that predicted a preference for their wives to have an orientation to children versus work were: a lower rating to the marriage value of Financial Security and higher ratings to Children, to the occupational value of Security, and to the parenthood value of Friendship; and a tendency to view the responsibility to earn a salary that supports a family as predominantly that of the man in the family.

The combination of predictor variables for females and males on the J-C scale differs as it did for the IL scale. For females, this time there were variables related both to children and to work. Only one variable appeared as a predictor for both scales—years of full-time work by age 41—and it appears with opposite-signed weights for the two scales. For males, the variables that predicted the child orientation on the J-C scale were, with one exception, from the three sets of values. And two of the variables, the marriage values of Financial Security and the "Earning Salary . . . ," appeared in sets of predictors for both IL and J-C, for males. The values were the major group of predictors for males for the J-C scale. There is a tendency for males who prefer their wives to have children and not work (the higher end of the J-C Scale) to hold values that emphasize the role of children in a marriage, have security as a value in deciding on an occupation, to view friendship with their children as an important reason to decide to become a parent and reject the idea of gaining financial security in marriage.

Number of Children Desired

Using the variable Number of Children Desired, another set of regression analyses was carried out that is of interest in the context of the job-child tradeoff. These analyses used as the dependent variable the number of children eleventh-grade students stated they desired. Again, the analyses were conducted separately by sex, because the three-way ANOVA for the sample groups showed the main effect of sex to be the only significant factor ($F_{1,549} = 9.77$, pr $> F = .0019$). The mean number of children desired by females was higher than that for males, 2.94 versus 2.63.

Table 7.5 presents the summary of the step-wise regression analyses. The multiple Rs were .339 ($R^2 = .115$) for females and .390 ($R^2 = .152$) for males. The variables that predicted the number of children desired by

TABLE 7.5   Summary of Step-wise Regression-Number of Children

	Females (N = 271)				
Variable	*B*	*Beta*	*Standard Error B*	*F*	*R Each Step*
Circle: Number of segments for children	.13991	.17211	.04871	8.25	.229
Involvement Level Scale	.12875	.16503	.04538	8.05	.288
M-Children	.01926	.14115	.00816	5.57	.318
School Average (9 = High)	-.08049	-.11902	.03902	4.26	.339
(Constant) 1.01827					
	Males (N = 282)				
Job-Child Scale	.13947	.23752	.03265	18.25	.263
M-Your Own Home	.01393	.12301	.00639	4.76	.311
M-A Feeling of Leadership	-.01860	-.17129	.00610	9.28	.341
Family Activity: Mowing the Lawn	.16396	.11153	.08623	3.62	.371
Family Activity: Reading to Children	-.41709	-.12400	.18869	4.89	.390
Family Activity: Mending Clothes	-.18780	-.11513	.09417	3.98	.406
(Constant) 3.0114					

females were higher values for: Circle—Number of segments for Children; the IL scale; the marriage value of Children; and a lower school average. The J-C scale was entered in the analysis, but was not among the variables significant in the step-wise prediction.

More variables entered the prediction equation for males. A greater number of children was predicted by the variables: child orientation on the J-C scale; a higher rating on the marriage value of Your Own Home and a lower rating on the marriage value of A Feeling of Leadership; and more traditional views of the family activities of Mowing the Lawn, Mending Clothes, and Reading to Children. For example, Mowing the Lawn has a positive weight, indicating that this activity is viewed as more of the man's responsibility. Eagly and Anderson (1974) had combined the family activity ratings into a single scale. This single score was also entered into the analyses for males but it entered the regression equation after the individual items and was not significant. It did not enter at all for females. As discussed in Chapter 8, the number of underlying dimensions of the activities may mitigate against the usefulness of a single score for this set of items.

Of the three dependent variables examined so far in this chapter, the variable best predicted was that of the Job-Child Scale. This is perhaps understandable since many of the questions in the study were designed to examine attitudes and values in the area of work and family (marriage and children). The IL scale is independent of the J-C scale and appears to be more concerned with a general personality style or commitment into an active life. It has a higher correlation with number of years of full-time work to age 41, as seen in the next section. The lower multiple Rs for the Number of Children Desired may reflect several factors. For example, one factor may be that eleventh-grade students have not considered realistically the *number* of children they desire, as opposed to a general expectation of having children. In fact, some female students reduced the number of children desired when they completed the time lines. The time lines have a distinct effect on student views of "how to put it all together," work and children. Results of a survey would be greatly affected by the placement of the time line questions. Another factor may be that the relationships with number of children are nonlinear and that prediction may vary for several subpopulations of women not identified here. SES and ethnic groups are not the basis of these groups, at least for the students in this sample.

Relative Importance of Work and Family

One other task in the interview examined the relative importance of work, marriage, and children for students. The importance or weight given to children was an important predictor of the number of children desired for girls in this study. Students were presented with a circle and asked to give the importance of work, marriage, children and "other" to them by dividing the circle into four parts. The number of segments assigned to each of the four areas was counted to give a "score" for each.[1] Three-way ANOVAs were carried out using each of the four areas as dependent variables. For Marriage, only one main effect was significant and no interactions appeared. The weights for Marriage differed for ethnic groups ($F_{2,588}$ = 16.52, pr > F = .000). The mean and SD for the ethnic groups were: White, mean 6.0 and SD 1.7; Black, mean 5.1, SD 1.9; and Hispanic, mean 6.0, SD 1.7. The black students in this sample tended to assign a lower weight (number of circle segments) to the area of Marriage in relation to work, Children and "other."

The ANOVA for Children showed one two-way interaction to be significant. The Sex by SES-group interaction was significant: $F_{1,588}$ = 4.73, pr > F = .030. The means and SDs for these groups were: middle SES—female, mean 5.0, SD 1.5; and male, mean 5.3, SD 1.7. For low-SES groups the means were: female, mean 5.3, SD 1.8; male, mean 5.0, SD 1.7. The means show that the pattern of weights or importance assigned to Children was the opposite within the SES groups. In the middle SES group females gave a lower weight than males to Children; in the low-SES group females gave a higher weight than males to Children.

The ANOVA for Work weights showed a significant main effect, ethnic group, and a two-way interaction, sex and SES: Ethnic, $F_{2,588}$ = 11.38, pr > F = .000; and Sex x SES, $F_{1,588}$ = 3.58, pr > F = .059. The means for the ethnic groups were: white, 5.6 (SD 2.1); black 6.5 (SD 2.4); and Hispanic 5.8 (SD 1.9). The means for the middle-SES groups were: female 6.1 (SD 2.2) and male 5.8 (SD 2.0). The means for the low-SES groups were: female 5.8 (SD 2.2) and male 6.1 (SD 2.4). These means show black students giving higher weight to the Work segment than white or Hispanic students, consistent with other data in this and related studies. And, as with the Children segment, the order of importance for the Work segments changes for females and males within the SES groups. There is a tendency for middle SES females to give more weight to work than low-SES females.

The weights for the "other" segment did not vary significantly between groups. For the total sample, the range of weights varied from 0-11 for Marriage, 0-11 for Children, 1-15 for Work, and 0-12 for "other." The "scores" for the Circle weights are ipsative, but the inclusion of the "other" segment for rating may have partially compensated for this characteristic by allowing more independence in assigning weights to the other three areas.

The Circle task showed small, but significant differences for Work, Marriage, and Children. Black students tended to assign more importance to Work and less to Marriage than did the other ethnic groups. Middle-SES female students weighted Work as slightly more important than did male students, but this order was changed for low-SES students. As noted, the weight for Children had significant predictive value for females when number of children desired and the Job-Child Scale were examined. It was a significant predictor for males when they gave their preferences for their wives' overall involvement in the job and children domains (the IL Scale).

The weights for children also entered as a significant predictor in number of years of full-time work planned to age 41. The relationship of the circle, the values, and other variables to the degree of planned full-time labor force participation is described next.

Full-Time Labor Force Participation to Age 41

The variable Number of Years of Full-Time Work to Age 41 (NYFT) is similar to a variable that has been analyzed extensively within the National Longitudinal Survey of the Educational and Labor Market Experience of Young Women (Parnes data). In that national survey, young women ages

14 to 24 have been asked to give their work plans for age 35. In the present study the variable NYFT is taken directly from the time line where the ages for planned major life events were recorded. Because the other events include education (including postsecondary education), marriage, ages at which children are born, and both full-time and part-time work plans, NYFT includes a variety of patterns of labor force participation (some of which are illustrated in Chapter 9). The range on this variable was 23 years. The mean was 16.3 (SD = 5.8), and as described in Chapter 8, there were sex and ethnic group differences, as well as sex X ethnic and sex X SES interactions. The means for females and males were 10.2 and 17, respectively. In the analyses described here the predictors of NYFT are examined for young women only, but include regression analyses for all of them as well as the ethnic subgroups.

The regression analyses were conducted in several stages because the three value sets as well as other variables related to sex roles are of interest as predictors. In the first stage the occupational values were entered along with a series of variables that showed simple r's with NYFT. Each of the other value sets were entered separately. Then the three value sets were entered jointly with the other variables as predictors. These two stages were carried out for all girls (N = 296), for white females (N = 97), for black females (N = 99), and for Hispanic females (N = 100).

The regression analyses are summarized in Table 7.6. Table 7.6 presents the predictors and the sign of the weights for each predictor variable for the analyses. Appendix Tables 6.5, 6.6, 6.7, 6.8, and 6.9 have full data for several of the regression analyses—all females with the occupational values and all three value sets, and each ethnic group with all value sets entered in the step-wise regressions.

As shown in Appendix Table 6.6, the variable that enters the prediction equation first for all the girls is the Involvement Level (IL) Scale, which has a simple r of .36 with NYFT. The J-C scale has a negative weight, as do the variables Working Pattern: Continuous-Briefly (negative because 1 = continuous, 4 = briefly), M-Children, and M-Someone to Rely On. Career Pattern: Full-Time also is positively weighted. The description that emerges for young women who are likely to have a preference for more years of full-time work includes a commitment to work *and* children, more orientation toward a job than children, plans for a continuous work pattern, a higher preference for a full-time career (as opposed to a job, part-time career, or not working), and a tendency to give lower ratings to the marriage values of Children and Someone to Rely On.

The predictors vary somewhat for the three ethnic groups. For the white females, the variable entering first is Career Pattern: Full-Time, with a simple r of .39. Number of Circle Segments allocated to Work enters

TABLE 7.6 Summary of Regression Analyses and Sign of Weight: Number of Years of Full-Time Work to Age 41

	Total Sample[1]				Sample Group White[2]				Black[3]				Hispanic[4]			
	With OV	With MV	With PV	With All	With OV	With MV	With PV	With All	With OV	With MV	With PV	With All	With OV	With MV	With PV	With All
IL Scale	+	+	+	+					+	+	+	+	+	+	+	+
J-C Scale	−	−	−	−					−	−	−	−		−		−
Working Pattern: Continuous-Briefly	−	−	−	−	−	−	−	−					−		−	−
Career Pattern: Full-Time	+	+	+	+	+	+	+	+								
Career Pattern: Not working																
Circle: No. Segments for children			−						−						−	
Circle: Work Segments					+	+	+	+								
Family Activity: Earning salary to support family	−								−			−		−		

172

TABLE 7.6 (Continued)

	Total Sample[1]				Sample Group White[2]				Black[3]				Hispanic[4]			
	With OV	With MV	With PV	With All	With OV	With MV	With PV	With All	With OV	With MV	With PV	With All	With OV	With MV	With PV	With All
Wife responsibility to earn money									−	−	−	−				
Husband responsibility to keep house									+	+	+	+		−		−
O-Security									+			+				
O-Variety								−								
O-Helping Others									−			−			.	
M-Children				−												−
M-Someone to rely on		−		−		+		+						−		−
M-A Helpmate													−		−	
M-Your own home																
R	.507	.522	.507	.522	.534	.552	.534	.579	.625	.577	.577	.625	.391	.544	.391	.544
R²	.257	.273	.257	.273	.286	.304	.286	.335	.391	.333	.333	.391	.153	.296	.153	.296

[1] N = 296.
[2] N = 97.
[3] N = 99.
[4] N = 100.

173

next (simple r = .38), then two variables given negative weights—Working Pattern: Continuous-Briefly, and the occupational value of Variety. The marriage value of A Helpmate enters last with a positive weight. These young women are more likely to have a preference for career and work commitment (three variables), to rate the occupational value of Variety lower and the marriage value of A Helpmate higher, than young women who do not plan to spend as many years of full-time work before age 41.

The black females (Appendix Table 6.8) had as the first predictor a family activity, Earning Salary to Support Family (simple r = -.40). The IL scale entered next (r = .37), then the J-C scale (r = -.34). The occupational value of Helping Others also received a negative weight, as did the Wife Responsibility to Earn Money (Q 56). The Husband Responsibility to Keep House was weighted positively, as was the occupational value of Security. These predictors are generally consistent, with the exception of the negative weights for the family activity of Earning Salary to Support Family and the Wife Responsibility to Earn Money. The negative weight for the family activity indicates a rating more toward the nontraditional end of the scale, but the negative wieght for the Wife Responsibility item can be interpreted as toward the more traditional view. The contradiction may be caused by the wording of the two questions.[2]

The overall picture of young black women who are planning to spend more years of full-time work in the labor force includes a more egalitarian attitude toward either the man or the woman earning the salary to support a family, a higher level of commitment to the total domain of work and children, more preference toward a job (as opposed to children and no job), a lower rating for the occupational value of Helping Others, a preference for the husband to accept more of the responsibility for keeping house, but less responsibility for the wife to earn money.

Hispanic females who are likely to have more years of full-time work by age 41 are identified by a somewhat different set of variables. The first predictor is the marriage value, Someone to Rely on (negatively weighted), with the simple r = -.27. Negative weights also appear for the Work Pattern: Continuous-Briefly, the Career Pattern: Not Working, and the marriage values of Children and Your Own Home. The one positively weighted variable is the IL Scale. These young Hispanic women with greater work plans can be described as having a higher commitment into the total work and children domain (IL scale) and a preference for working continuously. They are likely to give lower ratings to the career pattern of not working and to the three marriage values—Someone to Rely On, Children, and Your Own Home—as reasons to decide to marry.

The patterns of predictors vary for the three ethnic groups, but there is one overall pattern apparent in Table 7.6: The predictors for the black females include two of the occupational values but not the marriage values, contrary to the entry of marriage values for the Hispanic students (and one for the white students). There is also a cluster of items that tends to reflect the nontraditional end of several attitudes toward the responsibilities of females and males for earning money and keeping house. For the Hispanic students three marriage values have negative weights, indicating *lower* ratings to Someone to Rely On, Children, and Your Own Home as reasons to decide to marry are predictive of more time in the labor market. And for both the black and Hispanic students the IL Scale is a predictor of NYFT. Thus the patterns that emerge show some overlapping of variables but also some clear differences for these three ethnic groups.

Although the earlier analyses of group differences on the values showed few ethnic group differences[3] (and no sex X ethnic interactions), there were three occupational values and three marriage values that entered the regression analyses for NYFT. The IL Scale is a predictor for two groups and the J-C Scale is for one group. Preferences for work and career patterns are also predictors for two groups. Only the marriage value (children) was a predictor of number of children desired for females, and the R was not as high as for NYFT. It is of considerable interest that the occupational value of Security was positively weighted for black females, and the R was highest for this group of young women. This value did not show sex differences for the total sample. The general research evidence is for black females to be more realistic of educational and occupational plans (e.g., Roderick & Kohen, 1976, p. 20). It may be occupational values can emerge as predictors only when there are high expectations and commitment to work and the world of work is not seen to be in conflict with the adult roles of marriage partner and parent. These expectations may also be tied to the expanded responsibility of men for the homemaking and parental roles. It would be interesting to examine whether female adolescents' preferences for NYFT changed under varying degrees of responsibilities for homemaking and parenting undertaken by males.

One other analysis examines the relationship of the values to other career decision-making and adult life-style variables. If the values show some sex differences, as found in the pilot study and in the Norris, Katz, and Chapman (1978) study, then these values can be used to form "sex-typical" and "sex-atypical" groups for both females and males. The four groups can then be compared for their similarity and differences on a number of other variables in the study, particularly those related to women's traditional sex roles. These data are of interest because the analyses of females and males often mask the overlapping distributions of the sexes that occur for any psychological variable studied. Further "refinement" of the types of females and males offers opportunity to understand how occupational and educational choices are conditioned by membership in different groups and, theoretically, could help with varying the approaches to counseling and guidance as a function of the individual's status and group membership. Particularly the content or substantive areas considered as part of career decision-making could vary according to the match between educational and work aspirations and planning for marriage, parenthood, and homemaking.

SEX-TYPICAL AND SEX-ATYPICAL VALUE
GROUPS AND OTHER PREFERENCES

Earlier analyses found sex differences on the values within each of the three sets of values—occupational, marriage, and parenthood. Sex differences were also found on a number of variables related to adult life style, for example, number of children desired and Coombs's Job-Child Orientation Scale. To examine the extent to which differences in the nonvalue variables might be accounted for by different values, sex-typical and sex-atypical groups were formed on the basis of the values. The newly formed groups were then used to examine the extent to which differences on the other variables might be due to sex-typical or sex-atypical values.

DEFINING THE GROUPS

The method of forming the sex-typical and sex-atypical groups followed that described by Norris, Katz, and Chapman (1978). The general approach was to run a regression analysis in which sex, scored dichotomously, was the dependent variable. Predictor variables were the values. For the present study, the regression analyses were done for each of the three value sets separately, so there were three prediction equations.

From the regression analysis predicted sex "scores" were computed. The distribution of predicted sex scores was split to match the actual sex distribution in the sample (50-50). Scores above the cutoff score were designated "predicted male" and those scores below the cutoff score were designated "predicted female." The classification of students into four groups was based on the match or mismatch of the actual sex and predicted sex. The four groups were:

Predicted Sex	Actual Sex Male	Female
Male	Male Sex-typical (MT)	Female Sex-atypical (FA)
Female	Male Sex-atypical (MA)	Female Sex-typical (FT)

A stepwise regression procedure was carried out using the standardized ratings for the 10 occupational values. The same procedure was followed for the 11 marriage values and the 12 parenthood values. The regression equations for each value set are given below. Each equation consists of three variables. The equations were the highest order solutions for which all beta weights were significant. Sex was the dependent variable in each case, with 1 = female and 2 = male.

Occupational Values Equation:

Sex = 2.0610 − .0107 (Helping Others) − .0066 (Variety) +

   .00748 (Leadership)

   R = .31

Marriage Values Equation:

Sex = 2.57594 − .00556 (Financial Security) − .006508

   (Emotional Support) − .009365 (Prestige)

   R = .24

Parenthood Values Equation:

Sex = 2.13855 − .00829 (Variety) + .008477 (A Stable

   Marriage) − .010404 (A Chance to Express Love)

   R = .31

The predictors in each equation are values for which there were high F values when sex differences between groups were analyzed. The number of students classified into each of the sex-typical and sex-atypical groups ranged from 106 to 194 (see Ns given in Appendix 6.1). The proportions of females and males classified as typical and atypical are almost the same in each instance. Because the three value sets are relatively independent, it was expected that the individuals classified as sex-typical and sex-atypical on the basis of each value set would differ. This expectation occurred to a considerable degree. For example, of 194 females classified as typical using the occupational values, 82 (42.3%) were classified as female atypical on the marriage values. Similarly, of 193 males classified as male typical on the occupational values, 84 (43.5%) were male atypical on the marriage values. Similar percentages occurred comparing the groups formed using occupational and parenthood values and when comparing groups formed using the marriage and parenthood values.

The groups formed by each value set were also compared for SES and ethnic group differences. Only the sex-typical/atypical groups formed using the occupational values had a significant chi-square for SES (χ^2_3 = 7.59, p = .0552). None of the comparisons were significant for the ethnic groups.

The analyses for the non-value variables were 2 X 2 ANOVAs, using actual sex by predicted sex as factors. The analyses were intended to determine whether there was any understanding of the sex differences to be gained by using classifications that differentiate female and male students on the basis of either the occupational, marriage or parenthood values. The analyses that follow discuss the findings on the basis of the value sets used to form the groups. A summary of the variables showing significant interactions and means for the four groups is given in Appendix 6.

OCCUPATIONAL VALUES

The variables for which the sex-typical/atypical analyses showed a significant interaction are: number of children desired; the Job-Child Orientation Scale of Coombs; the estimate, How good a student are you?; number of children in family; the marriage values—A Helpmate, A Permanent Companion and A Feeling of Leadership, and the parenthood value, Variety.[4]

The mean number of children desired by sex-atypical females, 2.67, was close to the mean number of children desired by both groups of males (MA 2.67, MT 2.62) and less than the number of children desired by the group of sex-typical females (3.09). Because the occupational values on which the groups were differentiated were negatively weighted for Helping Others and Variety, and positively weighted for Leadership, the sex-atypical females who tended to desire fewer children were more likely to give a higher weight to Leadership and lower ratings to the other two values (i.e., be more like the male typical group).

The means for the groups on the Job-Child Orientation Scale were: FA 3.75; FT 4.32; MA 4.88; and MT 4.80. On the J-C scale a higher score means the person is more child oriented than job oriented; a lower score means more oriented toward a job than children. (For this question, males were to answer in terms of what they would like for their wives to have; females were to respond in terms of what they would like for themselves.) Here the atypical females, as differentiated by the occupational values, tend to have lower scores on the scale, indicating somewhat more of an orientation toward job than children. (The scale range is 1-7, and the mean for the atypical females is about at the middle of the score scale.) The sex-atypical males (MA) have the highest mean overall, indicating a higher preference for their wives to be more oriented toward children than toward a job.

The means for the groups on the variable, number of children in (own) family were: FA 3.03; FT 3.46; MA 3.55; and MT 3.05. Here the FA mean of 3.03 is very close to the mean of the MT group, 3.05. The means for the FT and MA groups are closer, and higher, indicating that on the average these groups came from larger families, and are more likely to desire more children and to be more child oriented on the J-C scale of Coombs.

Group differences were also noted on the question, How good a student are you? Responses to this question fell into four categories: 1 = One of the best students in my class; 2 = Above middle of the class; 3 = In the middle of my class; 4 = Just good enough to get by. The means were: FA 2.39; FT 2.61; MA 2.58; and MT 2.52. The FA group reported the lowest responses (2.39, but the higher rank in class), although the averages for all the groups fell between the categories of 2 and 3. The FT had the highest of the means (2.61, the lowest rank).

For the marriage values with group differences, the means were: A Helpmate (MV), FA 46.56, FT 48.85, MA 48.93, and MT 46.81; A Permanent Companion (MV), FA 54.62, FT 56.64, MA 57.11, and MT 55.74; and Feeling of Leadership (MV), FA 42.56, FT 39.50, MA 39.82 and MT 43.72. There was one parenthood value, Variety, for which there were also group differences. The means were: FA 51.05, FT 52.06, MA 50.10, and MT 46.75. Examining the three marriage values, the means for the FA group are closer to the MT group means than to the other two groups. For example, the FA and MT groups have the lowest means for the values A Helpmate and A Permanent Companion, and the highest means for the value, A Feeling of Leadership. The means for the parenthood value of Variety do not follow the same pattern.

When the occupational values are used to form "types"—typical and atypical for gender—there are several other life-style variables that distinguish the groups. The sex-atypical females were identified by three occupational values: these girls tended to give higher ratings to Leadership and lower ratings to Helping Others and Variety. They desire somewhat fewer children, are more job than children oriented, come from somewhat smaller families, are slightly better students, are less likely to give higher ratings to A Helpmate or A Permanent Companion as a reason to marry, and higher ratings to A Feeling of Leadership in Marriage, and a higher rating to the parenthood value of Variety, as a reason to decide to become a parent. The opposite of these statements provides a characterization of the sex-typical female as based on the occupational values. A different characterization emerges when the marriage values are used as the basis of forming groups.

MARRIAGE VALUES

The marriage values that predicted sex-typical and atypical groups were all negatively weighted: Financial Security, Emotional Support, and Prestige. Males are less likely than females to want Financial Security, Emotional Support, and Prestige via marriage, whereas females are more likely to rate these values as important reasons for marriage.

There were several variables upon which the sex-typical/sex-atypical groups formed on the basis of sex differences in the marriage values were differentiated: number of children; the Job-Child Orientation Scale of Coombs; part-time job as a work pattern; the occupational values of Prestige and Variety; and the parenthood values of A Sense of Pride and A Stable Marriage.[5] The means for the FT and MT groups were almost identical; the FA group desired a larger number of children than did the FT group. The FT group had the lowest mean on the J-C scale, which can have values from 1 through 7, indicating somewhat less of an orientation to children than the other groups had. The FT mean was about midpoint of the scale between an orientation to children versus preference for a job. The FA group was above the midpoint of the scale, moving more towards the preference for children that both groups of males stated was what they would like for their wives to have.

The work pattern Part-time Job was one of a group of five descriptions to be ranked/rated by students, where the descriptions distinguished between a career and a job, full-time and part-time work, and a no work description (see Table 5.8). Ratings could range from 0 to 8. Students were asked how much each situation appealed to them, from 0, I would dislike this very much, to 8, I would like this very much. The FA group gave higher ratings to Part-time Job. In the interview, students did distinguish between the definitions of a career and a job, in terms of a career as work you do because you really like to do it and a job as something you do mostly for money. Thus the FA students are rating their preference of a part-time job higher than other students, and again are close to the FT group. When compared with the FT students, the students in the FA group here have expressed a preference for a greater number of children, a greater orientation toward children as opposed to a job, and for a part-time job, an even more "traditional" female role orientation. The FA students expressed a lower rating for Prestige of an occupation, as a characteristic important in selecting an occupation, and a higher rating for Variety in an occupation. The mean for the FA is close to the MT group, and lower than the FT rating for Prestige. On the Variety value, the FA group is the highest, the FT and MT are next in order of means, and the MA gave this value the lowest rating of the four groups. It is possible to speculate that the FA group, with their higher ratings for number of children and slightly greater orientation to children, do not place a high value on a particular occupation, but, as with the ratings for Part-time Job and Variety, seek an occupation that allows them to focus on children but would still be stimulating at least to some extent, as indicated by the Variety rating.

The parenthood values with significant interactions were A Sense of Pride and A Stable Marriage. The MT and FT means for A Sense of Pride fall between the two means for the atypical groups, with the FA group being closer to the MT group in giving this value a rating at the mean of the scale. The FT and MA groups gave A Sense of Pride a higher rating as a value important in deciding to become a parent. Although A Stable Marriage was given ratings at or below the mean by all four groups, the FT group gave it the lowest rating as a reason or need anticipated in deciding to have children. The MT group rated this slightly below A Sense of Pride.

Reviewing the relationship between the prediction of the sex-typical/atypical groups and reducing the differences between the sexes by means of these groups it appears the marriage values do not define sex typical and atypical in the same manner that the occupational values do. The use of the marriage values to separate the sexes by a regression equation resulted in all negative weights, implying "something is not" rather than a combination of positive and negative weights as occurred for the occupational values. The FA and MT groups are also not as consistently ordered (closely related) in the same way they were for the occupational values. These results may occur for a number of reasons.

One reason the results may differ is that stereotypes or views of appropriate behaviors or satisfactions in marriage for males and females or their values are highly consistent within each sex. That is, although the rankings and ratings of the marriage values have variability, these distributions are not as rectangular as are those for the occupational values. Alternatively, the marriage values developed here require revisions, using either a better conceptual view, or statistical procedures, or both. Another interpretation is that these concepts related to marriage are not well-differentiated *in general*; individuals thinking about marriage may have only a vague or general perspective on the values or needs to be met by marriage which are not well articulated beyond a general emotional component. Thus, the results may reflect both a "state of thinking about marriage" as well as a "state of assessing values about marriage."

The pattern of means for the sex-atypical females as identified by the marriage values "fit" together, however. These girls, who did not give as high ratings as the sex-typical females to Financial Security, Emotional Support, and Prestige as satisfaction through marriage, present an even more "traditional" female role. They desire more children, are more children than job oriented, prefer a part-time work pattern, give less importance to obtaining prestige in an occupation and more importance to variety, and are less likely to have A Sense of Pride or A Stable Marriage as important values in deciding to become a parent. Yet another perspective is provided by the parenthood values.

PARENTHOOD VALUES

There were a large number of variables differentiated by the sex-typical/sex-atypical groups formed on the basis of sex differences in parenthood values.[6] The parenthood values that predicted sex were: (-) Variety, (-) A Chance to Express Love, and (+) A Stable Marriage. Males were more likely than females to want A Stable Marriage through parenthood, and less likely to satisfy needs for Variety and A Chance to Express Love through deciding to become a parent.

Two variables were concerned with the level of student achievement: How good a student are you? and the high school grade average. The first used a scale with 1 = One of the best students in the class, 2 = Above the middle of the class, 3 = In the middle of the class, and 4 = Just good enough to get by. The HS average was on a scale of from 1 = D (69 or below) to 9 = A (93-100). Both variables were self-reported by students. For both variables the trends are the same. The FA and MT groups have lower estimates of school achievement when compared to the other two groups. These data are also reflected in differences in the Planned Level of Education, Occupational Level (Roe), and the Occupational Score (Census). The planned level of education is highest for the FT and MA groups.

Similarly, the means for these groups show a higher level of occupation most likely to do (Roe categories) and of the Census occupational scores. For the Work pattern ratings the FT and FA groups are most oriented toward a part-time career or part-time job (as defined by the A/T groups formed by the three parenthood values). The part-time career pattern is given the highest rating by the FT and FA groups, followed by the MA and MT groups. Full-time job received the highest mean rating from the MT group, then the FA, FT, and MA groups. The part-time job pattern was given its highest rating by the FA group, and lowest by the MA group.

Three of the variables on the time line also had significant interactions: age at completing education, age at marriage, and age at time of second child. (The means for these variables for the four groups are also given in Appendix 6.) The mean ages for completing education are somewhat higher for the FT and MA groups. For age at marriage and age at second child, there were sex main effects but the general trend is for the FA group to have the lowest mean age for the four groups. The MA group plans to be oldest at marriage and time of second child, in line with plans for completing education at an older (mean) age. The FA group is closest to the MT group for age at completing education, but then becomes closer to the FT group for the marriage and second child ages.

Four occupational values showed significant interaction effects for the four groups: Helping Others, Variety, Leisure, and Early Entry. For two of the values, Helping Others and Variety, the means for the two female groups are closer than either is to the typical male group, with both female groups rating Helping Others and Variety higher than did either of the male groups. The FA group gave the lowest rating (of a set of ratings below the mean) to Leisure, and the highest of a set of generally low ratings to Early Entry.

Three marriage values had significant sex X A/T interactions: Emotional Support, A Close Physical Relationship, and A Normal Life. The means for these marriage values follow the pattern of FA and MT group means being most similar in magnitude. The typical females tended to give higher ratings to Emotional Support and A Close Physical Relationship, and a lower rating to A Normal Life as a value to consider in deciding to become married. As with the other values, the ratings among all four groups tended to be in the same general range, but to differ within these ranges.

Over the set of variables which were examined for changes in sex differences that might be accounted for by a set of parenthood values used as predictors of sex (1 = female, 2 = male), the FA and MT groups tended to be closer in numerical value than did the FA and FT groups. The FT and MA groups tended to be better students, to plan for higher levels of education and occupations, to desire a career rather than a job, and to plan to marry and have children at later ages than the FA group. The FT group tended to rate slighly higher traditional female occupational values, Helping Others and Variety, but to give a lower rating to Early Entry, in agreement with their educational and occupational aspirations. They also tended to place a higher value on the marriage values Emotional Support and A Close Physical Relationship and a lower value on A Normal Life.

The parenthood values, in terms of selecting predictors and defining sex-typical and sex-atypical groups, also functioned in the same general manner that the occupational values did. That is, the patterns of interactions were more consistent in the relationships among the four groups than they were for the marriage values.

Another view of these data was obtained by rerunning the analysis using extreme groups, that is, the 200 at each end of the predicted sex distribution. The same variables were identified (with minor exceptions) as reported in Appendix 6. In addition, the interaction terms were examined for the value set used to form the regression equations. These latter interactions help to clarify the "types" formed by the regression analyses.

The occupational values used to form the sex-typical and sex-atypical groups in the first analysis were Helping Others (-), Variety (-), and Leadership (+). The sex-atypical females had lower scores than typical females and atypical males on Helping Others and Variety, and higher means on High Income, Prestige, and Leadership; these means were very similar to the typical male means. Conversely, the atypical male means were high on Helping Others and Variety and lower on Leadership and High Income (see Appendix 6.2). There are, within this extreme case analysis of the occupational values, about one-third of the females who have occupational values more "typical" of males, and in this sense are nontraditional in their values (see Appendix 6.2).

The "nontraditional" characterization fits with the variables described earlier: Somewhat fewer children desired and more orientation toward a job (on the J-C scale), higher self-ratings on "How good a student are you?" and lower ratings for the marriage values of A Helpmate and A Permanent Companion, with a slightly higher rating for "A Feeling of Leadership."

The "atypical" females in the marriage values present a different picture. These women students are the more "traditional" women (see Appendix 6.3). The sex-atypical females have higher means on these values as reasons for deciding to become married: to have Your Own Home, Someone to Rely on, Children, A Permanent Companion, A Normal Life, and A Helpmate. With the exception of their lower means on Financial Security and Prestige, these data present a more traditional view of women's reasons for marrying, in accord with more traditional male views (males do not view financial security or prestige as important values in deciding to marry).

The "more traditional" set of values also appears in the variables described earlier. The sex-atypical women had the highest mean for number of children desired, were more oriented toward children than a job (on the J-C scale), had the highest ratings for the work pattern of a part-time job, and gave lower ratings to the occupational value of Prestige and a higher rating to Variety as an occupational value. They also had a somewhat higher rating for the parenthood value of A Stable Marriage and a lower mean for A Sense of Pride.

The means for sex-typical and sex-atypical groups on the parenthood values are presented in Appendix 6.4. The "character" of the parenthood values differs from both the occupational and marriage values. The values that distinguish the sex-atypical and sex-typical females are on a dimension that may tentatively be called maturity, or a less conforming response to the expectations of others. The sex-atypical females had higher means on the parenthood values of Respect of Others, A Stable Marriage, Confidence as a Man or Woman, and A Sense of Importance. These values center around "others" views of the woman as a reason to decide to become a parent. The sex-atypical women had lower means on A Sense of Pride, Variety, Friendship, A Chance to Express Love, and Joy. These values, as reasons to decide to become a parent, are more centered on the perceived satisfactions to the individual, rather than responses to social pressures or expectations.

The variables associated with the sex-atypical females were: lower averages in high school and self-ratings of How good a student; and lower planned level of education, and occupation. They were less likely to prefer a part-time career, and more likely to prefer a full-time job or part-time job. They were also more likely to complete education, marry, and have a second child earlier.

IMPLICATIONS FOR COUNSELING

The implications for counseling suggested here are tentative, but the occupational, marriage, and parenthood values do provide different definitions of sex-typical and sex-atypical students. The identification of "nontraditional" value orientations for the sex-atypical females on the occupational values suggests counselors can be supportive by encouraging examination of nontraditional occupations for these women. For those women who have sex-typical occupational values, there is a need to assist them in distinguishing the occupational values as based in the general role of women as helpers of others (in the role of wife and parent) versus the professional or occupationally based role that includes helping others.

Most of the eleventh graders expect to marry (and these expectations agree with population statistics). The sex-typical women tended to rate Financial Support and Prestige higher as reasons to marry. Can counselors help these women to distinguish their own attainments and need for an independent basis for each of these values, rather than through another, as the typical males do with these values? The sex-atypical females tend to rate higher the need of Someone to Rely on, A Permanent Companion, Children, Your Own Home, and A Normal Life, as reasons for deciding to marry. These girls present a different "type" and it may be useful to discuss and clarify the relationship of these values to the general independence goal of adolescents. Also, these values can be viewed as similar to those of the sex-atypical females in deciding to become a parent. These needs or values can be described as more conforming in perspective than the others and perhaps characterized as at the conforming stage of ego development (Loevinger, 1976; Swensen, 1980). Here the counselor has a more general task, that of facilitating self-awareness and a move to a higher level of ego development. The values based on the sex roles of wife and parent (mother) can be used to structure the self-awareness. Are these ratings based on the individual's own values, or the expectations of others?

All three sets of values provide the basis for the exploration of values and needs in relation to the adult roles of worker, marriage partner, and parent. The sex-typical and sex-atypical groups suggest that individuals will differ in their general orientation to each set of values, requiring an adaptation of the process and content of the counseling approach.

NOTES

1. Means and SDs for the total sample for the four parts of the circle were: Marriage, M = 5.7, SD = 1.8; Children, M = 5.1, SD = 1.7; Work, M = 6.0, SD = 2.2; Other, M = 3.2, SD = 1.7. There were 20 segments marked on the circle.

2. In the first instance, there is a midpoint that is the option, Could be either person's responsibility, and the black students in the sample were more toward this midpoint of the scale than either the white or Hispanic students. The directions for the responsibility item do not have such an option. The questions asked are: What do you think is the best arrangement for dividing up these responsibilities? For example, What percentage of the responsibility should the husband accept? and the wife? The mean for black females on percentage responsibility for the wife was 39.6, SD = 13.7; the mean for all females was 36.5 (SD = 15.1).

3. Of the values used as predictors here, only the marriage value of Children showed a significant ethnic group main effect.

4. All F values had pr > F .044 or less.

5. All F values had pr > F .023 or less. See Appendix 6 for means.

6. All F values had pr > F .038 or less. See Appendix 6 for means and listing of variables.

Chapter 8

PERCEPTIONS OF SEX ROLES

Career decisions made by women appear to take into account their expectations for marriage and children (Psathas, 1968). According to Bernard (1976) these expectations for marriage and children are influenced by social norms for the behaviors appropriate for females and males, that is, their sex roles. Sex-role attitudes in the area of the family and responsibilities for earnings are critical for both sexes. The relationship of the IL scale to number of years of full-time work before 41 for women suggests an "additive" view of how women can participate in the domain of occupations. That is, the role of worker is "added on" to the traditional adult roles of homemaker and mother responsibilities. Unless there is a corresponding expansion of men's family roles, particularly responsibilities, most women's needs and satisfactions in the occupational domain will remain contingent on marriage and parenthood until middle adulthood.

Perucci, Potter, and Rhoads (1978) found that the socialization-ideology hypothesis received the greatest support in accounting for a husband's participation in 12 selected household child-care activities. Contemporary sex-role ideology has also been found to be related to expected number of children ($r = -.22$) for a sample of girls in seven suburban high schools in Atlanta (Wrigley & Stokes, 1977). These studies, among others, suggest the influence of sex-typing of activities on participation in family roles and fertility. In the present study, sex-typing of activities did not relate to number of children desired for females but did for male students. Sex-typed family activities, however, did relate to labor force plans to age 41. Here we examine eleventh-grade students' perceptions of sex roles in more depth, particularly to explore whether there are different clusters of activities among those that are commonly used in studies and whether questions on financial responsibility and child care remain sex-role stereotyped.

Sex roles were examined in two series of questions during the interview. The first was a list of activities for families with children drawn from the work of Eagly and Anderson (1974) and modified slightly for the present study. The activities included in the list are those traditionally assigned to either a man or woman by virtue of their sex. For example, cleaning the house and teaching children sports are two such activities.

The second set of questions related to sex roles asked students to assign the percentage of responsibility the husband or wife should accept for three main responsibilities in a family: earning money, keeping house, and caring for children. Related questions asked about the circumstances under which a husband or wife should not work and how a husband or wife might feel if her/his spouse earned more money (than the husband or wife). The last questions described in this chapter asked students to indicate the ages at which they expected to be in school, marry, have children, work full-time, and work part-time. These questions bear on the continuation of the phenomenon of returning or reentry women.

Sex Roles and Family Activities

Students rated 22 activities for families with children on the 1 to 5 scale, from Only a Woman's Responsibility to Only a Man's Responsibility. Appendix 7.1 presents the frequencies given to each responsibility alternative by the total sample of eleventh-grade students. Examples of items with traditional allocation of sex roles are the activities Mending Clothes and Repairing Household Appliances. Mending Clothes was assigned mainly to women (55.3%) or only to women (14%); Repairing Household Appliances was considered to be mainly a man's responsibility (55.8%) and only a man's responsibility (13.3%). Three activities were checked only as being either person's or the woman's responsibility: Cleaning the House, Washing Clothes, and Caring for Baby.

GROUP PATTERNS

Each of the 22 activities was analyzed using a 3-way ANOVA to examine group differences.[1] Only a few questions had very high percentage for one alternative. For example, the activities Reading to Children, Taking Children to Doctor, Deciding to Move to Another City, Helping Children with Homework, and Deciding to Buy a Large Item: color TV, washing machine, were rated as "could be either the man's or the woman's responsibility" by 80% or more of the students. These activities were essentially perceived as egalitarian, or equally able to be done by either the man or woman. On the other hand, mending clothes was perceived in that manner by only 30% of the students.

The three-way ANOVA's for all the activity items are summarized in Table 8.1. For each activity the significant main effect or interaction is indicated. Although there are significant differences in the means for the groups, the actual differences in mean ratings are not large. The direction and consistency of the differences are of interest, however, and are discussed here for the series of items significant for each main effect.

The means for items with group differences are reported in Appendix 7.2. Examining the direction of the differences on the items with significant sex main effects shows that the ratings given by females are less traditional, that is, less sex-role stereotyped. For example, females had a higher mean (less strictly women's responsibility) for the activity of Cleaning the House, 2.7 versus 2.5. And females had *lower* means (less strictly men's responsibility) for the remainder of the activity items that had sex differences. For example, the female and male means for Managing Family Money were 3.2 and 3.4, respectively; for Repairing Household Appliances the means were 3.7 and 3.9; for Mowing the Lawn the means were 3.7 and 4.1; and for Taking out Garbage the means were 3.4 and 3.6. There was only one item in which the sex differences appeared to be more stereotyped for females, Taking Children to Doctor. The mean for females was 2.8 and for males 2.9. The general trend for the girls to have less sex-role stereotyped views is consistent with other research on these attitudes.

Nine of the 13 items with sex differences also had statistically significant differences in the mean responses of the ethnic groups. The items with ethnic differences and the group means are also shown in Appendix 7.2. Differences among the ethnic groups are not as consistent as the differences between the sexes. For the activity Cleaning the House, the Hispanic and white groups are more traditional (tended to rate the activity as more the responsibility of the woman) than the black group. On the next item, however, Managing Family Money, the Hispanic group is more traditional than the black and white groups. And for the item, Fixing a Broken Lamp, the black students tended to rate the activity in accord with traditional sex roles in the family. These group differences do not have the consistent pattern the sex differences did.

TABLE 8.1   Summary of ANOVAs of Activities for Families with Children

	Significant Fs ($pr > F = .05$ or less) Main Effect			Interaction			
	Sex	Ethnic	SES	Sex/Ethnic	Sex/SES	Ethnic/SES	Three Way
Cleaning the house	X	X	X				
Mending clothes		X		X			
Managing family money	X	X					
Repairing household appliances	X	X	X				
Mowing the lawn	X	X					
Planning color scheme for home					X		
Reading to children						X	
Taking out garbage	X	X	X				
Washing the family car	X	X					
Washing clothes			X				
Caring for baby				X			
Taking children to doctor	X		X				
Earning salary that supports family	X	X	X.				
Doing family food shopping							
Deciding when car needs tune up	X		X				
Teaching children sports	X						
Cooking meals			X				
Fixing a broken lamp	X	X	X				X
Deciding to move to another city	X						
Helping children with homework							X
Staying home from work if a child is sick				X			
Deciding to buy a large item; color TV, washing machine, etc.	X	X					X

Ten of the activity items showed SES group differences. The SES group differences were very consistent. For each item the middle-SES students gave ratings that were less traditionally sex stereotypical. That is, if the item were traditionally a woman's responsibility, middle-SES students rated it more toward the middle of the scale, where it could be either person's responsibility. One example is the item Cleaning the House. Middle-SES students had a mean rating of 2.7 and low-SES students had a mean of 2.6, more toward the woman's responsibility end of the rating scale. Similarly, if the item was for an activity that has been traditionally the man's responsibility, middle-SES students would give it a lower rating, moving toward the middle of the scale where the activity could be either person's responsibility. For example, Deciding when a Car Needs a Tune-up was given a mean rating of 3.8 by middle SES students and a mean of 4.0 by low-SES students.

The sex by ethnic group interactions also had a consistent pattern. For three items with a significant sex X ethnic interaction, the disordinal differences between groups were that the female Hispanic students were the most traditional of the three female groups and the white male students were the most traditional of the three male groups. The means for these items were:

Means

Activity	Females			Males		
	W	B	H	W	B	H
Mending Clothes	2.3	2.3	2.0	2.1	2.2	2.2
Caring for Baby	2.6	2.7	2.5	2.4	2.5	2.6
Staying Home from Work if a Child is Sick	2.5	2.6	2.3	2.4	2.5	2.5

The Hispanic females had a mean rating of 2.0 for Mending Clothes, the lowest (most oriented toward a woman's traditional responsibility) of the groups of women, and the white males had a mean rating of 2.1, the lowest of the male ratings.

The one item with a sex X SES interaction, Planning Color Scheme for Home, had means indicating that middle-SES females had more of a tendency to say this activity could be either person's responsibility than did the other groups. The means were middle-SES female 2.8, males 2.7; low-SES female mean was 2.7, males also 2.7. The single item with an interaction between ethnic and SES groups was Reading to Children. The means were identical at 3.0, with the exception low-SES black students had a mean rating of 2.9, indicating a slightly more traditional (female responsibility) rating for this activity.

Although several three-way interactions were reported, the smaller sizes of these groups (N = 50 per group) and the small differences over all the groups do not warrant further description here. Of more interest is the examination of the activities in terms of their independence and overlap.

INDEPENDENCE OF THE ACTIVITIES

A factor analysis of the 22 items was carried out for the total sample, as well as for females only and males only (because over half of the items had sex differences in the mean ratings). Appendix 7.3 reports the six factors (using a criterion of eigen values of 1.00 or greater) and factor loadings for activities above .30 on each factor. The seven factors for the female sample are given in Table 8.2, and the six factors for the male sample in Table 8.3.

The main factors in each of the three analyses are similar, and appear to sample three general areas: homemaking, children, and family decision-making or the marital relationship. Two separate factors appeared that reflect traditional sex-role activities in homemaking for females and males, respectively. The traditionally female homemaking-role activities are on Factor 2 for the total group, and Factor 1 for the other two samples. Items such as Cleaning the House, Mending Clothes, and Cooking Meals have high loadings on the factors. For males, one additional item loads negatively on this factor, Earning Salary That Supports the Family, as opposed to the traditionally female homemaking support activities.

The traditional male homemaking activities are on Factor 1 for the total sample, Factor 3 for the female sample (four items identify this factor), and Factor 2 for the male group (seven items). The items in common which identify this factor are Repairing Household Appliances, Deciding When Car Needs Tune-up, Fixing a Broken Lamp, and Mowing the Lawn. The additional items that appeared on the male students' factor were Washing the Family Car, Teaching Children Sports, and Earning Salary That Supports Family. One bipolar factor that is defined at one end by traditional male and at the other end by traditional female sex-role activities appeared in the female sample (Factor 6).

Activities concerned with children were split between two factors in these groups. For example, in the female sample Factor 2 is a bipolar factor defined at one end by Caring for Baby and Helping Children with Homework, and, with a low loading, at the other end by Deciding When Car Needs Tune-up. Other items concerned with children appeared on Factor 4 for the female sample: Reading to Children and Taking Children

TABLE 8.2   Factors and Activity Item Loading—Females[1]

Activity	Loading
Factor 1	
Cleaning the home	
Mending clothes	.61
Washing clothes	.66
Doing family food shopping	.41
Cooking meals	.69
Staying home from work if child is sick	.56
Factor 2	
Caring for baby	.61
Helping children with homework	.80
Deciding when car needs tune-up	−.32
Factor 3	
Repairing household appliances	.69
Deciding when car needs tune-up	.59
Fixing a broken lamp	.78
Mowing the lawn	.31
Factor 4	
Reading to children	.80
Taking children to doctor	−.48
Doing family food shopping	.39
Factor 5	
Managing family money	.33
Planning color scheme for home	.81
Teaching children sports	−.35
Factor 6	
Taking out garbage	.69
Washing family car	.69
Taking children to doctor	.47
Mending clothes	−.32
Mowing the lawn	.49
Doing family food shopping	−.31
Deciding when car needs tune-up	.32
Factor 7	
Managing family money	.59
Earning salary that supports family	.42
Teaching children sports	.63
Deciding to move to another city	.73

[1] N = 291.

TABLE 8.3   Factors and Activity Item Loading—Males[1]

Activity	
Factor 1	Loading
Cleaning the house	.60
Mending clothes	.67
Washing clothes	.76
Earning salary that supports family	−.38
Doing family food shopping	.51
Cooking meals	.70
Staying home from work if a child is sick	.33
Factor 2	
Repairing household appliances	.65
Mowing the lawn	.66
Washing the family car	.39
Earning salary that supports family	.31
Deciding when car needs tune-up	.61
Teaching children sports	.53
Fixing a broken lamp	.74
Factor 3	
Caring for baby	.58
Helping children with homework	.81
Staying home from work if a child is sick	.56
Factor 4	
Reading to children	.76
Taking children to doctor	.75
Factor 5	
Reading to children	−.34
Taking out garbage	.72
Washing the family car	.45
Factor 6	
Managing family money	.61
Planning color scheme for home	−.65
Earning salary that supports family	.40
Deciding to move to another city	.54

[1] N = 288.

to Doctor (Doing Family's Food Shopping also has a moderate loading on this factor). For males the similar two factors are Factors 3 and 4. (In the total sample these items appear on Factors 4 and 5.) One factor has a different type of activity. Factor 6 in the male sample, Factor 7 in the female sample, and Factor 3 in the total sample have items that are concerned with decision-making or allocation of power in the family. These factors have the items: Managing Family Money, Earning Salary

That Supports Family, and Deciding to Move to Another City. (Teaching Children Sports appears on this factor in the female and total sample analysis.) All of these items showed sex differences in responsibility ratings, and all were rated more toward being a man's responsibility.

The clustering of the family activity items are fairly similar across the three samples. In terms of the factor analyses being limited by the items represented in the item pool, it can be noted that the traditionally sex-role stereotyped homemaking activities are well sampled, both for males and females, perhaps even oversampled. The items concerned with children appear to represent three areas, but with only one or two items in each: caring for very young children (one item), a caretaker function; reading to children or teaching children sports, a concern with their physical and mental development, perhaps more of a teaching role; and an item such as Taking Children to Doctor, which appears to represent the continuing caretaking responsibility, regardless of the age of the child. Future research could very well define these functions further, and add items to determine if in fact they are perceived as different types of family activities and allocated by traditional perspectives on adult roles of females and males.

The third area is concerned with the marital relationship, the traditional husband-wife role in terms of economics and decision-making. It was represented by three items, and could well be expanded to provide more definition of this area in future research. The three items were: Managing Family Money, Earning Salary That Supports Family, and Deciding to Move to Another City. Additional items could deal with other aspects of the trade-offs between the man's and the woman's occupational and family roles. The differences in factor composition and means for sex, SES, and ethnic groups also indicate that the activities should be used as single items in research, until further work is done on the item pool and confirmed by factor analyses.

Dividing Three Responsibilities:
Earning Money, Keeping House, and Caring for Children

Attitudes toward sex roles were examined in another question, What do you think is the best arrangement for dividing up these (Earning Money, Keeping House, Caring for Children) responsibilities? Students were asked, In terms of earning money, for example, what percentage of the responsibility should the husband accept? and the wife? or someone else? For the total sample the mean percents for earning money were: husband, 67.8 and wife, 32.1. The means for Keeping House were husband, 34.8, wife

63.6, and someone else 1.9. Caring for Children had means of 43.4 for the husband, 55.3 for the wife, and 1.2 for someone else.

The means follow the traditional patterns for Earning Money and Keeping House. All of the wives' percentages of responsibilities for Earning Money fell at 50% and below; none of the males responses were below 50%. An unexpected result was the nearly equal mean for Caring for Children. For the total sample, 379 (63.2%) stated 50% of the responsibility should be the wife's. (The percentages did not always sum to 100% across persons, because the students could assign the percentages independently to each person.) This 50-50 split was not found for the other two areas of responsibility. Nearly a third, however, allocated 50% of the responsibility for earning money to the husband and 50% to the wife. Similarly, slightly over one-third, 36%, allocated responsibility for keeping house equally to the husband and wife.

Responses to each of the three areas were examined by three-way ANOVAs. All three main effects were significant for the area of Earning Money. The F values for the main effects were, for husband's percentage: Sex, $F_{1,588} = 54.46$, pr $> F = .0001$; Ethnic, $F_{2,588} = 9.89$, pr $> F = .0001$; and SES, $F_{1,588} = 11.49$, pr $> F = .0007$. The means for the sex groups were females 63.4 and males 72.3. For ethnic groups the means were white 71.2, black 64.6, and Hispanic 67.6. SES group means were middle 65.8 and low 69.9. These differences indicate that females were giving a lower degree of responsibility to earning money for the family to the husband than the males were, again a less traditional view of the sex role. There was not, however, a fully equal allocation of responsibility for earning money.

The ethnic group differences indicated that the white students, as a group, allocated higher percentages of responsibility to males than did black or Hispanic students, reflecting a somewhat more traditional sex role view of this responsibility. Within the SES groups, the low-SES group allocated the higher percentage responsibility, the more traditional view.

There were two significant main effects for Keeping House as the husband's responsibility: Ethnic, $F_{2,588} = 4.15$, pr $> F = .0162$; and SES, $F_{1,588} = 6.15$, pr $> F = .0134$. There was one significant main effect for the wife's responsibility: SES, $F_{1,588} = 11.37$, pr $> F = .0008$. The means for the ethnic groups for husband's responsibility for Keeping House were: 32.0, white; 36.8, black; and 34.4, Hispanic. The black students assigned a slightly higher percent responsibility to the husband's role in housekeeping. The means for the SES groups were: 36.1, middle; and 32.7, low. The middle-SES group also assigned a slightly higher percentage responsibility to the husband. The means for the significant SES group difference for the wife's responsibility in keeping house were: 61.2, middle; and 66.0, low.

The means are in the same direction as for the husband's responsibility, with the middle-SES group assigning a lower percentage responsibility to the wife.

The three-way ANOVA for Caring for Children showed no significant main effects or interactions among the sample groups. As noted above, nearly two-thirds of the students stated that husbands and wives should share equally in the responsibility of caring for children. As was noted in the ratings of family activities, however, specific activities tend to be perceived along sex-traditional lines by many of the students.

The last questions that examined traditional or nontraditional attitudes toward the family were concerned with the circumstances under which a husband or wife should *not* work and how a wife or husband felt if their spouse earned more money than they did. The responses to the question, Are there any circumstances under which a *husband* should not work? were coded for analysis. Almost two-thirds of the students gave the circumstance of ill health (62%). For the circumstances under which a wife should not work, the predominant response was, If she has small children (63%), followed by Ill health (16%) and If she doesn't want to (6%). Analyses of the main groups by chi-squares showed no group differences for situations under which a husband should not work but significant differences between the sexes on the situations under which a wife should not work. More females than males cited Ill Health as a reason (20% vs. 11%).

Examples of the responses given by students to when a wife should not work included:

When she's pregnant; when the child is still young.
If it is a hazard to her health and if she sees that her children are not able to cope with the housekeeper and they really need her.
If she has an illness or if she doesn't want to.
If she wants to take off from work to care for her children, she should do it for a period of time.
Illness; during pregnancy and after the children are born; during the first couple of years so she can take care of them.

Rarely did students provide the answer for the husband of, "If he wants to be with his family," for circumstances under which a husband should not work. Sixteen students gave this response, as represented by the female student who said a husband should work, "Unless he's sick or taking care of the children." The reality of options (or rather, lack of options) remains traditional for males. For female students, as shown in the work plans later in this chapter, there is also an unreality, but in a different sense—the lack of knowledge of women's work patterns and the rapid return to work shown for labor force data from the National Longitudinal Survey of Young Women. The average woman in the sample stayed in the labor force until three or four months before the birth of the first child; 40% of white females and 60% of black females were back in the labor force within five months (Mott, 1978).

One of the attitudinal variables that appears fundamental to changing the power relationships within marriage is the attitude toward responsibility for earning money and the sense of power given by money. This attitude was tapped and labelled the Economic Equity theorist by Ellen Goodman (1980). The occasion for the definition was an earlier column, Mastering the Marital Two-step (1979). In this earlier column Goodman described "the grateful wife":

> In the beginning, this young wife was grateful to find herself married to a man who let her work. That was in 1964. . . . Later, the wife looked around her . . . and was grateful that her husband wasn't threatened, hurt, neglected, insulted—the multiple choices of the mid-60s—by her job.

> He was proud. And her cup overran with gratitude . . . (and through a decade of work and small children). If she was coming home late, he would make dinner. All you have to do is ask, he would say with a smile. . . . [But later] she began to realize that all the items of their shared life were stored in her exclusive computer. . . . The grateful wife began to wonder why she should say thank you when a father took care of his children and why she should say please when a husband took care of his house. She began to realize that being grateful meant being responsible. (Goodman, 1979).

The Economic Equity theorists were,

> dollar for dollar men. . . . The most vivid Eco-Husband from California put it this way, "I earn 75 percent of our family income. If I did 50 percent of the housework, then I would be contributing 62 percent. This is unfair. As long as I am the chief earner, my wife should be chief homemaker.[2]

How do eleventh graders perceive at least part of this issue which revolves around earning money?

The responses to the question, How do you think a wife (husband) feels if her husband (wife) earns more money than she (he) does? were coded Positive (responses typically said proud, feels good about it), Negative, or Doesn't matter. Table 8.4 presents the responses for these categories. The overall trend in these data was along the line of traditional sex roles.

Eighty-two percent of the sample stated the wife would be positive or accepting if the husband earned more money. Only 21% of the students stated that the husband's feeling would be positive or accepting (doesn't matter) if the wife earned more money than he did. About three-fourths said his attitude would be negative, reflecting the traditional sex-role expectations for the husband as major wage earner.

Chi-square analyses showed that the females and males differed in their responses to how a wife and husband would feel ($\chi^2_3 = 28.83$, $p = .0000$ and $\chi^2_3 = 17.62$, $p = .005$) but that the other main groups did not. More males than females stated a wife would feel negative if her husband earned more (16% vs. 5%) and more females said it doesn't matter (56% vs. 41%). On the husband's feelings, more females than males said he would feel negative (79% vs. 68%).

Of particular concern is the 74% of the sample who responded that the husband will feel negative if the wife earns more. Example of the types of responses given by both boys and girls were:

> He'll feel funny. He's supposed to make more.
> Doesn't like it. He feels cheap. Doesn't make him feel like a man.
> He would get jealous. It depends on education though.
> If I have a college degree I should earn more if he dropped out.
> Generally they would feel down, that they are not breadwinners. That depresses me that they would feel like that.
> Because it is usually his doing to support the wife and a lot of them don't like their wives to work.
> Feels like he has lost his manhood because they feel they should earn more.
> Terrible, cause a man should bring in more money.
> Neglected—she'll be spending more time on the job.
> Lousy, 'cause she's doing most of the work and he should be.
> Feels like a dummy—because she supports (him) and that's not right.
> Bad, because a woman should earn less.
> Not good because he'd feel he's not succeeding.

The first six of these responses were given by girls, the last six by boys. The girls' responses to how the wives would feel if their husbands earned more money than they did often reflect the expectations that men will have better jobs, be better educated, and traditionally are paid more than women:

> He's earning more money, he has the better job.
> She's probably just accept it; it's been that way for a long time. He might have had more education.

TABLE 8.4   Attitudes Toward One Spouse Earning More Money Than the Other

| Attitude | Wife's feeling if husband earns more | | | | | | Husband's feeling if wife earns more | | | | | |
| | F | | M | | Total | | F | | M | | Total | |
	N	%	N	%	N	%	N	%	N	%	N	%
Positive	102	34	99	33	201	34	14	5	23	8	37	6
Negative	14	5	47	16	61	10	236	79	205	68	441	74
Doesn't matter	167	56	123	41	290	48	29	10	60	20	89	15
Other	16	5	30	10	46	8	21	7	12	4	33	5
Total	299	100%	299	100%	598	100%	300	101%	300	100%	600	100%

Wouldn't care. If he's earning more money, he probably has harder job
and deserves it.

OK because wife takes care of kids more.

Secure, usually a man earns more.

Normal, she's not working.

It wouldn't bother her, that's how it's been.

She shouldn't feel upset because it is expected that he is the breadwinner.

The apparent inconsistencies in these responses in dividing responsibilities for earning money, child care, and keeping house have also been noted
in the study by Herzog, Bachman, and Johnston (1980) of a national
sample of high school seniors. In examining preferences for a wife's
participation in employment in settings with and without children, they
found that there are still many seniors who prefer a wife who works
half-time or not at all over one who holds a full-time job (even when there
are no children), and with preschool children the wife is very clearly the
one who is expected to drop out of the labor force or to change to
part-time employment. This latter finding is very consistent with the data
for these eleventh graders on how children will affect their work plans and
in the time lines described below.

Furthermore, Herzog et al. suggest that what appears to be a preference
for egalitarianism—in child care division of responsibilities, which for most
of their seniors was an equal division of responsibility—in fact still has the
final responsibility resting with the one partner who has traditionally held
that particular duty. Thus the wife is finally held responsible for child care
and the husband for economic support of the family. As these authors
summarized,

> Overall, there is an impressive lack of flexibility in the way the
> husband's employment responsibilities are viewed by both male and
> female seniors. Also, and this is particularly remarkable in this age of
> changing sex roles, absolutely no change in preferences regarding the
> husband's role has been registered during the last four years. (p. 20)

The levels of sex differences they did observe in their data were not
pronounced enough to predict widespread and fundamental disagreement
between the sexes about the proper roles for husbands and wives. This
conclusion is also echoed in the eleventh graders' reasons for how and why
husbands and wives will feel if their respective spouses earned more than
they did. Whereas they tended to appear more egalitarian in caring for
children and to suggest that wives should assume some responsibility
(about one-third) for earning money to support the family, the percep-

tions of the negative effects of a wife earning more money are held by the vast majority and the reasons given are very traditional. For many of these future husbands and wives, the underlying attitudes are reflected in expected ages for major life events.

Timing of Major Life Events

Questions designed to elicit student plans for education, marriage, children, full-time work, and part-time work between the ages of 16 and 41 were asked by means of time lines. Interviewers or students circled the age(s) at which they expected each event would occur. Appendix 7.4 presents the frequency distributions for each event.

The mean age at which students planned to complete high school was 17.5 and the expected age for completing education ranged from 17 to 34. The mean age anticipated for marriage was 25 years, with a range from 18 to 40. Student age at birth of first child ranged from 16 to 40, with a mean of 26.7 years.

Three-way ANOVAs were used to examine the data for group differences. Age at Finishing High School showed significant main effects for ethnic and SES groups: Ethnic, $F_{2,588}$ = 3.1, pr $>$ F = .0474; and SES, $F_{1,588}$ = 11.3, pr $>$ F = .0008. There were slight differences in the means for the ethnic groups: 17.43, white; 17.47, black; and 17.59, Hispanic. Means for the SES groups were: 17.4, middle; and 17.58, low. These mean ages reflect age differences in the sample that were noted earlier, with the Hispanic and low-SES students slightly older than the other groups.

Age at Completing Education also showed significant ethnic (F = 11.2, pr $>$ F = .0001) and SES (F = 36.0, pr $>$ F = .0001) group differences. Means for the ethnic groups were: 21.52, white; 22.44, black; and 22.56, Hispanic. SES group means were: 22.76, middle; and 21.58, low. The SES group differences reflect the lower educational aspirations of the low-SES group.

Age at Marriage showed all three main effects significant. The sex main effect was significant at the .0001 level (F = 44.59) and the mean age at which boys expected to marry was later than that for girls—25.81 vs. 24.17. The main effect for ethnic groups was significant at pr $>$ F = .041 (F = 3.22), and the means for the groups were: 24.74, white; 25.46, black; and 24.82, Hispanic. The F for the SES groups was 8.71 (pr $>$ F = .0033), and the means were: 25.36, middle; and 24.64, low. For these groups, males, black students, and middle-SES students expected to marry at later ages. These patterns are similar to those for age at completion of education. The patterns are more realistic for the male students than the female students. Age at first marriage for women was 21.8 and for males 24.2, in

1978 (Bureau of the Census, 1979). Thus, these eleventh-grade girls predict more delay in marriage than is likely to occur (even though the present sample is equally weighted with middle- and low-SES students).

For timing of children, the ages at which each student expected to have the first, second, or third child were circled. The three-way ANOVAs were calculated for all three, but the number of missing cases varied for each, as noted in Appendix 7.4. The overall mean age for first child was 26.7 years. Twenty-six students (4.3%) did not plan to have a child or did not respond. The ANOVA had significant sex ($F = 20.9$, $pr > F = .0001$) differences, with again the males showing a later mean age than females (27.2 vs. 26.1). The SES main effect was also significant ($F = 13.38$, $pr > F = .0003$) and the mean age for middle-SES students was later than for low-SES students (27.13 vs. 26.21).

For age at second child data were missing for 56 (9.3%) of the students (i.e., either they had no plans for a second child or did not respond). The sex main effect was significant ($F = 12.33$, $pr > F = .0005$) and the mean age for males was again higher than for females, 29.1 vs. 28.2. The SES main effect was significant ($F = 15.16$, $pr > F = .0001$) and the mean for middle-SES students was higher than for low-SES students, 29.14 versus 28.14. Responses for age of third child were given by less than half of the students, 277 or 46.4%, consistent with earlier data on number of children planned (45.5% planned 0, 1, or 2 children). The ANOVA for these students showed significant ethnic and SES effects. The F for the ethnic main effect was 4.27 ($pr > F = .0149$) and the means were: 30.26, white; 30.36, black; and 29.11, Hispanic. The F for the SES main effect was 6.42 ($pr > F = .0119$) and the means were 30.46 for middle SES students and 29.40 for low-SES students. The SES trend is consistent with the differences in ages at completion of education, marriage, and first child, because middle-SES students tended to expect to complete education and marry at later ages.

The expected ages for full-time and part-time work are of interest because they indicated a pattern whereby some students recognized they would be in the work force full-time and then would stop full-time work and would later resume it. Similarly, the distributions for part-time work indicated entry and exit from the work force for a small percentage of students. As shown in Appendix 7.4 the mean age at which all students expected to begin full-time work was 23.8, with a range from 17 to 40 years. Appendix 7.5 presents the frequency distributions of ages for work plans for females and males separately for part-time work and Table 8.5 presents the data for full-time work.

For timing of work plans, age was circled according to when and what type of work pattern students expected. This pattern could include entry,

TABLE 8.5   Frequency Distributions for Full-Time Work Expectations for Females and Males

| | Started full-time work | | | | Resumed full-time work | | | |
| | Female | | Male | | Female | | Male | |
Age	F	%	F	%	F	%	F	%
Missing/								
0	16	5.3	1	.3	80	60.0	289	96.3
16								
17	1	.3						
18	11	3.7	11	3.7				
19	14	4.7	11	3.7				
20	16	5.3	20	6.7				
21	27	9.0	22	7.3	2	.7		
22	41	13.7	47	15.7				
23	49	16.3	57	19.0	2	.7	2	.7
24	26	8.7	27	9.0	2	.7	1	.3
25	30	10.0	43	14.3	1	.3		
26	12	4.0	25	8.3	3	1.0		
27	11	3.7	17	5.7	4	1.3	1	.3
28	9	3.0	8	2.7	3	1.0		
29	5	1.7	7	2.3	9	3.0	2	.7
30	8	2.7	2	.7	8	2.7	1	.3
31	4	1.3			9	3.0		
32	2	.7			6	2.0		
33	4	1.3	1	.3	8	2.7		
34	2	.7			10	3.3		
35	5	1.7	1	.3	20	6.7		
36					8	2.7	1	.3
37	2	.7			7	2.3	1	.3
38	2	.7			6	2.0		
39					1	.3		
40	3	1.0			10	3.3	2	.7
41					1	.3		
Mean	24.1		23.4		33		30.7	
SD	4.3		2.7		4.4		6.5	

exit, and reentry for both full-time and part-time work between the ages of 16 and 41. As shown in Table 8.5, the distributions for the sexes show that more males expect to start full-time work at earlier ages, and it is primarily women who forecast a reentry to (or resuming of) full-time work at some age. Only 11 males forecast starting and later resuming full-time work. Although 80 of the females forecast this pattern, this underesti- mates the entry and exit patterns in employment because of the shifts to part-time work among the times planned for children. As might be expected, the age distribution of females doing part-time work is more scattered than that for males, with only a small percentage of males expecting to have part-time work after age 25. Of those anticipating starting part-time work a second time, 45 were female and 5 were male. And similarly for ending part-time work a second time, 44 were female and 3 male. The part-time work for males is predominantly during their education years, and for females part-time work continues on through the child rearing or family cycle.

ANOVAs for the work age variables were also calculated. Age at starting full-time work showed all main effects and one interaction were significant: Sex, $F_{1,571}$ = 5.89, pr > F = .0156; Ethnic, $F_{2,571}$ = 3.59, pr > F = .0283; SES, $F_{1,571}$ = 9.43, pr > F = .0022; and Sex x Ethnic, $F_{2,571}$ = 3.69, pr > F = .0257. The mean ages for the main groups were: Females 24.12; males 23.41; white 23.20; black 23.99; Hispanic 24.07; middle SES 24.21; and low SES 23.31. The mean ages for the interaction were: female–white 23.52, black 24.86, and Hispanic 23.95; male means were white 22.90, black 23.16 and Hispanic 24.18.

The highest mean age for starting full-time work was for black females and Hispanic males. The age resuming full-time work had responses from less than 25% of the sample (N = 131 students). Of this group, 120, or almost all, were females. There were no significant differences for ethnic groups but there were for SES groups (F$_{1,120}$ = 9.67, pr > F = .0355). The mean age expected for resuming full-time work was 33.90 for middle-SES students and 31.61 for low-SES students. When the means for females only were examined, however, the middle-SES group had a mean of 33.86 (N = 63) and the low-SES group had a mean age of 32.07 (N = 57).

Age at starting part-time work also differed by sex (F$_{1,411}$ = 55.40, pr > F = .0001). The Sex X Ethnic groups interaction was also significant (F$_{2,411}$ = 4.59, pr > F = .0107). Females expected to start part-time work at later ages than males (means of 23.31 and 19.40, respectively, N_F = 224, N_M = 199). The means for the subgroups were: Female–white 24.83, black 22.06, and Hispanic 23.01; for males the means were white 18.87, black 19.76 and Hispanic 19.71. Black females expected to start part-time work at an earlier age and white males expected to start somewhat earlier. Again, the sex differences in ages reflect different work patterns. Typically, the males expected to work while attending college, and the higher mean age for females reflects less expectation of working during college (perhaps less realistic expectations).

The pattern for ending part-time work also reflects a different pattern for the sexes and their different reasons for entering and leaving full-time and part-time work status. Only the sex main effect was significant (F$_{1,379}$ = 54.27, pr > F = .0001). The mean age for females was 26.73 (SD = 6.50) and that for males was 22.94 (SD = 2.75).

The data for the students who expected to start and end part-time work a second time were also analyzed. The data were examined for females only (typically, a pattern around the timing of children). Only the SES group differences were significant: For age at reentry to part-time work $F_{1,39} = 4.22$, pr $>$ F = .0467; the mean for middle-SES students was 33.62 and for low-SES students 30.67. For age at end of part-time work, $F_{1,36} = 6.79$, pr $>$ F = .0132; the middle-SES mean was 36.75 and for low SES the mean was 32.50. On the average, middle-SES females expected to reenter and leave part-time work at later ages than did low-SES females.

These data on work patterns are summarized in one variable, number of years of full-time work before age 41 (examined in Chapter 7 for relationships with the values and other variables). Each student's time line for full-time work was used to count the circled number of years for full-time work. The range of this variable for the total sample was 23 years. The mean was 16.3 (SD = 5.8).

The three-way ANOVA showed significant main effects for sex and ethnic groups, and interaction effects for sex X ethnic groups and sex X SES groups: Sex, $F_{1,585} = 357.96$, pr $>$ F = .0001; Ethnic, $F_{2,585} = 6.90$, pr $>$ F = .0011; Sex X Ethnic, $F_{2,585} = 12.64$, pr $>$ F = .0001; and Sex X SES, $F_{1,585} = 9.18$, pr $>$ F = .0026. The means for the sex groups were 20.21 for females and 17.02 for males. Other means were:

	Ethnic			SES	
	W	B	H	M	L
Females	8.15	11.87	10.63	10.57	9.84
Males	17.47	17.03	16.56	16.29	17.75
Total	12.81	14.46	13.63	13.44(N.S.)	13.83(N.S.)

The interaction of sex X ethnic groups reflects the fact that black females expected to have the largest number of years of full-time work by age 41 and white males differed slightly from the other two groups, expecting to have the greatest number of years of full-time work by age 41. For the small difference in means for SES groups, middle-SES females expected to have more years of work before age 41, as did the low-SES males.

Overall, the data on timing of major life events are likely to be most realistic for the males, although "unrealistic" in the plans for education and hence average number of years in the labor force to age 41. Their plans for years of work are not affected by marriage and children. For these eleventh-grade females, it is also likely that the number of years for education beyond high school are unrealistic. In addition, we noted earlier the disparity between their estimates for age at marriage and 1978 census estimates. If the NLS (Parnes data) are representative, then it is also likely that the number of years they plan to be out of the work force for childbearing are also overestimates for a sizeable proportion of these young women. These differences between the realities of women's labor force participation and their plans have often been described as important for counseling and interventions. They are critical to linking career education and career development to a meaningful theory of women's career development.

In the next chapter there are case descriptions of several female students. The time lines for girls with traditional and nontraditional occupational choices, and their values are examined to draw attention to the ambiguities and conflicts young women need to examine more openly and explicitly.

NOTES

1. The items were also summed to obtain a total score following Eagly and Anderson. For the total score sex and ethnic groups showed the only significant main effects (pr > F of .0001). There were no significant interactions.

2. See Goodman, 1979, for descriptions and analysis of individuals at different stages of change with respect to sex roles.

Chapter 9

CHOICES OF ADOLESCENT GIRLS:
Case Studies

Analyses of the frequencies and group responses to the interview questions and the values provide a convenient shorthand to define trends and project the variables of most interest for action and further research. The analyses do not convey the wealth of the experiences of adolescents and the ideas they have about their futures. The goal of this chapter is to provide a more wholistic perspective of the various facets of the study. In order to attain this goal, several interviews were taped and transcribed in their entirety. One of these interviews is presented here, including a summary of the demographic characteristics of the student. The focus is, however, upon the student's occupational goal, the values, work plans, other sex-role variables, and the time line. The remainder of the chapter contains shorter descriptions for several other students, with the selection of the students guided by the criterion of their occupational goal and time-line patterns— specifically, whether a different time-line pattern was combined with a traditional or nontraditional occupation for women. Because nontraditional occupational choices were not widespread, and virtually nonexistent for the nonprofessional field (only 6% or 18 students), these abbreviated case descriptions provide only hints of the possible relationships between traditional/nontraditional occupational choice, family patterns, and other measures.

The case material is presented only for adolescent females, and there is no attempt to judge the "appropriateness" of the occupational aspirations or to point out all of the inconsistencies in the student's responses from one question to the next. The levels of educational and occupational aspirations were sometimes inconsistent, and, to the outside observer, unrealistic in terms of reported high school grade-point averages. Similarly, the time line question may appear unrealistic or at least not consistent with current census data on ages of marriage and childbirth. The inconsistencies are realistic, however, and represent the stage of development of these adolescents and the general lack of prior discussions in the areas of career, marriage, and family decisions. They form the context within which career education, counseling interventions, or future research will occur.

The Interview
Sherri, a Nontraditional Occupational Choice

The young black woman whose transcript follows is 15 years old, was born in New York, and has spent most of her life there. Sherri's mother was born in Georgia, and she lives with both her parents. Both parents graduated from high school and both work. Her father is a trackman with the transit authority and is a supervisor; her mother is a payroll clerk with a major shoe retailer. Sherri's mother has always worked full-time, before she married and while her two children were growing up. Sherri says she is about a C student and expects to graduate from a four-year college. She attends a large urban public high school. The interviewer is asking about the jobs Sherri has considered doing:

I: What kinds of jobs have you thought of, what kinds of jobs would you like in the future?

S: At the college? I want to be a doctor.

I: And what other jobs have you thought about?

S: Nursing.

I: And what else?

S: Accountant.

I: Anything else?

S: That's it, really. I was interested in being a model, but I've thought about it, but after a while, when they don't want you anymore, then there's nothing you can do after that.

I: Are there other jobs you've thought about once that you don't want any more?

S: Lawyer and Secretary.

I: Which one are you most interested in doing now?

S: Doctor.

I: And what job do you think you actually will do?

S: Doctor.

I: Why do you think you actually will be a doctor?

S: I want to be a pediatrician, and I like children.

I: Anything else that makes you think you'll actually do that?

S: No, I just really want to go through that, that's really what I want to be.

I: Will you work for yourself or for somebody else?

S: For myself.

I: And what are the main duties or activities you'd have as a pediatrician?

S: Helping kids, maybe even deliver babies.

I: And what other kinds of activities?

S: They get involved with hospitals, and they have private practice, and they open up free clinics or something like that.

I: How did you decide on this job?

S: When I went to the doctor with my mother when I was small, and I saw the doctor working with the little babies, the new-born babies. . . .

I: Do you know anybody who is a pediatrician?

S: I have an aunt who's a nurse.

I: Who do you talk to about your occupational plans?

S: My parents, my family—my grandmother and my aunt.

I: Who do you talk to about your educational plans?

S: My parents.

I: And who do you talk to about your marriage plans?

S: My parents.

I: Has a teacher ever talked to you about any kinds of work for you?

S: No—oh yes, yes. The health career teacher was telling me how much school I'd have to go through, and how to take tests for medical school.

I: Has a counselor ever talked to you about kinds of work?

S: No.

I: What things do you consider important in deciding what kind of work you want to do?

S: Well, you really have to know what you want to do, and after you find out, you put your mind to it and do that thing. You have to have confidence in yourself.

I: Do you plan to have children?

S: Yes.

I: How many children would you like to have?

S: Four.

I: Will having a family make a difference in your plans for work?

S: No.

I: Why not?

S: 'Cause I'm doing this for me and my family.

I: If by some chance you were to get enough money to live comfortably, would you still work?

S: Yes [I'd still work]. Because I'm helping people and I shouldn't just stop.

I: Which of the following would you prefer if you had enough money to live comfortably without working?

S: To concentrate on home and family.

I: What adult do you know personally who's living a life you'd like to have?

S: My aunt.

I: How old is your aunt?

S: She should be about 20 now.

I: What do you like or admire most about your aunt?

S: She's free and does what she wants. She has a family and everything, but she works, and still has time to go out and time for her family.

I: How would you like to be like your aunt?

S: Have her energy. Have the power she has just to keep on doing everything for yourself and for your family.

I: So your aunt's married?

S: Yes.

I: And how many children?

S: One child.

I: And what kind of work does she do?

S: She's a secretary.

I: Does she work full-time?

S: Yes.

I: I'd like to ask you some questions now about work, marriage, and children that are related to career decision-making. These cards describe ideas people have about careers and jobs. . . .

Sherri gave her two highest ratings, 8 and 6, to Full-Time Career and Full-Time Job, and her lowest rating (2) to No Job. Her involvement level score was 5, slightly below the average for black females of 5.3, but above the means for white (4.1) and Hispanic (4.8) females. Her next activity was with the cards for the occupation values. Her rank order was (high to low): Prestige, Helping Others, High Income, Variety, Field of Interest, Independence, Security, Leadership, Leisure, and Early Entry. Among her highest values are these typically ranked higher by females (Helping Others and Variety) and typically ranked highest by males (High Income and Prestige). The reasons she gave for her preferences follow.

I: Tell me a little bit about why you put them in this order.

S: Prestige, I think—if you don't have people's respect, then you really don't have anything cause you can't go on, you can't work without the respect of others. And what I want to do is really help others, so that would be my second one. High Income—everybody likes money—I'd like to have a high income. And Variety—I wouldn't want to go through the same monotony of everything everyday, but have different things, variety. Work in main Field of Interest would be science, because I want to be a doctor. And Independence, cause I want to make my own decisions, and not have always somebody leading me, but be able to do what I want.

I: But now these are less important to you.

S: Yes. Security, I won't really need security, since usually I'll be working on my own. And Leadership, I wouldn't like leading other people; I just want my independence, everybody else should have theirs. Leisure—I guess I'll be working most of the time and I won't have time, but work is more important than leisure and work shouldn't interfere with that, but you should have time for both. And Early Entry—I want to finish college first, I don't just want to jump into any job.

For the marriage values, Sherri's rank order was: 1—Emotional Support, then Prestige, Someone to Rely On, Children, Permanent Companion, A Normal Life, A Close Physical Relationship, Financial Security, A Help

Mate, Your Own Home, and A Feeling of Leadership. Sherri's high rankings for Emotional Support and Someone to Rely On are typical of these young women, although her high ranking of Prestige is less typical.

I: Why are some higher and some low?

S: Emotional Support is needed when you have problems, you can talk out the problems with each other, and it brings you closer; Prestige— you'd be proud of each other and proud of your success and that gives you more courage to go on and you're proud enough and you're relying on someone—you know, here's somebody here to protect you and take care of you. Children—everybody wants to have children, and you can provide for them. A Permanent Companion is somebody who's always there—you have somebody to come home to, your companion's always there. A Normal Life—with family and friends and children. A Close Physical Relationship— when you're close and whatnot. And Financial Security—I think it's important, but as long as you have your own job you're both secure, and you're secure in each other; one isn't secure in just one. He's not really there to help you pay your bills, you're there to help each other, and everybody sharing the work and whatnot. And a Help Mate—you don't want to be the boss, because then you'd have all the power and he'd be afraid of you, and there's really no relationship there. And Leadership—I don't like leadership, you know, where one guy's elected.

I: Tell me again about Your Own Home.

S: Because you don't want to be your own boss; it's not really your own house, but you're sharing it with somebody else too, and you can't really take over.

I: Is there anything that would influence your decision to get married that isn't on the cards?

S: No. Nothing besides love.

Sherri's ranks for the parenthood values were: 1—Sense of Accomplishment, then Friendship, A Sense of Pride, A Tie to the Future, A Chance to Express Love, Variety, Joy, A Stable Marriage, Future Security, A Sense of Importance, Confidence as a Man or Woman, Respect of Others.

I: Tell me again why some are high and some low.

S: A Sense of Accomplishment is like raising your child, and when you see that you have accomplished something good it makes you feel proud because your child has done very good, and it's not good just to be parent and child; it's good to be Friends because it's closer and

you can always count on your child to come to you with problems
and whatnot. A Sense of Pride—you know, like they say, that if your
child is very successful you feel proud because you know you have
raised this child and they've grown very successful. And a Tie to the
Future is when you're a parent and you have given life to one and
that one has given life to another and you're leaving part of you
behind, and it's giving you a chance to show that you can love and
be loved by another, and a child gives you Variety in life—you see
him growing and whatnot, and from a little baby to a teenager to a
grown-up. He brings you laughter (Joy) and whatnot because you
see him everyday, and you're there, keeping him well and whatnot.
A Stable Marriage doesn't always have to be with children, because
people who don't have children often have very stable marriages, and
you don't usually have to use your children for your Future Security
because your children, you take care of them when they were small,
it's not really necessary for them to take care of you; you're not
going to force them to take care of you. It's like being on an ego
trip, feeling really important; you know, your children are really
important to you but it's not really to feel a sense of importance
because you have children. And your children don't have to give you
Confidence in being a Man or Woman, you give yourself that
confidence. Being a parent, you don't need the Respect of (Others)
your family or friends to become a parent, you give that respect to
yourself.

Sherri next completed the Job-Child Scale, selecting first B, 1 child, 3/4
time job, then C, 2 children, 1/2 time job, then A, No children, full time
job, resulting in a scale score of 3, below the total sample mean of 4.1, and
below the mean for black females of 3.65.

I: Can you tell me a little about your choices on these, why you picked
these?

S: I like to work full-time but I also want to have children.

I: That's the closest combination (B). How about these two choices?
Which would you like best?

S: C.

I: Why C?

S: Because I'm working, and I'll also have time to spend with my
children.

I: Which of these two?

S: A, cause I think I'd rather work than just stay home all day.

On the Circle task Sherri's division of the circle into segments for work, marriage, children, and other reflected the emphasis on work, then children. Nine of the 20 segments were for the importance of work, 5 each to marriage and children, and 1 to "other," which Sherri said included leisure, vacation, free time at home, and watching TV. The weight of 9 for work was above the total sample mean of 6 (SD 2.2) and above the mean for black students of 6.5 (SD 2.4), which was the highest of the three ethnic groups.

Sherri's ratings of the female/male responsibilities for families with children tended to be about average, and somewhat egalitarian; that is, she gave 13 of 22 ratings of "3," the activity could be either person's responsibility. Four activities were rated as mainly a woman's responsibility, and five as mainly the man's, as discussed below. (The discussion took place after Sherri had completed rating the activities.)

I: [Say why you marked it, e.g., cleaning the house.]

S: Well, you should share the housework; it shouldn't be just one person's job.

I: Mending the clothes?

S: I don't think men really know how to sew.

I: Managing family money?

S: Women seem to have problems when it comes to managing money.

I: Repairing household appliances?

S: Men seem to be good at repairing things.

I: Cutting the grass . . . mainly the male?

S: You always see it like that anyway, the men always mowing the lawn.

I: Planning the color scheme for the house?

S: Women seem to be good at decorating.

I: Reading to children?

S: A parent should be close to the children and read to them.

I: Taking out the garbage?

S: You shouldn't have to wait for someone to take out the garbage; if it gets full, just take it out.

I: Washing the family car?

S: If it's the family car, they're both going to use it, so they should take turns washing it.

I: Washing the clothes?

S: Men don't usually wash clothes very good, when it comes to bleach and whatnot.

I: Caring for baby?

S: Either person should care for the baby; either person should take the children to the doctor. Either person who earns a salary can support the family. I think the woman should do all the shopping 'cause men just pick up anything at the store. My father, he picks up anything, he doesn't care. Man should decide when the car needs a tuneup, cause I don't think the woman really knows. The wife may be good at sports, too. They both could cook.

I: Do you think fixing the lamp is mainly a man's job?

S: Yes, since he's good at repairing things, he should fix the lamp. If they move to another city, I think it should be done together. They both can help the children with their homework. Either one can stay home if the children are sick.

I: Why do you think that?

S: Cause they both work, and the wfe can't always stay home, so the husband can stay home, too, sometimes. They should discuss about whether they should buy a large item, since they might not need it.

The interview continues with work decisions for self and for spouse.

I: On this page are some choices you have about work after school. . . . You will work?

S: Yes.

I: What will your working hours be, which choice?

S: Mostly full-time.

I: Why?

S: Cause doctors are always on duty, on call.

I: And what will your work pattern be?

S: Mostly continuously.

I: Do you think you'll change work often?

S: (start in one field, remain in this field through working life) cause I like children, and I think I'll stay working with children.

I: How will you combine work and family? Work before marriage?

S: Yes.

I: Work before children?

S: Yes.

I: Work while children are 1-3?

S: No.

I: 3-5?

S: Yes.

I: 5-12?

S: Yes.

I: Over 12?

S: Yes.

(The response for not working while the children are 1-3 is not consistent with the time line, below.)

I: Now think about what you might expect your husband to do. . . . What kind of education will your husband have?

S: College.

I: Will he work?

S: Yes.

I: What will his working hours be?

S: Full-time.

I: Why do you think full-time?

S: Because mostly all men work full-time because they feel they have to provide for their family.

I: What will his work pattern be?

S: Mostly continuously.

I: Why?

S: He'll probably take off for vacation. [Sherri did not expect her husband's work to be affected by having children.]

I: Tell me the ages at which you expect to do these activities [the time lines]. When will you graduate from high school?

S: 16.

I: When will you be in college?

S: 17, 12 years if I want to be a doctor. I'll be in school a very long time!

I: When do you expect to get married?

S: 25.

I: When might you have children?

S: 26.

I: While you're still in medical school?

S: Yes.

I: The second child?

S: 29.

I: Third? (Sherri had said she wanted four children earlier in the interview.)

S: I have to have a third? I've changed my mind—when I look at this, I'll be too old to have kids. 31 and 32.

I: Well, I'm not saying you have to do it. Put what you think you'd like.

S: That's it, because I don't think I want kids in my thirties.

I: When will you be working part-time?

S: During medical school and during college.

I: Each one of these years, part-time. What about here? [ages 25 and 26]

S: No.

I: And here?

S: Yes, between 27 and 28.

I: And part-time here? What about here? [at age 30, after second child at age 29]

S: Then I should be working full-time.

I: And the rest of this will be full-time? Yes, full-time [to age 41].

I: There are three main responsibilities in a family—what is the best arrangement of dividing these. . . .

S: 50-50, because if they're both working, they should both help in paying the bills, and the house and rent.

I: Keeping house?

S: 40-60. Cause most likely the wife will keep the house better than her husband, but he can help.

I: And caring for children?

S: 50-50, because both husband and wife should care for children, not just one.

I: Are there any circumstances under which a husband shouldn't work?

S: If he has an illness.

I: Are there any circumstances under which a wife shouldn't work?

S: Illness; during pregnancy and after the children are born, during the first couple years, so she can take care of them.

I: How do you think a wife feels if a husband earns more?

S: She shouldn't feel anything, because any job he does, a man will automatically earn more than a woman does anyway.

I: Why is that?

S: That's just the way it is, I don't know. Men just make more money than women in jobs. They feel the man is more capable.

I: How does the husband feel?

S: If they have a close relationship it shouldn't bother him. If she has a good paying job she is helping with the family; it shouldn't really bother him.

Sherri's responses in the interviews reflect the apparent options that women have in choices among timing of education, work and family. The time line, as mentioned earlier, puts all these decisions together in one visual whole. Sherri changed from wanting four children to two, and presents also an unusual pattern of marriage and child-bearing while completing education. This is, in the main, an atypical pattern for these adolescent girls as it may well be even among women medical students.

In the remainder of the chapter there are descriptions of some of the time lines and the values for other girls with nontraditional, and traditional, professional occupational choices. Other descriptions for traditional, nonprofessional occupations are also given.

Planning a Semiprofessional, Traditional
Occupational Field
Helen

Helen is one of two children in a white middle-class family; her mother is not presently working and her father works for a major TV network, as manager of the news. He completed three years of college and her mother completed an MA in art and design. When her mother worked she was a codirector of fashion for a major women's national retail chain. Her mother has worked off and on, and did not work until after the children were in elementary school. Helen considers herself a B student and plans to graduate from a four-year college. She works part-time for Avon. The career she plans is as a fashion coordinator—a person who coordinates clothes for professional women. She would work for herself, and her grandmother is employed in this field. She has planned a work/family pattern that she thinks is possible because of the flexibility in working hours and location. She plans to have six children and to work at home, not leaving the children when they are young.

Helen's time line shows college attendance from 18-21, with part-time work during this period. She plans to work full-time from 22 to 26, to marry at 26 and to have her first child the next year. The years between 27 and 34 will be spent in closely timed child-bearing. Part-time work will resume at 34, continue through age 39, and full-time work will resume at age 40. Helen's attitudes toward the responsibilities of men and woman in family activities is more traditional (for example, than Sherri's), and she rates earning salary that supports the family as mainly a man's responsibility. Also, the child care planned is for at home, by the wife, until the youngest child is 10 (here inconsistent with her time-line return to full-time work when the youngest child is about 6). Her career pattern preference is for a part-time career, and job-child scale score is 5 as is the involvement level score.

In accord with her occupational choice, Helen gave the highest ranking to the occupational value of Prestige, then Independence, High Income, Helping Others, Leisure, and Security. She distinguished between Helping Others as a personal satisfaction and as occupational value:

Helping Others—I worked three years in a nursing home, volunteer work, and I got a lot out of it. I felt good because I did it, a lot of satisfaction from it. But I couldn't go around helping people my whole life. I love doing things like that, and I'd have to do it on my free time but I wouldn't make an occupation out of it.

Helen ranked the marriage values in this order: Children, Someone to Rely On, Emotional Support, A Help Mate, Financial Security, Prestige, A Close Physical Relationship, A Permanent Companion, A Feeling of Leadership, A Normal Life, and Your Own Home. The high preference for Children as a reason for deciding to get married fits with the prediction of number of children desired and the Job-Child Scale, and a lower number of years of full-time work to age 41. Her discussion of the values of Children, Someone to Rely on, Emotional Support, and a Help Mate, included:

Children—children are very important. It's not that they make a marriage. Marriage depends on love and caring and the whole thing, but children make the marriage grow. . . .

Someone to Rely On—Because I feel that your husband should protect you even from . . . if he really feels that you are wrong, to criticize you, but to be there when you need [him]. Like if he says, "Now that was really dumb of you, I'll be here but that was really stupid," and let him tell me why because I have to learn from my mistakes.

Emotional Support. Trust is, if you can't trust your husband I don't know who you can trust. I think that is neck in neck with love.

A Help Mate. I am not lazy. I will get up and do it, but my husband is not going to sit down with the newspaper and say, "Sweetheart, do this and do this." He is going to be there and helping me. . . . This isn't a one-way thing.

Three of her top-ranked marriage values were characteristic of the sex-atypical group formed by the marriage values (Chapter 7) and these adolescents tended to have a high number of children desired, to be higher on the J-C Scale, and to be higher on part-time work, characteristics that match some of Helen's goals and attitudes also.

Helen ranked the parenthood value of Friendship first, followed by A Chance to Express Love, Joy, Future Security, Variety, A Sense of Pride, Accomplishment, A Stable Marriage, A Tie to the Future, Respect of Others, Confidence as a Man or Woman, and A Sense of Importance. Here she describes her reason for ranking Friendship first:

Friendship—I feel that it is so important for the parents and the children to have a really close relationship. If you can't talk to your parents and you can't talk to your friends, or you can talk to your friends—still, when you come home you can have like a knot in your stomach. I think that's the most important thing, to get along with their parents because you can't get rid of them. You're not going to murder them off or anything.

The parenthood values that are high for Helen tended to overlap with those that identified the sex-typical girls defined by the parenthood values (Chapter 7). As noted there, these values appeared to be more centered on the perceived satisfactions to the individual in becoming a parent, rather than responses to social pressures or expectations.

Planning a Traditional Female Occupation
Rose

Rose was born and grew up in New York. She lives with one sibling and her mother (her parents are divorced). Her father is a plant manager in a basic industry and is responsible for about 70 employees. He also had some college, but did not graduate. Her mother attended high school, but did not graduate. Her mother is not presently working, has not worked since the two children were born, but did work as a wrapper in a department store before she married. The family is supported by the father. Rose has a B+ average and plans to graduate from a four-year college. She has worked part-time as a secretary and plans on this as a -full-time occupation, perhaps as an executive secretary in a law firm. When she has children she plans to raise them herself. The adult she most admires is a friend who is 23 and working full-time as a secretary. Rose ranked a full-time career as her first preference. She has a score of 3 on the IL scale and 7 on the Job-Child Scale. She also gave Children the highest weight in the Circle task (7) and a weight of 5 to work and 5 to marriage. She has fairly traditional ratings for the activities for families with children, stating that Earning Salary that Supports Family is only a man's responsibility. She plans to have four children and to take care of them at home until the youngest child is 7 or 8. These responses fit closely with the time lines, where Rose plans to be in college and working part-time until age 22. She plans to marry at 23, to have children at ages 25, 27, 29, and 31. She does not plan on full- or part-time work during any of this time. She plans to work full-time from age 38 on.

The ranks Rose gave to the occupational values were: Field of Interest (personal contact) first, then Helping Others, Variety, Leisure, Independence, Security, Prestige, Leadership, Early Entry, and High Income. Her highest occupational values are not the ones associated with higher educational aspirations; they are more like the ones rated higher by the "typical" girls on the occupational values, and her plans for four children and the highest score at the children end of the Job-Child scale are in agreement with the variables identifying that group. She ranked the marriage value of A Close Physical Relationship as number one, then the values Someone to Rely On, Emotional Support, Children, A Permanent Companion, Financial Security, A Help Mate, Your Own Home, Prestige, A Feeling of Leadership, and A Normal Life. Her highest rank for the parenthood values was given to A Chance to Express Love, then Joy, Friendship, A Sense of Accomplishment, A Sense of Pride, Variety, A Tie to the Future, Future Security, A Sense of Importance, A Stable Marriage, Respect of Others, and Confidence as a Man or Woman.

The relatively high placement given the marriage values of Someone to Rely On and Children fit the pattern of a lower number of years of full-time work to age 41 (although the high rating to the career pattern choice of full-time does not). The high ratings for the parenthood values of A Chance to Express Love, Joy, and Friendship also fit with the sex-typical group on these values. Many of Rose's attitudes towards sex roles are "traditional," as are her occupational choice, level of aspirations, and many of the occupational, marriage, and parenthood value patterns.

Planning a Traditional Profession
Frances

Frances was born in New York, but her mother was born in Cuba. Spanish is spoken at home, and Frances lives with her mother (who has been separated from her father for four years). There are two other children at home. Her father is an automotive technician, completed grade school, and runs the service department for a car dealer. Her mother had some technical training after high school for her work as a hair colorist. Frances says that her mother worked before her marriage but did not work until the divorce. The youngest child was about 9 years old at that time. Frances has an A- average and plans to graduate from a four-year college. She has had work experience in the summer as a camp counselor and has done part-time clerical work. She is most interested in being a play therapist. She has worked for four years with children, read about play therapy, and thinks she has a good idea of what it would be like. A teacher suggested this occupation to her.

Frances plans to have three children, and would have to go to school or work on a part-time basis if she had a family. Her most admired adult is a teacher, married, about 27, and working part-time. She most admires the teacher's ability to work and take care of her child, too—of being able to handle the situation of working and family combined. Her Involvement Level score is a 2 (low involvement in the work and child total domain) and the Job-Child score is a 2, toward the job rather than children end of the scale. Frances gave a weight of 8 to Work in the Circle task, 6 to Marriage, and 3 to Children. She gave all the activities for a family with children a rating of 3 (could be either person's responsibility), plans to remain at home when the children are young (1-3) and plans to share the responsibilities for earning money, keeping house, and caring for children with her husband.

The time lines show seven years of education beyond high school, marriage at 25, full-time work from 25 to 28, a first child at 28, part-time work for three years, a second child at 32, part-time work for two years, and then continuous full-time work. When doing the time line, she changed her number of children desired from three to two.

Frances's rankings of the three sets of values (from high to low) were:

Occupational Values: Helping Others, Field of Interest, Independence, Variety, Security, Leadership, Prestige, Leisure, High Income, and Early Entry.

Marriage values: A Permanent Companion, Children, Someone to Rely On, Emotional Support, A Normal Life, Financial Security, A Close Physical Relationship, A Help Mate, Prestige, Your Own Home, and A Feeling of Leadership.

Parenthood values: A Chance to Express Love, Friendship, Accomplishment, Joy, Variety, Confidence as a Man or Woman, A Sense of Pride, A Tie to the Future, Respect of Others, A Sense of Importance, A Stable Marriage, and Future Security.

The occupational values tend to be those rated more highly by the girls than the boys in this group of adolescents. The higher rating for Independence is associated with higher level of educational aspirations for this sample. The lower ratings for Leadership, Prestige, and High Income were associated with the sex-typical occupational group (although the low Job-Child scale score is not consistent with this group's pattern). The high ratings on the Marriage Values of Children, and Someone to Rely On were associated, for the Hispanic girls, with a lower number of years of full-time work to age 41 (along with a low IL score). Frances had 10 years of full-time work planned, slightly below the average for Hispanic females in the sample (M = 10.6). The parenthood values ranked at the top also tend to be those typical of the girls in the sample, and were more likely to be ranked higher by the young women than the young men.

Frances presents an interesting contrast in values, attitudes, and plans. Her ratings of the family activities were totally "egalitarian" and she has a very low rating (less emphasis on children) on the Job-Child scale. Her occupational choice and pattern of combining work and family, however, appear generally traditional at this stage, although not as traditional as those for Sharon.

Planning a Traditional Profession
Sharon

Sharon also was born and grew up in New York. Her father owns a car business and attended college but did not graduate. Her mother completed high school and attended secretarial school. She is presently employed part-time, and has been continuously employed on a part-time basis since she started work, except for the years when the two children had not yet entered elementary school. Sharon has a C+ average and plans to graduate from a four-year college. She has part-time work experience in accounting. She knows she wants to teach, but has not given much thought to her occupational choice. She would like to have three children and would not go back to work until the children were in school. Her most admired adult is an aunt who "has got a nice house, doesn't work, has 2 kids, and a dog." Sharon's most preferred career pattern card is the one for part-time career. On the IL scale, she has a preferred choice of no children, no job (score of 1). On the Job-Child scale she had a score of 7, three children, no job. Many of her ratings on the activities for families with children reflect traditional roles, particularly for women; only Mowing the Lawn and Earning Salary That Supports Family are assigned as mainly a man's responsibility. On the Circle task, Sharon gave a weight of 4 to work, 7 to marriage, 6 to children, and 3 to other (working in the community).

Sharon's time lines show college from ages 18 through 21, marriage at age 22, part-time work at ages 22-24, child bearing at ages 24, 26, and 28, and then full-time work beginning at age 35 and continuing. Her pattern for combining work and family includes three years of part-time work prior to age 35, and then full-time, continuous work.

Sharon rated the three sets of values as follows:

Occupational values: Leisure, Helping Others, Security, High Income, Independence, Prestige, Variety, Field of Interest, Early Entry, and Leadership.

Marriage values: Emotional Support, A Permanent Companion, Someone to Rely On, Children, A Close Physical Relationship, A Normal Life, Your Own Home, Prestige, Financial Security, A Help Mate, and A Feeling of Leadership.

Parenthood values: A Chance to Express Love, A Tie to the Future, Future Security, Joy, Confidence as a Man or Woman, Variety, A Sense of Accomplishment, Friendship, Respect of Others, A Stable Marriage, A Sense of Pride, and A Sense of Importance.

The high ranking of the occupational value Leisure is in agreement with the low IL-scale score. The high ranking of Helping Others, lack of definition of career choices, and work patterns all appear to reflect a low work commitment and a traditional view of women's adult roles. The appearance of A Permanent Companion, Someone to Rely On, and Children as high marriage values also are more characteristic of the sex-atypical group (and more traditional group) defined by the marriage values. These adolescents had high Job-Child scores and high part-time work ratings, as well as a tendency to rate the occupational values of prestige and variety lower. These ratings also characterize the students tending to have a lower number of years of full-time work to age 41. The parenthood values rated highly (after A Chance to Express Love) include the two security-oriented values, Joy and Confidence as a Man or Woman. In contrast with Sharon's views, Kathy plans both a nontraditional (for women) career and a nontraditional family plan: to be childless.

Planning a Nontraditional Career
Kathy

Kathy is 16 years old and a native New Yorker. She lives with her parents and they both completed high school. Her father is the head of a fabric manufacturing company, with plants in several states. Her mother works part-time as a bookkeeper in a law office. Her mother worked before her marriage, but did not return to work until the youngest of her two children was in elementary school (about five years ago). Kathy reports being an A− student, and plans to attend professional or graduate school. She has had work experience as a summer counselor and part-time office work. She has considered the occupations of lawyer, writer, veterinarian, and business management. She is most interested in, and is planning toward, a career in business management, and plans to work for herself. She does not plan to have children and intends to marry "at a later age." Her most admired adult is a 30-year-old teacher, who is single and works full-time: "She's very independent; has a job, no family, and does what she wants." Kathy would like to be like her by having "her kind of independence."

Kathy has a score of 5 on the Involvement Level scale (for the total domain of work and children) and a 1 on the Job-Child scale (no children, full-time job). On the Circle task, she has three sections, work (a weight of 12), marriage (3), and other (5). The Other sector includes friends, traveling, and socializing. Kathy rated all but 5 of the activities for families with children as, Could be either person's responsibilities. The two rated mainly a woman's responsibility were Mending Clothes and Caring for Baby. The three rated mainly a man's responsibility were Mowing the Lawn, Deciding When Car Needs Tune-up, and Fixing a Broken Lamp. She plans to work full-time, continuously, to start in one field, change to a new field at some time, and has the same expectations for her future spouse. Her time lines show postsecondary education from age 19 through 24. She plans to work full-time and continuously from age 25 on, and to marry about age 30.

The rankings of the three sets of values were (from high to low):

Occupational values: Independence, Variety, Leadership, Prestige, Leisure, Field of Interest, Helping Others, High Income, Security, and Early Entry.

Marriage values: Emotional Support, Someone to Rely On, A Permanent Companion, A Help Mate, A Close Physical Relationship, Financial Security, Your Own Home, A Feeling of Leadership, Prestige, A Normal Life, and Children.

Parenthood values: A Chance to Express Love, Friendship, Joy, Variety, Future Security, A Sense of Pride, A Tie to the Future, A Sense of Importance, A Sense of Accomplishment, Respect of Others, A Stable Marriage, and Confidence as a Man or Woman.

The occupational values appear to fit well with the plans for a career in business management: high ranking to the values of Independence, Leadership, and Variety. The high ranking for Variety also indicates that this value probably means something different to Kathy than to Rose, according to the role of Variety as a predictor—with a negative weight—for number of years of full-time work to age 41. All the other predictors of a greater number of years of full-time work for white females are a part of Kathy's responses in the interview: Work Pattern—Continuous; Full-time Career ranking; and a higher weight to the Work sector of the Circle task, including a fairly high ranking for the marriage value of A Help Mate. Her lowest ranking of Children as a reason to decide to marry is a relatively rare response (29 of the 600 students, 5%, gave this ranking). Kathy's rankings of the parenthood values appear to emphasize those of the "sex-typical" group of women described in Chapter 7, and are values that are more centered on the perceived satisfactions to the individual in the relationship, rather than on the choice of parenthood as a response to social pressures or expectations.

Summary

In this chapter there has been an attempt to present a more integrated view of the values and other variables for a few of the adolescent girls interviewed. The cases were selected to represent different types of occupations and family/work patterns. For all the young women in the sample, about 6% chose nonprofessional nontraditional (for females) occupations, for example, computer operator, probation officer, police officer, and photographer. Another 37% chose traditional, nonprofessional occupations such as stewardess, secretary, dental hygienist, and beautician. About one-fourth also had traditionally female professional occupations. These were almost entirely in three categories: teacher, nurse, and social worker. There was considerably more diversity in the professional, nontraditional occupations named by the remaining 26% of the sample (another 6% did not name any occupation). These included doctors (all but one listed pediatrician), lawyers, accountants, one dentist, business administration, one aerospace engineer, and a few scientists (one each in zoology, marine biology, meterology).

Both Sherri and Kathy, who chose nontraditional professional occupations, tended to be more egalitarian in their attitudes toward the responsibilities of men and women. Both presented unusual patterns of combining work, marriage, and family. For the girls who chose more traditionally female occupations, Helen, Frances, and Sharon, the reverse patterns appeared. The three value sets were used here in a somewhat different manner than they would be in actual practice. Their use was based on some of the "normative" data provided by the sample of 300 boys and 300 girls. That is, to what extent did the highly ranked values reflect some of the sex differences or ethnic group differences? These latter differences were not apparent for most of the group comparisons on the values, but did appear for the variable, Number of Years of Full-time Work to age 41. The comparison of the cases to the sex-typical and sex-atypical analyses (Chapter 7) is another example of group comparisons that would not be made in practice. The intention in their use here has been to highlight some of the possible dimensions along which the values differ and to alert the user to some patterns of responses that may be informative for practice. It should be remembered that all of the distributions by sex, ethnic, and SES groups are highly overlapping.

Taken altogether, the information each student has provided on their values and plans provides a starting point to encourage further exploration of both occupations and other adult roles. A primary concern for all of these students is their lack of awareness of the wide scope of occupations that are available, and an uncertainty of the extent to which they recognize where their values in all three areas—work, marriage, and parenthood—are taking them, as Katz would say. More particularly, to what extent are they consciously aware of their values in relation to their plans? This question provides an impetus both to further research and practice (interventions) as discussed in Chapter 10.

Chapter 10

CONCLUSIONS

In this study there has been an attempt to expand the types of information related to the career development of women. The expansion of information has been into the areas of marriage and parenthood values, other sex-role-related attitudes, and the plans adolescents have for combining these three areas in adulthood. The expansion has its impetus in the continuing discrepancy between the type of occupations and earnings of men and women. Although there are many changes in women's workforce participation and in ages of marriage and fertility rates, these have not been reflected thus far in the desegregation of occupations and equity in earnings.

The Bureau of the Census (1979) reports that age at first marriage has increased to 22.1 years for women and 24.4 for men and there have been increases in the percentages of young adult women delaying or entering marriage. In 1979 about 49% of women 20-24 years old were still single, compared with only 28% in 1960. The proportion of women aged 25 to 29 who had never married also showed a marked increase since 1960, from 11 to 20%. Divorce rates have increased and families not maintained by a married couple increased by 50% in the last decade. Current projections are that only 1 in 4 married women will be a full-time homemaker and mother by 1990 (Smith, 1979). The current figure is about one-third. By

1990 it is estimated that 45% of preschool children (10.5 million children) will have working mothers.

Bronfenbrenner (1979) has argued that there is an increased need for large-scale programs of substitute care for children of working parents, as well as use of other solutions, such as released time from work for parental obligations and flexible work schedules. Almost all modern industrial nations are active in these programs. Interviews with working women (Working women speak, 1979) stress the lacks in child care, education, training, and in their own attitudes, as well as active sex discrimination as obstacles to upward mobility. These women in "blue and pink" collar jobs comprise some 80% of all American working women. There appears to be increasing public support for improving the status of women. Results of the 1980 Roper Poll for Virginia Slims (National NOW Times, 1980, p. 15) show that 64% of both men and women support the efforts to strengthen and change women's status (1970 figures were 40% of women and 44% of men). Changing views of marriage were also reported: A majority of women (52%) perceived marriage as a responsibility to be equally shared by both partners (earning salaries and sharing family and household responsibility), as did almost half of the men (49%). The figure was higher for younger women, 66%. Data on financial assets are changing slowly. Overall, 28% of the women had savings or checking accounts in their own names, compared to about 15% in 1972. Among single women, the rates are about 62% now, versus about 40% eight years ago. Few women have installment, mortgage or personal bank loans in their own names (7%, 5%, and 4%, respectively).

Although there are some changes in enrollment patterns in college majors as well as in college attendance, by far the majority of women students are in traditional, female-intensive professions (Cerra, 1980). According to 1978 figures, the average female college graduate working full-time earned 60% of the salary of a man with the same education working full-time. It is projected that by 1987, for example, 71% of all doctoral degrees earned by women would still be in such fields as education, library science, fine and applied arts, English, and foreign languages. About two-thirds of the adolescent girls in the present study had tentative occupational choices in traditionally women's fields. Girls with professional-level aspirations were about evenly divided between traditional and nontraditional occupations; within the nonprofessional occupations, however, only 14% gave nontraditional occupational choices (18 of 128 girls).

These data on increases in labor force participation and occupational segregation suggest that guidance and counseling, as well as other parts of the educational system, must contribute more actively to assisting women to become aware and explore the domain of occupations more realistically. It is argued here that one of the keys to planning more realistically is to provide both data and techniques to explore individual values in relation to occupations, marriage, and parenthood. Thus the development of the marriage and parenthood values was designed to provide such a technique and the research provides data on responses to the values. In this chapter the major findings are summarized briefly, and there are discussions of the implications of the findings for further research, practice, and evaluation of guidance programs. One section, reflections on the values, reconsiders the marriage and parenthood values in the light of other work on values, as well as the present data.

Major Findings
Educational, Occupational, and Family Plans and Expectations

The sample of 600 urban eleventh graders represented equally sex, two levels of socioeconomic status (middle and low), and three ethnic groups (white, black, and Hispanic). The majority of these adolescents were 16 years old, and 80% were born in New York. Students as a group had relatively high educational aspirations: half of the sample thought they would graduate from a four-year college and another 26% stated they would have professional or graduate education. There were no sex differences in educational aspirations, although there were SES and ethnic group differences. Black and Hispanic students had somewhat higher aspirations than the white students in this sample. Level of occupational aspirations also did not show sex differences, although (using the Bureau of the Census level scores) there was a sex X ethnic group interaction, with the higher aspirations for white and black females and for Hispanic and black males.

Student work expectations were examined in several questions—in preferences for career (career vs. job and full-time vs. part-time vs. not working) and work expectations. Ratings on career-job choices differed by sex on all choices except part-time job. For example, male students rated full-time career slightly higher than female students, and female students rated part-time career slightly higher than did the male students. Both the black and Hispanic students rated full-time work higher and not working lower than the white students. For the work pattern question (continuously, mostly continuously, off and on—stopping for periods of one year or more and briefly, less than four years altogether), significant sex and ethnic group main effects were found. More males than females expected to work continuously, and black students expected to work somewhat more continuously than white students. Expectations for changing their type of work did not vary by group: over half the students (58%) expected to start in one field and remain in this field through their working life; almost a third (29%) expected to start in one field, change to a new field at some time; and 10% expected to try a variety of different jobs, not all in one field.

Student marriage plans were highly similar: almost all students said they would like to be married (only 5% said they would not). Family plans differed by sex, however, with girls desiring a larger number of children than boys. The mean number of children desired by girls was 2.94 and by boys 2.63. (The mean number of children desired was uncorrelated with the number of children in the students' own families.) And, more females than males thought that having a family would make a difference in their plans for work.

A question about how to combine work and family indicated that 57% (343) of the students expected to work continuously regardless of marriage/children (63 of the 343 were females). A second part of the question examined when students would work in relation to the ages of their children. These data were analyzed for females only. Only 6.5% (15 girls) expected to work when their children were 1-3 years old; 37% when their children were 3-5 years old; 42% when children were 5-12 years old; and the remaining 14% when children were 12 years or older. Thus, 79% of these female students expected to work when the children were between 3 and 12 years old.

After students answered the set of work decision questions for themselves, they were asked to answer the same set for their spouses. Overall, 73% thought their spouse would have a college education, 6.5% noncollege further education, and 19% a high school education. Somewhat more females than males thought their spouse would have a college education (78% vs. 70%); more blacks expected their spouses to have a college education; and more middle-SES students had that expectation. A majority (94%) stated their spouses would work and of the males 24 or 9% predicted that their wives would work full-time. This last percentage stands in contrast to the earlier self-response to the same question, where 117 (39%) of the female students expected to work full-time. Another 20% of the male students, however, expected that their wives would work mostly full-time.

The questions on marriage, family, and work patterns show some differences among the groups in the study. Sex differences in number of children desired showed that women wanted a slightly greater number of children than men (2.94 to 2.63) and women anticipated a greater affect on their work plans from having children than did men. What is most noticeable, however, is that about 40% of the female students said that having a family would *not* influence their plans for work. The reasons given for this response show that at least some proportion of those responding *no* are aware of divorce statistics, the economy, and the intrinsic satisfaction that can come from work. Rankings of work patterns tend to be similar across groups but a comparison of ratings shows that the traditional pattern of sex differences in preferences—females preferred part-time work or lower work commitment—can still be found looking at the sample as a whole. These differences also reflect the views of the 50% of the girls who stated that Yes, having a family would affect their plans for work.

The average number of jobs students had considered as future occupations was 3.1 (standard deviation of 1.2). Eleventh-grade students have not considered many jobs, and this finding does not differ for either sex, the three ethnic groups, or the two SES categories. Given the data on number of jobs students have considered, and in anticipation that these data would reflect few occupations considered, questions were included on persons students talk to about their educational, occupational, and family plans, and whether or not counselors or teachers talk to them about specific work or occupations. Students talked about their educational and occupational plans with their parents, relatives, friends, and a wide variety of persons. Only a small number of students stated they did not talk to anybody about these plans. For the marriage and family plans, however, a third of the students said they did not talk to anyone. A majority of students reported that no teachers or counselors had talked to them about work possibilities (65% for teachers and 73% for counselors).

A further question examining influences on plans was, What adult do you know personally who is living a life you would like to have? Almost a third of the sample (32%) did not identify an adult they wished to be like in some aspect. Of 396 students who clearly identified an adult, 84% liked or admired an adult of the same sex. There were slightly more female students who identified adult models of the opposite sex (22% vs. 11% for males). Aspects of the adult life students wanted to emulate were coded for work, family, personality, or combinations thereof. Taking into account the combinations, 49% of the students mentioned the adult's work pattern, 24% the family pattern, and 54% the adult's personality. The main aspects of adult life cited alone or in combination were the adult's personality and work pattern. Aspects of family life were not cited as often by these eleventh-grade students. The adults were typically a relative in the immediate or close family. Somewhat more females than males identified an aspect of the family pattern (21% vs. 9%).

The focus on personality and work patterns may reflect the immediacy of these aspects of adolescent development. The lack of focus on family patterns again may reflect the lack of discussion and examination of alternative choices for the parts of adult life that will particularly affect women's career and employment planning. In the next section the occupational, marriage, and parenthood values are presented. The characteristics of student responses to the values and their relationships to education and occupational decisions are summarized.

OCCUPATIONAL, MARRIAGE, AND PARENTHOOD VALUES

This section reports findings for all 600 students and for the main sample groups. The group differences are of interest from two perspectives: (1) to what extent are results common or generalizable across these groups of concern in the use of the values in practice; and (2) to what extent do any group differences provide useful information on issues— stereotypes or unexamined views—that are important for either sample representativeness in further research or working with individuals in career development? *All* of the frequency distributions are highly overlapping for all the groups in this study, and it is important to remember this fact in the discussions that follow.

Ten *occupational values* were rank ordered and rated by students: High Income, Prestige, Independence, Helping Others, Security, Variety, Leadership, Field of Interest, Leisure, and Early Entry (Katz, 1973), Major criteria for the values were that high school students would discriminate among the value terms and would vary in the relative weights assigned to them. These characteristics of the occupational values have been demonstrated in other settings and were found again in the present study. The frequency distributions for the ranks for each value are fairly rectangular in form. The most important value for the eleventh-grade students in thinking about choosing an occupation was major Field of Interest. The least important was Early Entry, defined as starting work right away, rather than spending time, effort, and money for more education. A multivariate analysis of variance using the main factors of sex, ethnic group, and SES and the 10 occupational values as dependent variables was run on the unstandardized ratings. Significant main effects were found for each factor, with no interactions.

Univariate ANOVAs on the standardized ratings were then computed. Sex main effects were significant for six values: High Income, Helping Others, Variety, Leadership, Field of Interest, and Leisure. Female students gave higher ratings to Helping Others, Variety, and Field of Interest. Males gave higher ratings to the remaining three values. Similar findings for some of the values were reported by Norris, Katz, and Chapman (1978), with sex differences on High Income, Leadership, and Helping Others.

Differences in the findings are probably due to the age differences as well as the location of their sample (at five two-year community colleges and at one four-year college in various parts of the country) compared to the sample of urban eleventh-grade students described here.

In the present study SES group differences were found for three values: High Income (M > L), Helping Others (L > M), and Early Entry (L > M). Only one ethnic group main effect was significant for the 10 values: Leisure, and black students gave this value a lower rating than white and Hispanic students. Group differences were most pronounced for females and males, less pronounced for SES groups and least pronounced of all for ethnic groups.

The *marriage values* were developed for the present study. The 11 values that students ranked and rated were: Financial Security; Emotional Support; A Helpmate; A Close Physical Relationship; Prestige; A Normal Life; A Permanent Companion; Children; Your Own Home; Someone to Rely On; and A Feeling of Leadership. Students were asked to consider the values for their relative importance in deciding to get married (or have a permanent companion). Each marriage value received all of the possible ranks and ratings, but the distributions were not as rectangular as they were for the occupational values. For example, Emotional Support was given the highest rank by 45% of the sample, resulting in a highly skewed distribution of ranks.

The most important values in deciding to get married, as given in this set of values, were: Emotional Support, A Permanent Companion, and A Close Physical Relationship. The least important values were: A Normal Life and A Feeling of Leadership. All three main effects were significant. Female students gave higher ratings to Financial Security, Emotional Support, and Prestige. Male students gave higher ratings to A Normal Life, Your Own Home, and A Feeling of Leadership. SES main effects were significant for four marriage values: Emotional Support (M > L), A Close Physical Relationship (M > L); A Normal Life (L > M); and Your Own Home (L > M). Only two values showed significant ethnic group differences: Financial Security and Children. Black students gave higher ratings to Financial Security than did the other two groups, and Hispanic students gave higher ratings to the marriage value of Children than did the other two groups.

The marriage values met the criteria described for values, but not as satisfactorily as did the occupational values. Although the rankings and ratings covered the entire range of all possible numbers for each marriage value, the distributions were not as rectangular as they were generally for the occupational values. Nevertheless, students did rank and rate the values and some systematic (but typically small) group differences were found.

Twelve *parenthood values* were defined for this study. The values were: A Sense of Accomplishment; A Sense of Pride; Variety; Friendship; The Respect of Others; A Stable Marriage; A Chance to Express Love; Confidence as a Man or Woman; Joy; Future Security; A Tie to the Future; and A Sense of Importance. Each parenthood value, with one exception, received a complete set of possible ranks (A Chance to Express Love did not receive any ranks of 12, although it did receive all possible ratings). Several of the parenthood values had very skewed distributions (Friendship, A Chance to Express Love, and Joy). The values rated highest as important in deciding to have children were A Chance to Express Love, Joy, and Friendship. Least important were the values of The Respect of Others, Confidence as a Man or Woman, and A Tie to the Future.

There were significant sex, ethnic, and SES group main effects. Sex differences were found for these six values: Variety (F > M); Friendship (F > M); Respect of Others (M > F); A Stable Marriage (M > F); A Chance to Express Love (F > M); and A Tie to the Future (M > F). SES main effects were significant for five values: Variety (M > L); Friendship (M > L); Confidence as a Man or Woman (L > M); Joy (M > L); and A Sense of Importance (L > M). Significant ethnic group effects were found for two values: A Sense of Pride (B > W > H); and A Chance to Express Love (W, H > B).

For the parenthood values, the majority of differences were found for females and males, with the number of SES group differences also high. Only 2 of the 12 values had different mean ratings for the 3 ethnic groups.

An overall characterization of the distribution and group differences data for the three sets of values is that they met two criteria: high school students varied in the relative weights (importance ratings) assigned to the values; and high school students discriminated among the terms. This latter criterion was initially demonstrated by the rank orderings and ratings, and again in the next section by the factor analysis of the 33 values. Also, subgroups of the sample did differ in the importance assigned to the values, with sex differences the most frequently found group difference for this sample. There were no interactions among the sex, SES, or ethnic groups; and the smallest number of group differences in ratings of the values was found for the ethnic groups.

FACTOR ANALYSES OF THE VALUES

The number of values which had significant sex differences in the mean ratings suggested that further analyses of the data should be carried out separately by sex. The smaller number of SES and ethnic group differences indicated that these distinctions did not need to be maintained in most analyses, although SES should be considered in some cases. Thus the factor analyses that examined the underlying structure for the total set of 33 values were carried out on the female students, the male students, and the combined sample. At this stage the factor analyses are important primarily to indicate that there are a number of dimensions that underlie the occupational, marriage, and parenthood values, and that there is independence as well as some overlap among the values in the three areas.

There were 14 separate factors for each of the three factor analyses (using a criterion of an eigen value of 1.00 or higher to retain a factor). The factor analyses demonstrated that there are both common and unique meanings between the value sets, for example, when a factor may consist of values from only one of the three sets. One particularly interesting finding is that several of the occupational values formed bipolar factors for males, but did not cluster as uniquely for females. For females, the occupational values were always combined with marriage or parenthood values. One interpretation of this finding is that it reflects the traditional separation of sex roles in our culture: Males are identified with occupational roles and females with homemaking and motherhood. The traditional separation of roles for adults by sex may mean that males more readily separate the values satisfied by occupations from those satisfied in marriage and parenthood. Females apparently have more difficulty in this separation, as illustrated in the loading of the occupational value, Helping Others, on several factors.

THE RELATION OF VALUES TO EDUCATIONAL AND OCCUPATIONAL DECISIONS

Level of educational aspiration and level of occupational aspiration were examined by forming groups on the basis of each of these variables and using discriminant analyses to determine the extent of the prediction of group membership that was possible using each of the value sets. These analyses were exploratory and conducted separately for females and males, as well as the total sample.

Level of educational aspiration. As described earlier, there were no sex differences in level of educational aspirations, but there were sex differences in weights assigned to about half of the values in each set. Extreme groups were formed to determine if the values discriminate between groups. Two groups were established:

Group 1 = High school + technical school after high school + graduate
from a two-year college + some college but less than four years;
Group 2 - Professional or graduate school.

The values that provided the best discrimination between the educational groups differed somewhat for females and males. Group 2 females, for example, were likely to give higher ratings to the occupational values of Independence and Leadership (in contrast to the values for Group 2 males of Variety and Field of Interest). The percentage of grouped cases correctly classified was 75% for both the female and male students.

The marriage values provided some discrimination between groups with different educational goals, although there was no a priori reason to expect the marriage values to provide high discrimination. The percentage of grouped cases correctly classified for female students was 62%, and for male students 74%. The parenthood values provided discrimination between groups similar to the occupational values (72% correctly classified for female students and 75% for male students). Sample values discriminating Group 1 and 2 female students were: Women with higher educational goals tended to rate more highly the values Joy, A Sense of Accomplishment, and Friendship; women with lower educational goals tended to rate the values of A Stable Marriage and Future Security more highly.

Level of career aspiration. Roe (1956) provided an analysis of level of occupation within each of her types or groups of occupations. Two groups were formed using her level scores (1-6) applied to occupations that students stated were ones they were likely to actually do. Group 1 was comprised of levels 1 and 2 (1 is the highest level), and group 2 of levels 3-6. Analyses were carried out for the total sample, for female students, and for male students. For the occupational values the percentage of grouped cases correctly classified by the discriminant function was 63%; it was 60% for the marriage values and 52% for the parenthood values. These findings are not summarized here, because the groups were not well discriminated. Separate analyses by sex did not show much improvement in percent of cases correctly classified. It may be that further refinement of the level of career aspiration measure would yield an improvement in discrimination, because the use of extreme groups for the educational goals resulted in an improvement in classification. It may also be that the occupations are further into the future and hence are not well-differentiated by students themselves.

CHILDREN, WORK, AND VALUE PREFERENCES

Involvement level and Job-Child Scales. Two scales were used to examine the preference students had for their level of commitment to the areas of having a job and raising children (the Involvement Level (IL) Scale) and their emphasis toward one or the other of these activities (the Job-Child— JC—Scales). Both scales were developed by Coombs (1979). The IL scale ranges from 1, a preference for least involvement to 7, a preference for most involvement in the total job and child domain. The JC scale ranges from 1, greatest preference for a job to 7, greatest preference for children, the job versus child-orientation domain. Female students responded to the choices (derived from a paired comparison study) in terms of what they would prefer for themselves, assuming the children were under 10 years of age and the job was for pay outside the home. Males were asked which combinations they would most like for their wives to have (given the same assumptions).

An ANOVA for the IL scale showed sex, ethnic, and sex X ethnic effects. Female students preferred a greater degree of total involvement in the entire job and child domain than male students said they wanted for their wives (means of 4.72 and 4.01, respectively). For the JC scale there were significant sex, ethnic, and ethnic X SES effects. Males preferred a higher degree of child orientation than females preferred for themselves (means of 4.83 and 4.12, respectively). Within ethnic groups, white students had a greater preference toward children than black students. The interaction occurred when middle-SES Hispanic students had the highest degree of preference for children (compared to a job), and for low-SES students, white students had the higher preference for children. Correlation between the IL and JC scales is low, -.123 for the total sample, and nonsignificant when computed within sex groups (-.080 for females and -.097 for males).

Further analyses of the Coombs's scales involved examination of the variables that might predict each scale. These analyses were carried out separately by sex. Using a combination of variables (work pattern of full-time career, number of years of full-time work before age 41, age completing education, expected working hours, and the occupational value High Income), a step-wise multiple regression yielded a multiple R = .447 for females. Different variables were identified as predictors for males, and the multiple R was .392. The variables predictive of the IL scale for women centered on work and occupational variables. The combination of variables differed for males, involving both work patterns for their spouses and their own ratings for children, as well as Financial Security (a marriage value) and A Sense of Pride (a parenthood value).

The variables that predicted the Job-Child Orientation Scale differed for females and males, and the prediction was better for females (multiple R = .609) than for males (multiple R = .388). For female students the variables that predicted a child orientation (high end of the JC scale) as opposed to a job orientation were: A higher number of weights (Circle segments) for children; fewer number of years of full-time work by age 41; a lower percentage of responsibility for the wife to earn money in a family with children; higher ratings to the marriage values of Children and A Permanent Companion; and a higher rating to the work pattern, Not Working. For the JC scale, predictor variables included variables related to both children and work, as opposed to the findings for the IL scale. For males, the variables that predicted the JC scale were, with one exception, from the three sets of values: the marriage values of Financial Security and Children, the occupational value of Security, the parenthood value of Friendship, and a view of the responsibility to earn a salary that supports a family as predominantly that of the man in the family.

Number of children desired. A variable related to the job-child trade-off is the number of children desired. Further sets of regression analyses were carried out for number of children as the dependent variable. The multiple R for female students was .339 and was .390 for male students. The variables entering the prediction equation for female students were: Number of weights (Circle segments) for children; the IL scale; the marriage value of Children; and a lower school average. Predictor variables for males were: a child orientation preferred for their spouse on the JC scale; a higher rating on the marriage value of Your Own Home and a lower rating on A Feeling of Leadership; and more traditional views on the female-male responsibilities for the family activities of Mowing the Lawn, Mending Clothes, and Reading to Children.

Number of years of full-time work to age 41. Data from the time lines were summarized into one variable, number of years of full-time work planned to age 41. Separate regression analyses were carried out for girls in the three ethnic groups because an ANOVA showed sex and ethnic group differences, as well as sex X ethnic and sex X SES interactions. The three value sets as well as other sex-role related variables were entered into the analyses. Only the occupational and marriage values were retained in any of the final stepwise regressions.

The best predictors for black students were the IL scale (+), the J-C scale (−), the family activity responsibility to earn money (−), two of the three husband-wife responsibilities—wife responsibility to earn money (−), and husband responsibility to keep house (+), the occupational values of Security (+) and Helping Others (−). The best predictors for Hispanic girls were the IL scale (+), the work pattern continuous (low value) to briefly (−), the career pattern not working (−), and the marriage values Children (−), Someone to Rely On (−), and Your Own Home (−). The best predictors for white females were the work pattern continuous-briefly (−), the career pattern full time (+), and the Circle task work segments (+), along with the occupational value of Variety (−) and the marriage value A Help Mate (+).

It is possible to speculate that for the black students, for example, there is a more realistic orientation toward work, regardless of family status, and thus the occupational values are able to enter the prediction equations—and the low weight for Helping Others is contrary to the usual high weights for the value given by females. The three marriage values that enter the equation for Hispanic females are those that suggest more independence in perspective—both from a marriage partner and from parents (Your Own Home as a reason to marry). Whereas the marriage value of A Help Mate was originally intended as a value men might more frequently endorse, for white females it enters as a predictor of more years of full-time work.

Overall, the values have been examined for group differences, for their interrelationships, and their relationship to educational and occupational decisions, two scales relating to work and children, to number of children desired, to number of years of full-time work to age 41, and for sex-typical/sex-atypical groups formed on the basis of each value set. The latter analyses were intended to provide further understanding of some issues that might be identified more for females or males and variables that might relate to them.

The values, particularly the occupational and parenthood values, do discriminate extreme groups on level of educational aspirations. Similar effectiveness in discrimination was not found for the level of occupational aspiration, using any of the three value sets. The likelihood is that whereas educational aspirations are close to being implemented and planned, the occupational aspirations are very tentative at this grade level. The pattern in which the different types of values enter into predictions for the children and work variables is of interest. For number of children desired, only the marriage values enter for both girls and boys. For the IL scale, only an occupational value enters for females; for males both a marriage and a parenthood value enter. For the J-C scale, only two marriage values entered for females but two marriage values, an occupational value and a parenthood value enters for males. For number of years of full-time work, only the marriage values enter for all 300 girls, but for the ethnic groups there are different patterns. Two occupational values enter for black females, three marriage values for Hispanic females, and one occupational and one marriage value for white females. These different patterns of relationships provide further substantiation of the need for the three value sets and the fact that they tap different dimensions.

SEX ROLES, FAMILY ACTIVITIES AND RESPONSIBILITIES, AND TIMING OF FAMILY AND WORK

Findings for sex-role attitudes are based on the responses to a list of activities for families with children that were rated on a 5-point scale from only a woman's responsibility to only a man's responsibility (adapted from

Eagly & Anderson, 1974). Another question asked students to allocate percentages to family responsibilities. The last series of questions asked the ages when students expected to be in school, work, marry, and have children.

Sex roles and family activities. Twenty-two activities were rated, for example, Mending Clothes and Repairing Household Appliances, on the 1 to 5 scale. Many items showed traditional allocation of sex roles. Mending Clothes was assigned mainly to women (55%) or only to women (14%); Repairing Household Appliances was considered to be mainly a man's responsibility (56%) or only to men (13%). Although there were often significant differences in the means for the groups, the actual differences in mean ratings were not large. There was, however, a direction and consistency to the differences, and some group differences were found for every activity item.

The direction of the differences on the 13 items with significant sex main effects showed that the ratings given by female students tended to be less traditional, that is, less sex-role stereotyped, than those given by male students. Differences among ethnic groups were not as consistent (nine items had differences among ethnic groups). SES group differences for the ten activity items with differences were very consistent. Middle-SES students gave ratings that were less traditionally sex stereotypical. Three items with sex X ethnic group interactions also had a consistent pattern: female Hispanic students were the most traditional in responses of the three female groups and white male students were the most traditional of the three male groups.

Division of family responsibilities. Attitudes toward sex roles were also examined by the question, What do you think is the best arrangement for dividing up (earning money, keeping house, caring for children) responsibilities? The means (of percentages assigned to the husband and wife) followed traditional patterns for Earning Money and Keeping House. An unexpected result was the nearly equal allocation of responsibility to husband and wife in Caring for Children. All three main effects were significant for the area of earning money, with female students, black students, and middle-SES students less traditional or more egalitarian in their responses.

Timing of family and work. Student plans for education, marriage, children, full-time work, and part-time work between the ages of 16 and 41 were elicited by means of time lines. The mean age estimated for completion of high school was 17.5, and the age of completing education ranged from 17 to 34. The mean age for marriage was 25 years, with a range from 18 to 40, and the mean age at birth of first child ranged from 16 to 40, with a mean of 26.7 years. Ethnic and SES group differences were found for age of high school graduation, completing education, and marriage, with sex differences found for the latter variable also. Mean age expected for marriage was 25.81 for boys and 24.17 for girls. Middle-SES students and black students also expected to marry at later ages than the other groups.

The mean age at which these eleventh-grade students expected to begin full-time work was 23.8, with a range from 14 to 40 years. More males expected to start full-time work at earlier ages, and it was primarily women who forecast a reentry or resuming of full-time work at some age. The age distribution for part-time work was more scattered for females than males, with only a small percentage of males expecting to do part-time work after age 25.

The data on work patterns on the time lines are summarized in one variable, number of years of full-time work before age 41. Sex, ethnic, sex X ethnic, and sex X SES group effects were found. The mean number of years of full-time work before age 41 was 17 for male students and 10.2 for female students. White females expected to have the fewest number of full-time work years, and Hispanic males expected to have the fewest years (in agreement with their later expected age at graduation, and so on). Low-SES females expected to have a lower number of years of full-time work than middle-SES females (9.84 vs. 10.57) and middle-SES males expected to have less time in full-time work than low-SES males (16.29 vs. 17.75).

Overall, the attitudes towards sex roles still exhibit many of the traditional views of the appropriate roles for females and males in the family setting. These attitudes are found to be more conservative for adolescent males than adolescent females, consistent with earlier research on adolescents and adults. Also, these adolescents do not report as egalitarian views of sharing responsibilities for earning money and family and household responsibilities as the 1980 Roper Survey of Adults (National NOW Times, 1980). If present trends continue, we can expect their attitudes to become more egalitarian and in agreement with statistics on labor force participation for women. In the meantime, however, girls are delayed in actively developing that part of their self-identity that is linked to work outside the home.

Among the psychological barriers to career development for women are those that relate to the development of the feminine identity centered primarily on the wife and mother roles and the accompanying delay in other definitions of the self. The result is apparent in the study of women's adult development, where writers from a variety of perspectives center on identity, for example, the identity confusion (Schlossberg & Waters, 1978), the quest for the postponed self (Sangiuliano, 1978), and the pursuit of an internally grounded identity (Rubin, 1979). In the responses to the time lines for these adolescent girls we see the same patterns planned as appear for the group of women who have been studied at midlife, as well as those who are returning to education or work in their twenties and thirties. Whereas the patterns appear in the time lines, for children and work, they are not related to the occupations chosen, particularly for the nontraditional professions and even for some of the traditionally women's fields (i.e., timing of certification and other professional barriers to returning to work).

Theories of career development do little to recognize the institutionalized barriers to labor force participation and how these may be interpreted in the planning and timing of the family cycle for women. Yet these are critical to planning to follow any areas of developed interests. Another major obstacle lies in the stereotyped view of adult roles for males, where there is also little planning of the relationship between worker and family roles, and no recognition of the possible effect of altering the dominance of the worker role in career planning. The patterns of the values in entering the relationships predictive of number of children desired and the Job-Child orientation desired for their wives suggests that the values may be useful to stimulate an examination of these different adult roles with adolescent boys.

Reflections on the Values

The May 1980 issue of *The Personnel and Guidance Journal* is devoted to a special issue on Values and the Counselor. Tyler (1980) suggests that many of the techniques described will be helping sensitize counselors to the possibility for developing and systematizing personal value systems. Among the techniques she emphasizes is the use of card sorts, with the content either provided or developed by the student, along with George Kelly's Rep Test. Rokeach and Regan (1980) describe Rokeach's definition of values and the terminal and instrumental values he has developed and now applied in practice. Rokeach reinforces Katz's interpretations of values: "A person's values represent, at one and the same time, the cognitive representations of societal demands and of individual needs, and each person develops through processes of socialization a value priority system" (p. 577). Rokeach argues for the measurement of human values at the generalized level represented in his Value Survey (e.g., A Comfortable Life, An Exciting Life, Equality, Family Security, Happiness, for the Terminal Values, and Ambitious, Broadminded, Cheerful, Clean, for the Instrumental Values.

The model followed in the present study of adolescent values has taken a different approach. Here the values are centered around those that are likely to be judged important in the choice of an occupation, the decision to marry, and the decision to become a parent. They are not presented at a generalized level. Katz (1973) provided a procedure and model in the occupational values, and through interviews, literature searching, and Kelly's Rep test we attempted to identify values related to the marriage and parenthood areas. Some of these "value" terms are also to be found (in a different wording) in Rokeach's lists of values.

The marriage and parenthood values are not as logically related to their decisions as the occupational values are. That is, Katz has classified occupations on the occupational values, and when the most important values are clarified for an individual, then the occupations that most closely match these values can be presented for more detailed consideration (Katz, 1973). The analogy does not hold for the marriage and parenthood values, because these values describe the attributes that may result in the decision between a few choices—to marry or not to marry, to become a parent or not. We would argue, however, that examination of the values should help to clarify the values that are entering into the choice and perhaps the underlying character of the type of marriage or type of parent the individual is assuming. This would, over time, assist in characterizing the type of marital relationship or parental interaction that might occur with a specific individual.

Viewed from this perspective, the marriage and parenthood values are thus a "draft" or first effort in clarifying the underlying dimensions that may characterize these relationships. The analyses of sex-typical and sex-atypical groups suggest that one dimension may relate to psychological maturity or level of ego development (Loevinger, 1976). The different factor structures for females and males reinforce the knowledge that these domains have different meanings for girls and boys. Factor analyses of the sets of values separately resulted in five or six factors each. When all 3 sets were analyzed together, there were 14 factors (reported in Appendix 4). Factor 1 for the girls shows that there is a parenthood factor identified primarily by Friendship (–) and Variety (–) values at one end, and Confidence as a Man or Woman (+) and A Stable Marriage (+) at the other end. We can hypothesize that for girls with a high score on this factor, their female identity centers on the role of mother. The girls with lower scores, emphasizing the values of Friendship and Variety as reasons to decide to become a parent, appear not to center their female identity on becoming a parent. There is a similar factor for males (Factor 6) but it included the marriage value of Someone to Rely On at the same end of the scale as Variety and Friendship. The addition of the marriage value may imply recognition of the traditional division of female and male responsibilities in parenting.

For males, Factor 3 consists of three marriage values: Permanent Companion (+), Normal Life (+), and Your Own Home (-). This factor appears to emphasize companionship and marriage as an expectation in adulthood. Conversely, Factor 13 is a factor for males that at one end emphasizes the expression of emotions. Both marriage and parenthood values are combined, M—A Close Physical Relationship (+) and P—A Chance to Express Love (+), with the other end of the scale defined by M—Your Own Home (-) and Respect of Others (-), a lower concern with the views of others. This combination of values does not appear as a factor for females.

The three value sets, then, appear to offer some potential for individuals and groups to examine values within the context of these three important decision options. Particularly for high school students, the value descriptions should serve to facilitate examination of these values before the decisions are made and to consider the decision options in relation to each other, a critical concern for women's career development. Further research and use of the values in practice will test these ideas.

Implications

FOR RESEARCH

There are a number of research implications following from this study of the values and related variables. The values have been proposed as a "technique" to increase exploration of adult roles and of the needs and satisfactions that arise in adult roles of worker, marriage partner, and parent. The values thus allow a focus on two of the three models of research and intervention discussed by Kanter (1976) as a means to reduce occupational segregation: the "temperamental model," which stresses women's character and personality in regard to socialization and sex roles and the "role-related model," which stresses the family and individual role conceptions. (The third is the social structural model, which examines the nature of organizational structures and work.) It may be possible in future research to relate personality concepts used in clinical and counseling settings for personal growth and development to the values and adult roles. A framework such as that of Jane Loevinger's for ego development may also result in reconceptualization and redefinitions of the marriage and parenthood values in relation to adult development.

Other avenues of research are in examining the meaningfulness of the values for groups of other ages, particularly with college-age students and adults in the 25-35 age range. Such studies would help to clarify the nature and definition of the marriage values particularly for their salience to individuals when the decision of marriage is closer in time. It would also be important to study the values in relation to measures of career development and family planning. Such studies could follow the path analysis approach taken by Harren et al. (1979), and add variables such as number of years of full-time work to age 41 and number of children desired, as influences on gender-dominant occupational choices (see Chapter 2 for more discussion of this area). This research should acknowledge that at present women *add on* roles. Appearance of the occupational values as predictors of the involvement level scale, for example, suggest that the occupational role is added on to the already accepted roles in parenthood and marriage. As Berryman (1978) put it, women choose flexibility to juggle marriage, work and, typically, children.

Phyllis Katz (1979) has written that adolescence offers one of the best times to examine attitudes toward sex roles and perhaps influence these attitudes in view of the reality of women's participation in the labor force. Her analysis suggests that the values should also be tried out for comprehension and discriminability among students in grades 9 and 10. The original choice of grade 11 as a starting point and the present results indicate that such a study may have similar results.

Turning to the measures of sex-role attitudes, the factor analysis of the activities for families with children suggest that future research may well develop scales that are more homogeneous. For example, 6 factors were identified for the 22 items. The main factors appeared similar in the analyses for the female and males samples, and represented three general areas: homemaking, children, and family decision-making or the marital relationship. The analysis indicates that the items in the area of homemaking activities were well sampled, for both females and males. Items concerned with children were less-well sampled, and could be expanded for better definition of the one or two factors that appear involved (a caretaker function and a developmental, teaching function). The third area of husband-wife roles in family economics and decision making could well be expanded. The methods of Herzog et al. (1980) would be useful for work here with youth, and the work of Scanzoni (1979a) for adults. Scanzoni's work also suggests that it is important to gain more perspective on negotiation and bargaining within the marriage or couple setting, which could be extended to work with adolescents.

The last area of consideration here is an examination in greater specificity and a shift of focus from general attitudes about sex roles to a specific analysis of approaches to coping with the primacy of worker *and* parent roles, for both males and females. A better understanding of male adolescents' attitudes is critical here because changes in the woman's role means some shifts in men's roles. Research that shows a correlation between higher levels of ego development and less stereotyped conceptions of sex roles for adults (Nettles, 1979) can also be examined for adolescents.

FOR PRACTICE

The implications for practice based on the values must be speculative at this stage. The special issue of the *Personnel and Guidance Journal* (May 1980) provides specific suggestions for the use of similar values, particularly in the articles by Rokeach and Regan and by Tyler. More generally, the implications for practice reside in at least two areas: (1) further developing the process by which adolescents can identify their options and bring choices to the level of awareness; and (2) developing a recognition of the relationship between self-identity and work (careers, broadly conceived) in this culture. One example of the first area is provided by Jessie Bernard's (1974) study of motherhood: "I was 40 years old, says a suburban housewife, before it dawned on me that I really had had no choice about becoming a mother. Not that I didn't know all about contraception but that it had never occurred to me that anything else was possible (p. 24)." This quotation points to the practical need to integrate techniques such as the sex-role related values into present counseling perspectives. When the eleventh grade women students marked all their choices in a series of time lines, the difficulty in "putting it all together" became painfully evident to these adolescents. Hard choices would be required. They had many questions and were open to discussions with the interviewers. Data on who students talked to about their educational and occupational plans became very real. Recall that for the marriage and family plans one-third of the students said they did not talk to anyone. The low average number of occupational choices (3) is also a major source of concern.

Bice (1977) and Osipow (1979) have examined the link between career education and vocational education. Both see aspects of career education—awareness programs, exploration programs, and guidance and counseling—as part of vocational education. Thus the values and other variables examined in this study have applications in parts of vocational education programs. Evenson and O'Neil (1978) have suggested that career education has an important role to play in combatting occupational sex-role stereotyping and several authors have prepared curriculum or counseling materials for occupations for women in the work force (e.g., Vetter & Sethney, 1972; Birk & Tanney, 1973; and Hurwitz & White, 1977). Another group has tested practices to affect career choice or to increase sex-fair counseling (e.g., Goldstein, 1975; Gilbert & Waldrop, 1978; Miller, 1979; and

Motsch, 1980). Kahnweiler and Kahnweiler (1980) reported a dual career family workship for college students that appears adaptable to acquaint high school students with basic conflicts and issues in such relationships.

The separation of work and other adult roles in schooling, counseling, occupational planning, and career education is particularly devastating for women. The concepts of role strain and role proliferation so far apparently attach disproportionally to women. These findings and ideas stress the need for any program touching upon the career development of women to concern itself not only with the content or career that is chosen but also with the marriage and family expectations of men and women. The articulation of the various roles of adults—worker, marriage partner and homemaker, and parent—must be examined by students, guidance workers, and career educators, perhaps going so far as to model or simulate the manner in which trade-offs in role demands can be negotiated by marriage partners and conflicts resolved. The marriage and parenthood values can be used in practice with the occupational values to assist girls and women in particular to more clearly understand the individual and social needs they may be expecting to satisfy in each adult role. The assumption, untested as yet, is that use of the three value sets, along with other materials, will result in more effective career decision-making. The definition of effective is described below, in the section on evaluation.

FOR EVALUATION

The above paragraphs have argued for an expanded set of variables in career education, guidance, and counseling activities that include career development for women especially. Kutner and Brogan (1976) and Harway (1980) have described the general process and specific sex bias in education and vocational counseling. They provide examples of variables and criteria to be examined for sex discrimination and sex bias in these settings. Super and Hall (1978) and Krumboltz, Becker-Haven, and Burnett (1979) also provide examples of criteria for career exploration and for career decision-making skills. The Krumboltz et al. review includes alternative outcomes of career guidance: improvements in decision-making skills, such as self-knowledge, conducting career exploration activities, increased occupational information, number of alternatives considered, congruence among vocational aspirations, ability to perceive relationships between present actions and future choices, and so on; increases in career maturity, as assessed by Super's Career Development Inventory, Crites's Career Maturity Inventory, or Westbrook's Cognitive Vocational Maturity Test; the nature and quality of vocational choices, including consideration and/or choice of nontraditional occupations, career orientation, realistic choices, and so on; improved employment seeking skills and occupational adaptation.

The arguement, however, for an expanded set of variables in career development also applies to an expanded set of criteria for the evaluation of programs and activities in career guidance and education. In addition to examining programs for overt sex bias in materials and procedures, and using the outcome variables suggested by Krumboltz et al., an "effective" program for women (and men) can be defined as increasing the likelihood that more occupations, traditional and/or nontraditional for women, will be explored, that fertility and education plans will be related to preferred occupation and level of career, marriage and parenthood commitments, and that these plans will be in agreement with expectations for labor force participation, articulation of role cycles for husband and wife, and a definition of a marriage "partnership" with respect to homemaking and parenting. Part of defining the marriage and parenthood division of responsibilities might well include outcome variables such as "negotiating skills" in relation to a partner, the attainment of social competencies that are both agentic and communal (Richardson et al., 1979), and a reduction of sex-stereotyped views of all three adult roles.

The outcomes that include examining and planning for other adult roles in conjunction with that of worker are not "prescribed" for students in any manner. As the student responses to the values make clear, there is a diversity of values held and a diversity of plans for relating work, marriage, and family. Further diversity and choices will be available to students with the acquisition of skills and increased competencies included in arriving at a definition of a marriage and parenthood "partnership." Expanding the criteria included in evaluation can focus attention on the needed extension of career development theory and activities.

The values and sex-role related variables included in the present study illustrate the change in the scope of life decisions that career theories must encompass in order to be meaningful for adolescent girls and, increasingly, to adolescent boys. Some values in each of the three sets are related to the career-choice variables and other values are related to the family planning variables of number of children desired, job-child orientation, and number of years of full-time work to age 41. There are no judgments to be placed on individual choice. The goal of using the values in research and practice is, as Katz has suggested, to attain self-knowledge of values in the service of individual choice.

BIBLIOGRAPHY

Adelson, J. *Adolescent psychology today.* Version of a paper presented at the Annual Meeting of the American Psychological Association, New York City, September, 1979.

Albrecht, S. L. Social class and sex-stereotyping of occupations. *Journal of Vocational Behavior,* 1976, *9,* 321-328.

Albrecht, S. L., Bahr, H., & Chadwick, B. A. Public stereotyping of sex roles, personality characteristics, and occupations. *Sociology and Social Research,* 1977, *61,* 223-241.

Allen, W. Family roles, occupational statuses, and achievement orientations among black women in the United States. *Signs: Journal of Women in Culture and Society,* 1979, *4,* 670-686.

Almquist, E. M. *Minorities, gender, and work.* Lexington, Mass.: Lexington Books, 1979.

Almquist, E. M. Sex stereotypes in occupational choice: The case for college women. *Journal of Vocational Behavior,* 1974, *5,* 13-21.

Angrist, S. S. The study of sex roles. In C. Perrucci & D. Targ (Eds.), *Marriage and the family: A critical analysis and proposals for change.* New York: David McKay, 1974, 182-188.

Angrist, S. S., Mickelsen, R., & Penna, A. N. Variations in adolescents' knowledge and attitudes about family life: Implications for curriculum design. *Adolescence,* 1976, *11,* 107-126.

Angrist, S. S., Mickelsen, R., & Penna, A. N. Sex differences in sex-role conceptions and family orientation of high school students. *Journal of Youth and Adolescence,* 1977, *6,* 179-186.

Astin, H. S., & Myint, T. Career development of young women during the post high school years. *Journal of Counseling Psychology,* 1971, *18,* 369-394.

Atchley, R. C. The life course, age grading, age-linked demands for decision making. In N. Datun & L. Ginsberg (Eds.), *Life-span developmental psychology—Normative life crises.* New York: Academic Press, 1978.

Ball-Rokeach, S. J. Receptivity to sexual equality. *Pacific Sociological Review,* 1976, *19,* 519-540.

Bayer, A. E. Life plans and marriage age: An application of path analyses. *Journal of Marriage and the Family,* 1969, *31,* 551-558.

Beckman, L. J. The relationship between sex roles, fertility and family size preferences. *Psychology of Women Quarterly,* 1979, *4,* 43-60.

Benedek, T. Motherhood and nurturing. In E. J. Anthony & T. Benedek (Eds.), *Parenthood: Its psychology and psycho-pathology*. Boston: Little, Brown, 1970.

Bennetts, L. Doctors' wives: Many report marriage is a disappointment. *The New York Times*, May 7, 1979, B10.

Bernard, J. *The future of motherhood*. New York: Dial Press, 1974.

Bernard, J. *Women, wives, mothers: Values and options*. Chicago: Aldine, 1975.

Bernard, J. Change and stability in sex-role norms and behavior. *Journal of Social Issues*, 1976, *32*, 207-223.

Berryman, S. E. *Sex desegregation of jobs: Evaluation issues*. Paper presented at the annual meeting of the Evaluation Research Society, Washington, D.C., November, 1978.

Bice, G. R. *Vocational education and career education: The uncertain connection*. Washington, D.C.: American Vocational Association, 1977.

Birk, J. M., & Tanney, M. F. *Career exploration for high school women: A model*. 1973. (ED 079 662)

Blau, P. M., Gustad, J. W., Jessor, R., Parnes, H. S., & Wilcock, R. C. Occupational choice: A conceptual framework. *Industrial and Labor Relations Review*, 1956, *9*, 531-543.

Bloch, R. H. Untangling the roots of modern sex roles: A survey of four centuries of change. *Signs*, 1978, *4*, 237-252.

Block, J., Denker, E. R., & Tittle, C. K. Perceived influences on career choices of 11th graders: Sex, SES, and ethnic group comparisons. *Sex Roles*, (in press).

Brito, P. K., & Jusenius, C. L. A note on young women's occupational expectations for age 35. *The Vocational Guidance Quarterly*, 1978, *26*, 165-175. (a)

Brito, P. K., & Jusenius, C. L. Sex segregation in the labor market: An analysis of young college women's occupational preferences. In F. L. Mott, *Women, work and family: Dimensions of change in American society*. Lexington, Mass.: Lexington Books, 1978. (b)

Bronfenbrenner, U. Contexts of child rearing. *American Psychologist*, 1979, *34*, 844-850.

Brozan, N. New marriage roles make men ambivalent about fatherhood. *The New York Times*, 1980, B5.

Bureau of the Census. *Methodology and scores of socioeconomic status*. Working Paper No. 15. Washington, D.C.: U.S. Department of Commerce, 1963.

Bureau of the Census. Marital status and living arrangements: March 1978. *Current Population Reports*, Series P-20, No. 338, Washington, D.C.: U.S. Government Printing Office, May, 1979.

Burlin, D. The relationship of parental education and maternal work and occupational status to occupational aspiration in adolescent females. *Journal of Vocational Behavior*, 1976, *9*, 99-104.

Carew, P. F. An exploratory study of adolescents' career decision-making process and content. *Dissertation Abstracts International*, 1977, 37 (12A), 7540.

Cerra, F. Study finds college women still aim for traditional jobs. *The New York Times*, Sunday, May 11, 1980.

Cherlin, A. *Postponing marriage: The influence of schooling, working, and work plans for young women*. Paper presented at the annual meeting of the American Sociological Association, San Francisco, Ca., September, 1978. (ED 161 790)

Chodorow, N. *The reproduction of mothering: Psychoanalysis and the sociology of gender*. Berkeley: University of California Press, 1978.

Clifford, G. J. *"Marry, stitch, die or do worse": Educating women for work in the American republic.* Paper prepared for discussion at the conference on the historiography of education and work, Stanford University, August, 1979.

Coombs, L. C. The measurement of commitment to work. *Journal of Population,* 1979, *2,* 203-223.

Corcoran, M. The economic consequences of marital dissolution for women in the middle years. *Sex Roles,* 1979, *5,* 343-353.

Corder-Bolz, J. Sex role and occupational aspirations: Final report of data analysis for FY 78 to National Institute of Education. Austin: Southwest Educational Development Laboratory, March 1979.

Cosby, A. G., & Charner, I. (Eds.). *Education and work in rural America The social context of early career decision and achievement,* 1978. (ED 164 215)

Curry, E. W., Hotchkiss, H. L., Picou, J. S., Stahura, J. M., & Salomone, J. *Significant other influence and career decisions. Volume II. Black and white female urban youth.* Research and development Series No. 138, 1978. (ED 159 333)

Darley, S. A. Big-time careers for the little woman: A dual-role dilemma. *Journal of Social Issues,* 1976, *32,* 85-98.

De Almeida, E. E. A descriptive and analytical study of the early adult roles of black and white women. *Dissertation Abstracts International,* 1977, *38* (4-A), 2351.

Douvan, E. Employment and the adolescent. In F. I. Nye & L. W. Hoffman (Eds.), *The employed mother in America.* Chicago: Rand McNally, 1963.

Douvan, E., & Adelson, J. *The adolescent experience.* New York: John Wiley, 1966.

Duncan, B., & Duncan, O. D. *Sex typing and social roles: A research report.* New York: Academic Press, 1978.

Duncan, O. D. Indicators of sex typing: Traditional and egalitarian, situational and ideological responses. *American Journal of Sociology,* 1979, *85,* 251-260.

Eagly, A., & Anderson, P. Sex role and attitudinal correlates of desired family size. *Journal of Applied Social Psychology,* 1974, *4,* 151-164.

Eckland, B. K., & Wisenbaker, J. M. *National longitudinal study: A capsule description of young adults four and one-half years after high school.* Research Triangle Park, N.C.: Center for Educational Research and Evaluation, Research Triangle Institute, February, 1979.

England, P. Women and occupational prestige: A case of vacuous sex equality. *Signs,* 1979, *5,* 252-265.

Entwisle, D. R., & Greenberger, E. Adolescents' views of women's work role. *American Journal of Orthopsychiatry,* 1972, *42,* 648-656.

Evenson, J. S., & O'Neil, M. L. *Current perspectives on the role of career education in combatting occupational sex-role stereotyping.* San Francisco, Ca.: Far West Laboratory for Educational Research and Development, May, 1978. (ED 156 916)

Falk, W. W., & Cosby, A. G. Women's marital-familial statuses and work histories: Some conceptual considerations. *Journal of Vocational Behavior,* 1978, *13,* 126-140.

Falk, W. W., & Salter, N.J. The stability of status orientations among young, white, rural women from three southern states. *Journal of Vocational Behavior,* 1978, *12,* 20-32.

Feldbaum, E. G. *Effects of life situational factors on women's career patterns.* Paper presented at the Annual Meeting of the American Psychological Association, New York, September, 1979.

Fitzgerald, L. F., & Crites, J. O. Toward a career psychology of women: What do we know? What do we need to know? *Journal of Counseling Psychology,* 1980, *27,* 44-62.

Fogarty, M. P., Rapoport, R., & Rapoport, R. N. *Sex, career and family.* Beverly Hills, Ca: Sage, 1971.

Frost, F., & Diamond, E. E. Ethnic and sex differences in occupational stereotyping by elementary school children. *Journal of Vocational Behavior,* 1979, *15,* 43-54.

Gackenbach, J. The effect of race, sex, and career goal differences on sex role attitudes at home and at work. *Journal of Vocational Behavior,* 1978, *12,* 93-101.

Garnets, L., & Pleck, J. H. Sex role identity, androgyny, and sex role transcendance: A sex role strain analysis. *Psychology of Women Quarterly,* 1979, *3,* 270-283.

Giele, J. Z. *Women and the future.* New York: Free Press, 1978.

Gilbert, L. A., & Waldrop, J. A. Evaluation of a procedure for increasing sex fair counseling. *Journal of Counseling Psychology,* 1978, *25,* 410-418.

Ginzberg, E. Toward a theory of occupational choice: A restatement. *Vocational Guidance Quarterly,* 1972, *20,* 169-176.

Ginzberg, E. & Associates. *Life Styles of educated women.* New York: Columbia University Press, 1966.

Ginzberg, E., Ginsburg, S. W., Axelrad, S., & Herma, J. L. *Occupational choice: An approach to a general theory.* New York: Columbia University Press, 1951.

Glick, P. C. Updating the life cycle of the family. *Journal of Marriage and the Family,* 1977, *39,* 5-13.

Goldstein, R. L. Effects of reinforcement and female career role models on the vocational attitudes of high school girls. *Dissertation Abstracts International,* 1975, *36* (3A), 1304.

Golladay, A., & Noell, J. (Eds.). *The condition of education* (statistical report). National Center for Education Statistics. Washington, D.C.: U.S. Government Printing Office, 1978.

Goodman, E. *Turning points: How and why do we change?* New York: Fawcett Columbine, 1979. (a)

Goodman, E. Mastering the marital two-step. *Greensboro Daily News,* A6, December 8, 1979.

Goodman, E. Your turn to vacuum, dear. *Greensboro Daily News,* G4, January 20, 1980.

Gottfredson, L. A. *An analytical description of employment according to race, sex, prestige and Holland type of work.* Report No. 249. April, 1978. (a) (ED 156 780)

Gottfredson, L. S. *Race and sex differences in occupational aspirations: Their development and consequences for occupational segregation.* Report No. 254. Baltimore, Md.: Johns Hopkins University, July, 1978. (b) (ED 159 456)

Gould, R. The phases of adult life: A study of developmental psychology. *American Journal of Psychiatry,* 1972, *129,* 521-532.

Grant, W. V., & Lind, C. G. *Digest of education statistics 1977-78.* Washington, D.C.: U.S. Government Printing Office, 1978.

Grant, W. V., & Lind, C. V. *Digest of Education Statistics 1979.* Washington, D.C.: U.S. Government Printing Office, 1979.

Gurin, P., & Morrison, B. M. *Education, labor market experiences and current expectancies of black and white men and women.* Final Report. September, 1976. (ED 135 996)

Gutek, B. A., & Nieva, V. *Career choice processes in women.* Paper presented at the Annual Meeting of the American Psychological Association, Toronto, Canada, August, 1978.

Hamburger, M. *Realism and consistency in early adolescent aspirations and expectations.* Unpublished doctoral dissertation, Columbia University, 1958.

Hansen, L. S., & Rapoza, R. S. (Eds.). *Career development and counseling of women.* Springfield, Ill.: Charles C Thomas, 1978.

Hare-Mustin, R. T., & Broderick, P. C. The myth of motherhood: A study of attitudes toward motherhood. *Psychology of Women Quarterly,* 1979, *4,* 114-128.

Harmon, L. W. Anatomy of career commitment in women. *Journal of Counseling Psychology,* 1970, *17,* 77-80.

Harren, V. A. *A career decision-making model.* Paper presented at the Annual Meeting of the American Personnel and Guidance Association, Las Vegas, Nevada, April, 1979.

Harren, V. A., Kass, R. A., Tinsley, H.E.A., & Moreland, J. R. Influence of sex role attitudes and cognitive styles on career decision making. *Journal of Counseling Psychology,* 1978, *25,* 390-398.

Harren, V. A., Kass, R. A., Tinsley, H.E.A., & Moreland, J. R. Influence of gender, sex role attitudes and cognitive complexity on gender-dominant career choices. *Journal of Counseling Psychology,* 1979, *26,* 227-234.

Harway, M. Sex bias in educational-vocational counseling. *Psychology of Women Quarterly,* 1980, *4,* 412-423.

Hawley, P. Perceptions of male models of femininity related to career choice. *Journal of Counseling Psychology,* 1972, *19,* 308-313.

Herzog, A. R., Bachman, J. G., & Johnson, L. D. *Paid work, child care, and housework: A national survey of high school seniors' preferences for sharing responsibilities between husband and wife.* Ann Arbor, Mich.: Survey Research Center, University of Michigan, June, 1980.

Hetherington, E. M. Divorce: A child's perspective. *American Psychologist,* 1979, *34,* 851-858.

Hofferth, S. L. *High school experience in the attainment process of non-college boys and girls: When and why do their paths diverge?* Working paper 1303-01. Washington, D.C.: The Urban Institute, February 1, 1980.

Hofferth, S. L., & Moore, K. A. *The consequences of a first childbirth: Causal models.* August, 1978. (ED 164 701)

Hofferth, S. L., & Moore, K. A. Women's employment and marriage. In R. E. Smith (Ed.), *The subtle revolution: Women at work.* Washington, D.C.: The Urban Institute, 1979.

Hofferth, S. L., and others. The consequences of age at first childbirth: Labor force participation and earnings. August, 1978. (ED 164 699)

Hoffman, L. W. Maternal employment: 1979. *American Psychologist,* 1979, *34,* 859-865.

Hoffman, L. W., & Hoffman, M. L. The value of children to parents. In J. T. Faucett (Ed.), *Psychological perspectives on population.* New York: Basic Books, 1973.

Holland, J. L. *Making vocational choices: A theory of careers.* Englewood Cliffs, N.J.: Prentice-Hall, 1973.

Holter, M. *Sex roles and social structure.* Oslo, Norway: Universtitsforlaget, 1970.

Hurwitz, R. E., & White, M. A. Efect of sex-linked vocational information on reported occupational choices of high school juniors. *Psychology of Women Quarterly*, 1977, *2*, 149-156.

Huston-Stein, A., & Higgins-Trenk, A. Development of females from childhood through adulthood: Career and feminine role orientation. In P. D. Baltes (Ed.), *Life span development and behavior. Vol. I.* New York: Academic Press, 1978, 258-296.

Iglitzin, L. B. A child's eye view of sex roles. *Today's Education*, 1972, 61, 23-25.

Izenberg, S. D. Attitudes towards women's roles and grade and sex of adolescents. *Dissertation Abstracts International*, 1978, *38* (11A), 6536.

Jepson, D., & Dilley, J. Vocational decision-making models: A review and comparative analysis. *Review of Educational Research*, 1974, *44*, 331-349.

Johnson, F. A., & Johnson, C. L. Role strain in high-commitment career women. *Journal of the American Academy of Psychoanalysis*, 1976, *4*, 13-36.

Johnson, S. J., & Jaccard, J. *Career-marriage orientations in males and females: An analysis of perceived personal consequences and normative pressures.* Modified version of a paper presented at the Annual Meeting of the American Psychological Association, New York, September, 1979.

Kahnweiler, J. B., & Kahnweiler, W. M. A dual career family workshop for college undergraduates. *Vocational Guidance Quarterly*, 1980, *28*, 225-230.

Kamerman, S. Work and family in industrialized societies. *Signs: Journal of Women in Culture and Society*, 1979, *4*, 632-650.

Kanter, R. M. The policy issues: Presentation VI. Combatting occupational segregation. *Signs*, 1976, *1*, 282-291.

Kass, R. A. *Career decision making, sex-role attitudes and cognitive styles: Which influences which?* Paper presented at the meeting of the American College Personnel Association, Los Angeles, Ca., March, 1979.

Katz, M. A model of guidance for career decision-making. *Vocational Guidance Quarterly*, 1966, *15*, 2-10.

Katz, M. Career decision-making: A computer-based System of Interactive Guidance and Information (SIGI). *Proceedings of the 1973 ETS Invitational Conference.* Princeton, N.J.: Educational Testing Service, 1973.

Katz, P. A. The development of female identity. *Sex Roles, A Journal of Research*, 1979, *5*, 155-178.

Kelly, G. A. *The psychology of personal constructs, Vol. I. A theory of personality.* New York: W. W. Norton, 1955.

Kerckhoff, A. C., & Parrow, A. A. *Sex differences in early contingencies in attainment.* October, 1978. (WE 006 383)

Kirkpatrick, C. *The family as process and institution* (2nd ed.). New York: Ronald Press, 1963.

Kleiman, D. John Jay mirrors city's high schools. *New York Times*, B1, May 9, 1979.

Klemmack, D. L., & Edwards, J. N. Women's acquisition of stereotyped occupational aspirations. *Sociology and Social Research*, 1973, *57*, 510-525.

Komarovsky, M. *Women in the modern world: Their education and their dilemmas.* Boston: Little, Brown, 1953.

Komarovsky, M. *Dilemmas of masculinity: A study of college youth.* New York: W. W. Norton, 1976.

Kotcher, E. V. Sex role identity and career goals in adolescent women. *Dissertation Abstracts International*, 1976, *36*, (9-A), 5949.

Krumboltz, J. D., Becker-Haven, J. F., & Burnett, K. F. Counseling psychology. *Annual Review of Psychology*, 1979, *30*, 555-602.

Krumboltz, J. D., Mitchell, A. M., & Jones, G. B. A social learning theory of career selection. *The Counseling Psychologist*, 1976, *6*, 71-81.

Kutner, N. G., & Brogan, D. Sources of sex discrimination in educational systems: A conceptual model. *Psychology of Women Quarterly*, 1976, *1*, 50-69.

Levine, A. Educational and occupational choice: A synthesis of literature from sociology and psychology. *Journal of Consumer Research*, 1976, *2*, 276-289.

Levinson, D. J. *The seasons of a man's life*. New York: Alfred A. Knopf, 1978.

Lichtman, M., Rothschild, S.J.S., & Peng, S. *Educational attainment among females and minorities*. Paper presented at the Annual Meeting of the American Educational Research Association, San Francisco, April, 1979.

Lipman-Blumen, J. The implications for family structure of changing sex roles. *Social Casework*, 1976, *57*, 67-79.

Lipman-Blumen, J., & Tickamyer, A. R. Sex roles in transition: A ten year perspective. *Annual Review of Sociology*, 1975, *1*, 297-337.

Loevinger, J. *Ego development: Conceptions and theories*. San Francisco: Jossey-Bass, 1976.

Loevinger, J. The idea of the ego. *The Counseling Psychologist*, 1979, *8*, 3 5.

Loevinger, J. Some thoughts on ego development and counseling. *The Personnel and Guidance Journal*, 1980, *58*, 389-390.

Looft, W. R. Vocational aspirations of second-grade girls. *Psychological Reports*, 1971, *28*, 241-242.

Lopata, H. Z. *Occupation: Housewife*. London: Oxford University Press, 1971.

Lowenthal, M. F., Thurnher, M., Chiriboga, D. & Associates. *Four stages of life: A comparative study of women and men facing transitions*. San Francisco: Jossey-Bass, 1975.

Lowenthal, M. F., & Weiss, L. Intimacy and crisis in adulthood. In L. S. Hansen & R. S. Rapoza, *Career development and counseling of women*. Springfield, Ill.: Charles C Thomas, 1978.

Lunneborg, P. W. Sex and career decision-making styles. *Journal of Counseling Psychology*, 1978, *25*, 299-305.

Lybarger, W. M. A multivariate analysis of the occupational interest domain of twelve hundred college men and women. *Dissertation Abstracts International*, 1978, *39* (2-B), 957.

Maccoby, E. E., & Jacklin, C. N. *The psychology of sex differences*. Stanford: Stanford University Press, 1974.

Magarrell, J. Today's new students, especially women, more materialistic. *The Chronical of Higher Education*, January 28, 1980, 3-5.

Mahoney, J., Heretick, D.M.L., & Katz, G. M. Gender specificity in value structures. *Sex Roles: A Journal of Research*, 1979, *5*, 311-318.

Margenau, H. The scientific basis of value theory. In A. H. Maslow (Ed.), *New knowledge in human values*. New York: Harper & Row, 1959.

Marini, M. M. Sex differences in the determination of adolescent aspirations: A review of research. *Sex Roles*, 1978, *4*, 723-753.

Marini, M. M., & Greenberger, E. Sex differences in educational aspirations and expectations. *American Educational Research Journal*, 1978, *15*, 67-79. (a)

Marini, M. M., & Greenberger, E. Sex differences in occupational aspirations and expectations. *Sociology of Work and Occupations*, 1978, *5*, 47-78. (b)

Maslow, A. H. *Motivation and personality.* New York: Harper & Row, 1954.

Maslow, A. H. *The farther reaches of human nature.* New York: Viking Press, 1971.

Mason, K. O. *Women's labor force participation.* Research Triangle Park, N.C.: The Center for Population Research and Services, July, 1974.

Mason, K. O. & Bumpass, L. B. *Women's sex role attitudes in the United States, 1970.* A revised version of a paper presented at the Annual Meeting of the American Sociological Association, 1973.

Mason, K. O., Czajka, J. L., & Arber, S. Change in U.S. women's sex-role attitudes, 1964-1974. *American Sociological Review,* 1976, *41,* 573-595.

McLaughlin, G. W., Hunt, W. K., & Montgomery, J. R. Socioeconomic status and the career aspirations and perceptions of women seniors in high school. *The Vocational Guidance Quarterly,* 1976, *25,* 155-162.

Medvene, A. M., & Collins, A. M. Occupational prestige and appropriateness: The views of mental health specialists. *Journal of Vocational Behavior,* 1976, *9,* 63-71.

Meixel, C. H. Effects of social structure, social psychological and sex role factors on female and male adolescents' status expectations. *Dissertation Abstracts International,* 1976, *37* (11A), 7351.

Miller, C. B. The impact of group career counseling on career maturity and stereotypical occupational choice of high school girls. *Dissertation Abstracts International,* 1979, *39,* 5330 (A).

Moore, K. A., & Hofferth, S. L. *The consequences of age at first childbirth: Family size. July, 1978.* (a) (ED 164 697)

Moore, K. A., & Hofferth, S. L. *The consequences of age at first childbirth: Female headed families and welfare recipients.* August, 1978. (b) (ED 164 700)

Moore, K. A., & Hofferth, S. L. *The consequences of age at first childbirth: Final research summary.* August, 1978. (c) (ED 164 702)

Moore, K. A., and others. *The consequences of age at first childbirth: Educational attainment.* August, 1978. (a) (ED 164 696)

Moore, K. A., and others. *The consequences of age at first childbirth: Marriage, separation and divorce.* July, 1978. (b) (ED 164 698)

Moreland, J. R., Harren, V. A., Krimsky-Montague, E., & Tinsley, H.E.A. Sex role self-concept and career decision making. *Journal of Counseling Psychology,* 1979, *26,* 329-336.

Motsch, P. Peer social modeling: A tool for assisting girls with career exploration. *Vocational Guidance Quarterly,* 1980, *28,* 231-240.

Mott, F. L. *Women, work, and family: Dimensions of change in American Society.* Lexington, Mass.: Lexington Books, 1978.

Moyer, K. L. *Vocational aspirations and expectations of Pennsylvania eleventh grade students, 1978.* (ED 162 189)

Munley, P. H. Erikson's theory of psychosocial development and career development. *Journal of Vocational Behavior,* 1977, *10,* 261-269.

National Center for Education Statistics. *Withdrawal from institutions of higher education: An appraisal with longitudinal data involving diverse institutions.* Washington, D.C.: U.S. Government Printing Office, 1977.

National Institute of Education. *Abstracts: Projects funded under the education and work grants competition.* Washington, D.C.: Department of Health, Education, and Welfare, 1976.

National NOW Times. Roper Poll for Virginia Slims. June 1980, p. 15.

Nettles, E. J. *The relationship of ego development and sex-role conception.* Paper presented at the Annual Meeting of the American Psychological Association, New York, August, 1979.

Neugarten, B. L., & Datan, N. Sociological perspectives on the life cycle. In P. Baltes & K. Scaie (Eds.), *Life span developmental psychology–personality and socialization.* New York: Academic Press, 1973.

New Educational Directions. *Sex as a determinant in vocational choice.* Final Report. June, 1977. (ED 145 135)

Nolfi, G. J., Fuller, W. C., Corazzini, A. J., Epstein, W. H., Freeman, R. B., Manski, C. F., Nelson, V. I., & Wise, D. A. *Experiences of recent high school graduates: The transition to work or post secondary education.* Lexington, Mass.: Lexington Books, 1978.

Norris, L., Katz, M. R., & Chapman, W. *Sex differences in the career decision-making process.* Final Report NIE-G-77-0002. Princeton, N.J.: Educational Testing Service, 1978.

Nye, F. I., & Hoffman, L. W. *The employed mother in America.* Chicago: Rand McNally, 1963.

Oberle, W. H. Role models of Negro and white rural youth at two stages of adolescence. *Journal of Negro Education,* 1974, *43,* 234-244.

Oberle, W. H., Stowers, K. R., & Falk, W. W. Place of residence and the role model preferences of black boys and girls. *Adolescence,* 1978, *13,* 13-20.

Osipow, S. H. *Career decision making and career maturity: How much overlap?* Paper presented at the Annual Meeting of the American Personnel and Guidance Association, Las Vegas, Nevada, April, 1979.

Osipow, S. H. *Theories of career development* (2nd ed.). Englewood Cliffs, N.J.: Prentice-Hall, 1973.

Osipow, S. The bases for career education and vocational education. In G. R. Bice (Ed.), *Vocational education and career education: The uncertain connection.* Washington, D.C.: American Vocational Association, 1977.

Panek, P. E., Rush, M. C., & Greenawalt, J. P. Current sex stereotypes of 25 occupations. *Psychological Reports,* 1977, *40,* 212-214.

Parnes, H. S., Jusenius, C. L., Blau, F., Nestel, G., Shortlidge, R. L., Jr., & Sandell, S. *Dual careers: Volume 4. R & D Monograph 21.* Washington, D.C.: U.S. Department of Labor, 1976.

Peng, S. S. Trends in the entry to higher education. *Educational Researcher,* 1977, *6,* 15-19.

Peng, S. S., Wisenbaker, J. M., Bailey, S. S., & Marnell, D. *Tabular summary of the third follow-up questionnaire data.* Vols. I, II, III, and IV. Washington, D.C.: U.S. Government Printing Office, March 1978.

Perrucci, C. C., Potter, H. R., & Rhoads, D. L. Determinants of male family-role performance. *Psychology of Women Quarterly,* 1978, *3,* 53-66.

Peterson-Hardt, S., & Burlin, F. Sex differences in perceptions of familial and occupational roles. *Journal of Vocational Behavior,* 1979, *14,* 306-316.

Picou, J. S., & Campbell, R. E. (Eds.). *Career behavior of special groups.* Columbus, Ohio: Merrill, 1975.

Pleck, J. H. The male sex-role: Definitions, problems, and sources of change. *The Journal of Social Issues,* 1976, *32,* 155-164.

Pleck, J. H., Staines, G. L., & Long, L. Conflicts between work and family life. *Monthly Labor Review,* March, 1980, 29-32.

Prediger, D. J., Roth, J. D., & Noeth, R. J. Career development of youth: A nationwide study. *Personnel and Guidance Journal,* 1974, *53,* 97-104.

Psathas, G. Toward a theory of occupational choice for women. *Sociology and Social Research,* 1968, *52,* 253-268.

Rand, L. M., & Miller, A. L. A developmental cross sectioning of women's career and marriage attitudes and life plans. *Journal of Vocational Behavior,* 1972, *2,* 317-331.

Rapoport, R., & Rapoport, R. N. *Dual-career families.* Baltimore, Md.: Penguin Books, 1971.

Rapoza, R. S., & Blocher, D. H. A comparative study of academic self-estimates, academic values, and academic aspirations of adolescent males and females. In L. S. Hanson & R. S. Rapoza (Eds.), *Career development and counseling of women.* Springfield, Ill.: Charles C Thomas, 1978.

Richardson, M. S. Toward an expanded view of careers. *The Counseling Psychologist,* 1979, *8,* 34-35.

Richardson, M. S., Merrifield, P., & Jacobson, S. *A factor analysis study of the Bem Sex Role Inventory.* Paper presented at the Annual Meeting of the American Psychological Association, New York, September, 1979.

Richardson, W. B., & Owings, M. F. *Women vocational students: Plans, aspirations, and socioeconomic indicators.* Paper presented at the annual meeting of the American Educational Research Association, San Francisco, April, 1979.

Rivers, C., Barnett, R., & Baruch, G. *Beyond sugar and spice: How women grow, learn and thrive.* New York: G. P. Putnam's, 1979.

Rock, D. A., & Freeberg, N. E. *Causal influences on educational plans of high school seniors: A structural analysis by race.* RB-77-8. Princeton, N.J.: Educational Testing Service, 1977.

Roderick, R. D., & Kohen, A. I. *Years for decision: Volume 3.* R & D Monograph 24. Washington, D.C.: U.S. Department of Labor, 1976.

Roe, A. *The psychology of occupations.* New York: Wiley, 1956.

Rokeach, M. *The nature of human values.* New York: Free Press, 1973.

Rokeach, M. (Ed.). *Understanding human values: Individual and societal.* New York: Free Press, 1979.

Rokeach, M., & Regan, J. F. The role of values in the counseling situation. *The Personnel and Guidance Journal,* 1980, *58*(9), 576-582.

Rubin, L. B. *Women of a certain age: The midlife search for self.* New York: Harper & Row, 1979.

Russo, N. F. The motherhood mandate. *Journal of Social Issues,* 1976, *32,* 143-153.

Russo, N. F. Overview: Sex roles, fertility and the motherhood mandate. *Psychology of Women Quarterly,* 1979, *4,* 7-15.

Sanchez, B. S. *Marriage deferment and achievement: Antecedents and consequences among rural youth.* Unpublished Master's Thesis, Texas A & M University, 1978. (ED 162 813)

Sangiuliano, I. *In her time.* New York: William Morrow, 1978.

Sawhill, I. V. Economic perspectives on the family. *Daedalus,* 1977, *106,* 115-125.

Scanzoni, J. Sex roles, economic factors, and marital solidarity in black and white marriages. *Journal of Marriage and the Family,* 1975, *37,* 130-144.

Scanzoni, J. Sex role change and influences on birth intentions. *Journal of Marriage and the Family,* 1976, *38,* 43-58.

Scanzoni, J. *Sex roles, women's work, and marital conflict.* Lexington, Mass.: Lexington Books, 1978.

Scanzoni, J. Sex-role influences on married women's status attainments. *Journal of Marriage and the Family,* 1979, *41,* 793-800. (a)

Scanzoni, J. Work and fertility control sequences among younger married women. *Journal of Marriage and the Family,* 1979, *41,* 739-748. (b)

Schlossberg, N. K., & Goodman, J. A woman's place: Children's sex stereotyping of occupations. *Journal of Vocational Guidance,* 1972, *20,* 266-270.

Schlossberg, N. K., & Waters, E. B. Counseling: Shifting the balance from problem to possibility. In *Women in midlife—Security and fulfillment (Part I).* A compendium of papers submitted to the Select Committee on Aging of the U.S. House of Representatives, Ninety-fifth Congress. Washington, D.C.: Committee Pub. No. 95-170, December, 1978.

Sheehy, G. *Passages: Predictable crises of adult life.* New York: Dutton, 1976.

Shinar, E. H. Sexual stereotypes of occupations. *Journal of Vocational Behavior,* 1975, *7,* 99-111.

Smith, K. B., and others. *Career contingencies and the formation of educational plans: An analysis of white adolescent males and females in rural Louisiana.* Paper presented at the Annual Meeting of the Southwestern Sociological Association, April, 1976. (ED 119 943)

Smith, R. E. (Ed.). *The subtle revolution: Women at work.* Washington, D.C.: The Urban Institute, 1979.

Spaeth, J. L. Differences in the occupational achievement process between male and female college graduates. *Sociology of Education,* 1977, *50,* 206-217.

Stolzenberg, R. M., & Waite, L. J. Age, fertility expectations and plans for employment. *American Sociological Review,* 1977, *42,* 769-783.

Strong, E. K., Jr., & Campbell, D. P. *Strong Vocational Interest Blank Manual.* Stanford, Ca.: Stanford University Press, 1966.

Super, D. E. *The psychology of careers.* New York: Harper & Row, 1957.

Super, D. E. *Career development: Self concept theory.* New York: CEEB Research Monograph No. 4, 1963.

Super, D. E. *Is career decision making career maturity? A developmental perspective.* Paper presented at the Annual Meeting of the American Personnel and Guidance Association, Las Vegas, Nevada, April, 1979.

Super, D. E., & Hall, D. T. Career development: Exploration and planning. *Annual Review of Psychology,* 1978, *29,* 333-372.

Super, D. E., & Jordaan, J. P. *Predictors of young adult vocational behavior.* (Adapted from) Paper presented at the Annual Meeting of the American Educational Research Association, San Francisco, Ca., April, 1979.

Swensen, C. H. Ego development and a general model for counseling and psychotherapy. *The Personnel and Guidance Journal,* 1980, *58,* 382-388.

Thomas, M. B., & Neal, P. A. Collaborating careers: The differential effects of race. *Journal of Vocational Behavior,* 1978, *12,* 33-42.

Thornton, A., & Camburn, D. Fertility, sex role attitudes and labor force participation. *Psychology of Women Quarterly,* 1979, *4,* 61-80.

Tiedeman, D. V., Katz, M. R., Miller-Tiedeman, A., & Osipow, S. H. *The cross-sectional story of early career development as revealed by the National Assessment of Educational Progress.* Washington, D.C.: American Personnel and Guidance Association, 1978.

Tiedeman, D. V., & O'Hara, R. P. *Career development: Choice and adjustment.* New York: College Entrance Examination Board, 1963.

Tittle, C. K., & Denker, E. R. *Returning women students in higher education: Defining policy issues.* New York: Praeger, 1980.

Tobin, P. L. Conjugal role definitions, value of children and contraceptive practice. *The Sociological Quarterly,* 1976, *17,* 314-322.

Tuck, B. F., & Keeling, B. Sex and cultural differences in the factorial structure of the SDS. *Journal of Vocational Behavior,* 1980, *16,* 105-114.

Tyler, L. E. *Individuality: Human possibilities and personal choice in the psychological development of men and women.* San Francisco: Jossey-Bass, 1978.

Tyler, L. E. Values clarification—A reaction. *The Personnel and Guidance Journal,* 1980, *58*(9), 574-575.

U.S. Commission on Civil Rights. *Social indicators of equality for minorities and women.* Washington, D.C.: U.S. Commission on Civil Rights, 1978.

U.S. Department of Labor. *Workers of Spanish origin: A chartbook.* Washington, D.C.: U.S. Department of Labor, 1978.

Van Dusen, R. A., & Sheldon, E. B. The changing status of American women: A life cycle perspective. *American Psychologist,* 1976, *31,* 106-116.

Vernon, P. E., & Allport, G. W. A test for personal values. *Journal of Abnormal and Social Psychology,* 1931, *26,* 231-248.

Vetter, L. Career counseling for women. *The Counseling Psychologist,* 1973, *4,* 54-67.

Vetter, L., & Sethney, B. J. *Women in the work force: Development and field testing of curriculum materials.* December, 1972. (ED 072 175)

Vetter, L., & Stockburger, D. W. *Career patterns of a national sample of women.* Research and development series No. 95 (re-issue). Final Report, 1977. (ED 146 363)

Waite, L. J. *Recent change in demographic patterns: Implications for women.* Paper presented at the Annual Meeting of the American Educational Research Association, Toronto, March, 1978. (a)

Waite, L. J. *Projecting female labor force participation from sex role attitudes.* Paper presented at the Annual Meeting of the American Sociological Association, San Francisco, September, 1978. (b) (ED 159 460)

Waite, L. J., & Stolzenberg, R. M. Intended childbearing and labor force participation of young women: Insights from nonrecursive models. *American Sociological Review,* 1976, *41,* 235-252.

White, M. S. Measuring androgyny in adulthood. *Psychology of Women Quarterly,* 1979, *3,* 293-307.

Women's Bureau. *20 facts on women workers.* Washington, D.C.: U.S. Department of Labor, August, 1979. (mineo)

Working women speak: 80% in low-pay jobs. *Guidepost,* December 13, 1979, 9.

Wrigley, A. P., & Stokes, C. S. Sex role ideology, selected life plans, and family size preferences: Further evidence. *Journal of Comparative Family Studies,* 1977, *8,* 391-400.

APPENDICES

APPENDIX 1.1
A Revised Occupational Scale for Rating Socioeconomic Status[1]

Category	Level 1	2	3	4	5	6	7
I Professional	Doctorate Judges Doctor Lawyer	Bachelor's or master degree Nurse Teacher Editor Pharmacist	BA or less Librarian Minister Reporter Lab Tech.	--	--	--	--
II Semi-profess.	--	Undertaker Airline Pilot	Clothes designer Commercial artist Photograp. Computer Prog.	Lab tech. Draftsman Photograp. Sound Editor Chemistry tech.	--	--	--
III Business (Bus. Value)	$750,000+ (size of business)	$250,000 - $750,000 Hotel Mgr.	$50,000 - $250,000 Office Mgr.	$25,000 - $50,000	up to $25,000	--	--
IV Clerical	Top notch sales	Life Ins. Salesman	Auto sales Admin. Sec. Auditors Accountant	Bookkeeper Steno Teller Cashier Traveling Salesman Ass't Buyer	Ass't Book-keeper Keypunch Operator Typist Tele. Oper. Store Clerk Salesperson Secretary (H.S.)	Shipping Clerk Mail clerk A&P check. Office boy	--
V Manual	--	--	--	Highly skilled Printer Radio/TV repair Plumber Electrician Watchmaker Machinist	Journeyman Carpenter Construc. Factory (w. respon.) Tele. foreman	Semi-skilled Low factory Helpers w. Construc. Miners	Heavy labor to (not stable)

267

APPENDIX 1.1 (Continued)

Category	1	2	3	4	5	6	7
VI Protective and Service	Police Commissioner	High police official	Detective Supt. of Bldgs. Fire Dept. Inspect.	Paraprofess. Family Plan. Counselor (H.S.) Policeman Fireman Chef Custodian Tailor Army recruit. Sanitation Supervisor Hotel Mgr.	Bus driver Corporal Barber Baker Cook Prac. Nurse Butcher Waiter at fine rest. Transit worker	Soldier Night policeman Bartender Truck Dr. Taxi Dr. Shoe repair Sanitation Chauffeur Ambulance Driver Meter read.	Night watchman Porter Garbage coll. Messenger boy Dish washer

1. Hamburger, M. Realism and consistency in early adolescent aspirations and expectations. Unpublished doctoral dissertation, Columbia University, 1958.

Roe Two-Way Classification of Occupations[1]

Level	I. Service	II. Business Contact	III. Organization	IV. Technology	V. Outdoor	VI. Science	VII. General Cultural	VIII. Arts and Entertainment
1	Personal therapists, Social work supervisors, Counselors	Promoters	United States President & Cabinet officers, Industrial ty-coons, International bankers	Inventive geniuses, Consulting or chief engineer, Ship's commanders	Consulting specialist	Research scientists, University, college faculties, Medical specialists: MD, Museum curators	Supreme Court Justices, University, college faculties, Prophets, Scholars	Creative artists, Performers, great, Teachers, university equivalent, Museum curators, Writer
2	Social workers, Occupational therapists, Probation, truant officers (with training)	Promoters, Public relations counselors	Computer Prog. Certified public accountants, Business and government executives, Union officials, Brokers, average	Applied scientists, Factory managers, Ship's officers, Engineers	Applied scientists, Landowners & operators, large, Landscape architects	Scientists, semi-independent, Nurses, Pharmacists, Veterinarian	Editors, Teachers, high school and elementary, Lawyer, Minister	Athletes, Art critics, Designers, Music arrangers, Actor, Musician, Artist
3	YMCA officials, Detectives, police sergeants, Welfare workers, City inspectors	Salesmen: auto, bond, insurance, etc., Dealers, retail and wholesale, Confidence men	Accountants, average, Employment managers, Owners, catering, dry-cleaning, etc.	Aviators, Contractors, Foremen (DOT I), Radio operators	County agents, Farm owners, Fish, game wardens	Technicians, medical, X-ray, museum, Weather observers, Chiropractor	Justices of the Peace, Radio announcers, Reporters, Librarians, Interpreter	Ad writers, Designers, Interior decorators, Showmen, Sports, Fashion, Merchandising, Writer

APPENDIX 1.2 (Continued)

		Group						
Level	I. Service	II. Business Contact	III. Organization	IV. Technology	V. Outdoor	VI. Science	VII. General Cultural	VIII. Arts and Entertainment
4	Barbers Chefs Practical nurses Policemen Beautician	Auctioneers Buyers(DOTI) House canvassers Interviewers, poll	Cashiers Clerks, credit, express, etc. Foremen, warehouse Salesclerks Secretary Key Punch	Blacksmiths Electricians Foremen(DOTI) Mechanics, average	Laboratory testers, dairy products, etc. Miners Oil well drillers	Technical assistants	Law	Advertising Artists Decorators, window, etc. Photographers Racing car drivers
5	Taxi drivers General houseworkers Waiters City firemen	Peddlers	Clerks, file, stock, etc. Notaries Runners Typists	Bulldozer operators Deliverymen Smelter workers Truck drivers	Gardeners Farm tenants Teamsters, cowpuncher Miner's helpers	Veterinary hospital attendants	Teacher aide	Illustrators, greeting cards Showcard writers Stagehands
6	Chambermaids Hospital attendants Elevator operators Watchmen		Messenger boys	Helpers Laborers Wrappers Yardmen	Dairy hands Farm laborers Lumberjacks	Nontechnical helpers in scientific organization		

1. Roe, A. *The psychology of occupations.* New York: Wiley, 1956.

APPENDIX 2.1
Frequency and Percentage for Persons to Whom Students Talk About Their Occupational Plans

	Father		Mother		Parents		Sibling		Other Rel.		Friend		Myself		Profes.		Other Comb.		Nobody		Total	
	N	%	N	%	N	%	N	%	N	%	N	%	N	%	N	%	N	%	N	%	N	%
Sex																						
Female	9	3	58	19	38	13	6	2	5	2	15	5	-	-	14	5	132	44	23	8	300	100
Male	21	7	28	9	54	18	15	5	10	3	20	7	-	-	15	5	108	36	29	10	300	100
Ethnic																						
White	12	6	18	9	39	20	4	2	4	2	12	6	-	-	7	4	84	42	20	10	200	100
Black	8	4	39	20	21	10	8	4	8	4	10	5	-	-	12	6	78	39	16	8	200	100
Hispanic	10	5	29	14	32	16	9	4	3	2	13	6	-	-	10	5	78	39	16	8	200	100
SES																						
Middle	22	7	35	12	49	16	7	2	5	2	12	4	-	-	17	6	133	44	20	7	300	100
Low	8	2	51	17	43	14	14	5	10	3	23	8	-	-	12	4	107	36	32	11	300	100

APPENDIX 2.2
Frequency and Percentage for Persons to Whom Students Talk About Their Educational Plans

	Father		Mother		Parents		Sibling		Other Rel.		Friend		Myself		Profes.		Other Comb.		Nobody		Total	
	N	%	N	%	N	%	N	%	N	%	N	%	N	%	N	%	N	%	N	%	N	%
Sex																						
Female	12	4	67	22	72	24	6	2	4	1	13	4	-	-	14	5	96	32	16	5	300	100
Male	21	7	51	17	81	27	13	4	6	2	9	3	1	.3	13	4	78	26	27	9	300	100
Ethnic																						
White	12	6	26	13	71	36	5	2	2	1	7	4	-	-	6	3	59	30	12	6	200	100
Black	5	3	56	28	36	18	6	3	4	2	6	3	-	-	13	7	62	31	12	6	200	100
Hispanic	16	8	36	18	46	23	8	-4	4	2	9	5	1	.5	8	4	53	26	19	10	200	100
SES																						
Middle	24	8	52	17	79	26	9	3	4	1	8	3	-	-	12	4	99	33	13	4	300	100
Low	9	3	66	22	74	25	10	3	6	2	14	5	1	.3	15	5	75	25	30	10	300	100

APPENDIX 2.3
Frequency and Percentage for Persons to Whom Students Talk About Their Marriage and Family Plans

	Father		Mother		Parents		Sibling		Other Rel.		Friend		Myself		Profes.		Other Comb.		Nobody		Total	
	N	%	N	%	N	%	N	%	N	%	N	%	N	%	N	%	N	%	N	%	N	%
Sex																						
Female	1	.3	57	19	30	10	12	4	4	1	67	22	4	1	-	-	60	20	65	22	300	100
Male	7	2	35	12	34	11	5	2	5	2	38	13	2	.7	-	-	42	14	132	44	300	100
Ethnic																						
White	2	1	21	10	33	16	5	3	1	.5	40	20	1	.5	-	-	38	19	59	30	200	100
Black	1	.5	40	20	16	8	4	2	5	3	32	16	2	1	-	-	30	15	70	35	200	100
Hispanic	5	3	31	15	15	8	8	4	3	2	33	16	3	2	-	-	34	17	68	34	200	100
SES																						
Middle	4	1	44	15	43	14	6	2	5	2	48	16	3	1	-	-	60	20	87	29	300	100
Low	4	1	48	16	21	7	11	4	4	1	57	19	3	1	-	-	42	14	110	37	300	100

APPENDIX 3.1

Number and Percentage of Students Assigning Ranks to Ten Occupational Values

Occupational Values

Rank	High Income		Prestige		Inde- pendence		Helping Others		Security		Variety		Leader- ship		Field of Interest		Leisure		Early Entry	
	F	%	F	%	F	%	F	%	F	%	F	%	F	%	F	%	F	%	F	%
1	75	12.5	44	7.3	40	6.7	85	14.2	52	8.7	35	5.8	30	5.0	226	37.7	6	1.0	8	1.3
2	72	12.0	79	13.2	66	11.0	88	14.7	65	10.8	60	10.0	39	6.5	93	15.5	26	4.3	12	2.0
3	65	10.8	81	13.5	83	13.8	62	10.3	88	14.7	73	12.2	48	8.0	46	7.7	34	5.7	20	3.3
4	64	10.7	73	12.2	80	13.3	75	12.5	84	14.0	67	11.2	51	8.5	45	7.5	41	6.8	20	3.3
5	50	8.3	69	11.5	68	11.3	67	11.2	94	15.7	69	11.5	47	7.8	55	9.2	64	10.7	16	2.7
6	63	10.5	67	11.2	71	11.8	56	9.3	60	10.0	64	10.7	73	12.2	30	5.0	80	13.3	35	5.8
7	73	12.2	65	10.8	77	12.8	57	9.5	50	8.3	66	11.0	61	10.2	35	5.8	85	14.2	31	5.2
8	57	9.5	62	10.3	54	9.0	48	8.0	44	7.3	64	10.7	75	12.5	34	5.7	113	18.8	49	8.2
9	42	7.0	34	5.7	46	7.7	42	7.0	43	7.2	76	12.7	100	16.7	22	3.7	99	16.5	97	16.2
10	39	6.5	26	4.3	15	2.5	20	3.3	20	3.3	26	4.3	76	12.7	14	2.3	52	8.7	312	52.0
M(SD)	5.1	2.8	5.0	2.5	5.1	2.5	4.6	2.7	4.8	2.5	5.5	2.6	6.4	2.7	3.4	2.7	6.7	2.3	8.4	2.3

APPENDIX 3.2

Number and Percentage of Students Assigning Ratings to Ten Occupational Values

Occupational Values

Rating	High Income F	High Income %	Prestige F	Prestige %	Independence F	Independence %	Helping Others F	Helping Others %	Security F	Security %	Variety F	Variety %	Leadership F	Leadership %	Field of Interest F	Field of Interest %	Leisure F	Leisure %	Early Entry F	Early Entry %
8	109	18.2	76	12.7	86	14.3	138	23.0	153	25.5	70	11.7	53	8.8	301	50.2	30	5.0	24	4.0
7	41	6.8	53	8.8	70	11.7	71	11.8	67	11.2	71	11.8	49	8.2	81	13.5	53	8.8	23	3.8
6	129	21.5	128	21.3	141	23.5	130	21.7	171	28.5	111	18.5	72	12.0	104	17.3	98	16.3	32	5.3
5	67	11.2	68	11.3	85	14.2	73	12.2	63	10.5	91	15.2	77	12.8	44	7.3	104	17.3	20	3.3
4	141	23.5	158	26.3	124	20.7	16	19.3	82	13.7	128	21.3	112	18.7	46	7.7	145	24.2	86	14.3
3	25	4.2	25	4.2	30	5.0	30	5.0	27	4.5	35	5.8	50	8.3	14	2.3	53	8.8	36	6.0
2	52	8.7	65	10.8	47	7.8	34	5.7	24	4.0	76	12.7	110	18.3	7	1.2	83	13.8	134	22.3
1	15	2.5	17	2.8	7	1.2	6	1.0	6	1.0	10	1.7	32	5.3	1	0.2	14	2.3	84	14.0
0	21	3.5	10	1.7	10	1.7	2	0.3	7	1.2	8	1.3	45	7.5	2	0.3	20	3.3	161	26.8
M(SD)	5.0	2.1	4.9	2.0	5.2	1.9	5.6	1.9	5.8	1.9	4.9	2.0	4.1	2.3	6.8	1.6	4.4	1.9	2.4	2.3

APPENDIX 3.3
Number of 300 Females and 300 Males Assigning Ranks to Ten Occupational Values

Occupational Values

Rank	High Income F	High Income M	Prestige F	Prestige M	Independence F	Independence M	Helping Others F	Helping Others M	Security F	Security M	Variety F	Variety M	Leadership F	Leadership M	Field of Interest F	Field of Interest M	Leisure F	Leisure M	Early Entry F	Early Entry M
1	30	45	21	23	23	17	54	31	18	34	21	14	11	19	113	113	3	3	5	3
2	23	49	37	42	33	33	55	33	29	36	40	20	17	22	51	42	9	17	6	6
3	34	31	46	35	46	37	37	25	33	55	41	32	18	30	23	23	10	24	12	8
4	26	38	40	33	46	34	39	36	50	34	34	33	16	35	17	28	20	21	12	8
5	23	27	32	37	34	34	28	39	53	41	34	35	22	25	34	21	34	30	6	10
6	40	23	34	33	30	41	25	31	32	28	33	31	37	36	16	14	36	44	17	18
7	46	27	37	28	31	46	20	37	25	25	33	33	27	34	14	21	49	36	18	13
8	30	27	23	39	27	27	24	24	25	19	24	40	42	33	14	20	66	47	25	24
9	22	20	18	16	23	23	14	28	25	18	35	41	65	35	10	12	45	54	44	53
10	26	13	12	14	7	8	4	16	10	10	5	21	45	31	8	6	28	24	155	157
Mean Rank	5.5	4.6	4.9	5.1	4.9	5.2	4.1	5.2	5.1	4.6	5.1	5.9	6.9	5.9	3.3	3.5	6.9	6.5	8.4	8.5
SD Rank	2.7	2.8	2.5	2.6	2.5	2.4	2.5	2.7	2.4	2.5	2.6	2.6	2.6	2.7	2.6	2.7	2.1	2.4	2.4	2.2
Mean: Std Rating	49.1*	52.8*	49.0	49.7	51.4	51.5	55.8*	51.1*	54.5	55.3	51.4	48.5*	43.5*	47.5*	60.7	59.0*	46.5*	48.2*	37.2	36.4
SD: Std Rating	9.8	9.7	9.8	9.5	9.2	8.5	9.3	10.5	8.1	9.4	9.5	9.7	9.9	10.6	8.0	8.7	8.1	8.3	10.4	10.4

*Sex differences significant p < .01.

276

APPENDIX 3.4
Number and Percentage of Students Assigning Ranks to Eleven Marriage Values

Marriage Values

Rank	Financial Security F	%	Emotional Support F	%	A Helpmate F	%	A Close Physical Relationship F	%	Prestige F	%	A Normal Life F	%	A Permanent Companion F	%	Children F	%	Your Own Home F	%	Someone to Rely On F	%	A Feeling of Leadership F	%
1	54	9.0	272	45.3	18	3.0	60	10.0	13	2.2	22	3.7	101	16.8	14	2.3	15	2.5	25	4.2	10	1.7
2	41	6.8	119	19.8	52	8.7	95	15.8	43	7.2	10	1.7	94	15.7	45	7.5	20	3.3	72	12.0	10	1.7
3	38	6.3	72	12.0	50	8.3	100	16.7	47	7.8	14	2.3	88	14.7	64	10.7	32	5.3	79	13.2	16	2.7
4	36	6.0	47	7.8	54	9.0	110	18.3	41	6.8	10	1.7	86	14.3	87	14.5	23	3.8	83	13.8	22	3.7
5	49	8.2	30	5.0	59	9.8	70	11.7	57	9.5	29	4.8	66	11.0	85	14.2	35	5.8	88	14.7	30	5.0
6	45	7.5	24	4.0	64	10.7	52	8.7	67	11.2	31	5.2	46	7.7	86	14.3	67	11.2	74	12.3	45	7.5
7	55	9.2	12	2.0	80	13.3	36	6.0	65	10.8	47	7.8	38	6.3	62	10.3	87	14.5	58	9.7	62	10.3
8	66	11.0	8	1.3	79	13.2	39	6.5	68	11.3	65	10.8	37	6.2	46	7.7	81	13.5	44	7.3	67	11.2
9	62	10.3	7	1.2	60	10.0	15	2.5	75	12.5	80	13.3	20	3.3	43	7.2	98	10.3	82	5.3	106	17.7
10	67	11.2	4	0.7	52	8.7	18	3.0	71	11.8	105	17.5	15	2.5	39	6.5	91	15.2	30	5.0	109	18.2
11	87	14.5	5	0.8	32	5.3	5	0.8	53	8.8	187	31.2	9	1.5	29	4.8	51	8.5	15	2.5	123	20.5
M(SD)	6.7	3.3	2.5	2.1	6.3	2.7	4.3	2.4	6.8	2.8	8.6	2.7	4.2	2.6	7.4	2.6	7.4	2.6	5.2	2.6	8.3	2.5

APPENDIX 3.5
Number and Percentage of Students Assigning Ratings to Eleven Marriage Values[1]

Marriage Values

Rating	Financial Security F	%	Emotional Support F	%	A Helpmate F	%	A Close Physical Relationship F	%	Prestige F	%	A Normal Life F	%	A Permanent Companion F	%	Children F	%	Your Own Home F	%	Someone to Rely On F	%	A Feeling of Leadership F	%
8	80	13.3	244	40.7	58	9.7	145	24.2	39	6.5	39	6.5	169	28.2	109	18.2	81	13.5	156	26.0	21	3.5
7	40	6.7	97	16.2	66	11.0	97	16.2	56	9.3	30	5.0	103	17.2	82	13.7	44	7.3	97	16.2	43	7.2
6	104	17.3	163	27.2	108	18.0	192	32.0	107	17.8	56	9.3	147	24.5	166	27.7	113	18.8	150	25.0	68	11.3
5	65	10.8	40	6.7	67	11.2	71	11.8	72	12.0	51	8.5	65	10.8	92	15.3	73	12.2	68	11.3	63	10.5
4	123	20.5	41	6.8	148	24.7	61	10.2	134	22.3	110	18.3	72	12.0	73	12.2	119	19.8	68	11.3	112	18.7
3	41	6.8	8	1.3	49	8.2	15	2.5	44	7.3	65	10.8	16	2.7	20	3.3	45	7.5	28	4.7	54	9.0
2	71	11.8	3	0.5	65	10.8	12	2.0	79	13.2	86	14.3	20	3.3	30	5.0	71	11.8	20	3.3	93	15.5
1	31	5.2	1	0.2	19	3.2	4	0.7	32	5.3	48	8.0	3	0.5	13	2.2	25	4.2	6	1.0	60	10.0
0	45	7.5	3	0.5	20	3.3	3	0.5	37	6.2	115	19.2	5	0.8	15	2.5	29	4.8	7	1.2	85	14.2
M(SD)	4.4	2.4	6.7	1.4	4.7	2.1	6.1	1.6	4.3	2.4	3.3	2.4	6.1	1.8	5.5	2.0	4.6	2.2	5.9	1.8	3.4	2.3

1. One case missing, 0.2%.

APPENDIX 3.6
Number of 300 Females and 300 Males Assigning Ranks to Eleven Marriage Values

Marriage Values

Rank	Financial Security		Emotional Support		A Helpmate		A Close Physical Relationship		Prestige		A Normal Life		A Permanent Companion		Children		Your Own Home		Someone to Rely On		A Feeling of Leadership	
	F	M	F	M	F	M	F	M	F	M	F	M	F	M	F	M	F	M	F	M	F	M
1	31	23	136	136	11	7	34	26	11	2	8	14	48	53	3	11	3	12	13	12	4	6
2	23	18	70	49	22	30	46	49	22	21	4	6	39	55	17	28	11	9	42	30	4	6
3	23	15	36	36	26	24	41	59	31	16	2	12	50	38	27	37	16	16	39	40	9	7
4	25	11	23	24	23	31	52	58	22	19	5	5	52	34	36	51	12	11	40	43	9	13
5	32	17	13	17	33	26	44	26	28	29	10	19	30	36	34	51	16	19	48	40	11	19
6	23	22	7	17	30	34	28	24	31	36	13	18	22	24	52	34	34	33	36	38	24	21
7	28	27	6	6	45	35	18	18	30	35	17	30	16	22	32	30	49	38	31	27	28	34
8	35	31	5	3	45	34	18	21	31	37	30	35	21	16	31	15	30	51	22	22	33	34
9	33	29	3	4	22	38	8	7	36	39	40	40	10	10	25	18	58	40	13	19	52	54
10	24	43	0	4	24	28	7	11	37	34	57	48	7	8	25	14	53	38	5	10	55	54
11	23	64	1	4	19	13	4	4	21	32	114	73	5	5	18	11	18	33			71	52
Mean Rank	6.0	7.3	2.3	2.7	6.3	6.3	4.3	4.3	6.5	7.0	9.0	8.1	4.2	4.1	6.3	5.3	7.5	7.3	5.0	5.4	8.4	8.1
SD Rank	3.1	3.3	1.8	2.3	2.7	2.8	2.4	2.4	2.9	2.7	2.4	2.9	2.6	2.6	2.6	2.5	2.5	2.7	2.5	2.6	2.4	2.5
Mean: Std Rating	48.2*	45.5*	59.8*	58.4*	48.0	47.6	56.0	55.8	47.8*	44.3*	39.3*	42.1*	55.0	56.2	52.5	53.3	47.1*	49.0*	54.9	55.4	40.6*	42.3*
SD: Std Rating	10.3	12.5	7.1	8.3	9.8	9.5	8.3	7.4	9.3	9.9	11.3	11.8	8.4	8.9	10.0	9.2	9.5	9.7	8.4	8.6	9.6	10.1

*Sex differences significant p $<$ .05.

APPENDIX 3.7
Number and Percentage of Students Assigning Ranks to Twelve Parenthood Values

Parenthood Values

Rank	Accomplishment F	%	A Sense of Pride F	%	Variety F	%	Friendship F	%	Respect of Others F	%	A Stable Marriage F	%	A Chance to Express Love F	%	Confidence as a Man/Woman F	%	Joy F	%	Future Security F	%	A Tie to the Future F	%	A Sense of Importance F	%
1	109	18.2	53	8.8	17	2.8	87	14.5	4	0.7	28	4.7	151	25.2	9	1.5	118	19.7	4	0.7	12	2.0	7	1.2
2	61	10.2	93	15.5	50	8.3	101	16.8	8	1.3	18	3.0	116	19.3	9	1.5	112	18.7	11	1.8	15	2.5	8	1.3
3	49	8.2	78	13.0	72	12.0	97	16.2	10	1.7	33	5.5	97	16.2	22	3.7	92	15.3	15	2.5	21	3.5	13	2.2
4	52	8.7	92	15.3	96	16.0	92	15.3	14	2.3	36	6.0	65	10.8	21	3.5	59	9.8	22	3.7	30	5.0	19	3.2
5	72	12.0	87	14.5	76	12.7	53	8.8	13	2.2	48	8.0	54	9.0	26	4.3	56	9.3	28	4.7	40	6.7	49	8.2
6	77	12.8	65	10.8	62	10.3	50	8.3	25	4.2	35	5.8	51	8.5	34	5.7	58	9.7	31	5.2	51	8.5	60	10.0
7	58	9.7	48	8.0	64	10.7	34	5.7	28	4.7	60	10.0	31	5.2	41	6.8	29	4.8	57	9.5	80	13.3	71	11.8
8	38	6.3	27	4.5	60	10.0	33	5.5	45	7.5	70	11.7	9	1.5	54	9.0	26	4.3	63	10.5	89	14.8	84	14.0
9	28	4.7	21	3.5	56	9.3	22	3.7	80	13.3	62	10.3	17	2.8	69	11.5	20	3.3	79	13.2	69	11.5	78	13.0
10	23	3.8	19	3.2	17	2.8	19	3.2	80	13.3	73	12.2	6	1.0	101	16.8	18	3.0	81	13.5	76	12.7	91	15.2
11	20	3.3	10	1.7	18	3.0	9	1.5	117	19.5	77	12.8	3	0.5	96	16.0	6	1.0	102	17.0	68	11.3	73	12.2
12	13	2.2	7	1.2	12	2.0	3	0.5	176	29.3	60	10.0	--	---	118	19.7	6	1.0	107	17.8	49	8.2	47	7.8
M(SD)	5.0	3.1	4.7	2.6	5.7	2.7	4.2	2.6	9.7	2.5	7.7	3.2	3.4	2.3	8.9	2.8	4.0	2.7	8.9	2.7	7.9	2.8	8.2	2.5

APPENDIX 3.8

Number and Percentage of Students Assigning Ratings to Twelve Parenthood Values[1]

Parenthood Values

Rating	Accomplishment		A Sense of Pride		Variety		Friendship		Respect of Others		A Stable Marriage		A Chance to Express Love		Confidence as a Man/Woman		Joy		Future Security		A Tie to the Future		A Sense of Importance	
	F	%	F	%	F	%	F	%	F	%	F	%	F	%	F	%	F	%	F	%	F	%	F	%
8	94	15.7	100	16.7	69	11.5	214	35.7	29	4.8	90	15.0	284	47.3	44	7.3	280	46.7	60	10.0	46	7.7	63	10.5
7	66	11.0	70	11.7	71	11.8	117	19.5	29	4.8	55	9.2	115	19.2	43	7.2	112	18.7	47	7.8	68	11.3	51	8.5
6	131	21.8	165	27.5	141	23.5	151	25.2	63	10.5	108	18.0	129	21.5	74	12.3	125	20.8	87	14.5	100	16.7	122	20.3
5	80	13.3	97	16.2	120	20.0	49	8.2	57	9.5	61	10.2	40	6.7	76	12.7	36	6.0	69	11.5	94	15.7	77	12.8
4	138	23.0	102	17.0	118	19.7	37	6.2	117	19.5	82	13.7	21	3.5	101	16.8	34	5.7	121	20.2	127	21.2	118	19.7
3	35	5.8	30	5.0	32	5.3	15	2.5	57	9.5	37	6.2	3	0.5	49	8.2	5	0.8	50	8.3	66	11.0	44	7.3
2	35	5.8	22	3.7	35	5.8	10	1.7	126	21.0	71	11.8	2	0.3	92	15.3	6	1.0	79	13.2	50	8.3	52	8.7
1	12	2.0	8	1.3	10	1.7	3	0.5	39	6.5	35	5.8	2	0.3	33	5.5	1	0.2	34	5.7	24	4.0	37	6.2
0	9	1.5	6	1.0	4	0.7	4	0.7	83	13.8	61	10.2	4	0.7	87	14.5	1	0.2	53	8.8	25	4.2	36	6.0
M(SD)	5.2	1.9	5.5	1.8	5.2	1.7	6.5	1.6	3.4	2.3	4.5	2.3	6.9	1.4	3.7	2.4	6.9	1.4	4.2	2.3	4.6	2.1	4.5	2.2

APPENDIX 3.9
Number of 300 Females and 300 Males Assigning Ranks to Twelve Parenthood Values

Parenthood Values

Rank	Accomplishment F	Accomplishment M	A Sense of Pride F	A Sense of Pride M	Variety F	Variety M	Friendship F	Friendship M	Respect of Others F	Respect of Others M	A Stable Marriage F	A Stable Marriage M	A Chance to Express Love F	A Chance to Express Love M	Confidence as a Man/Woman F	Confidence as a Man/Woman M	Joy F	Joy M	Future Security F	Future Security M	A Tie to the Future F	A Tie to the Future M	A Sense of Importance F	A Sense of Importance M
1	44	65	23	30	8	9	51	36	2	2	10	18	88	63	6	3	62	56	0	4	2	10	3	4
2	31	30	37	56	31	19	51	50	5	3	5	13	60	56	4	5	65	47	4	7	5	10	4	4
3	26	23	37	41	37	35	60	37	3	7	8	25	53	44	11	11	45	47	7	8	7	14	5	8
4	26	26	47	45	59	37	44	48	4	10	15	21	31	34	13	8	30	29	11	11	11	19	8	11
5	41	31	45	42	42	34	28	25	5	8	24	24	22	32	15	11	23	33	12	16	25	15	18	31
6	40	37	43	22	40	22	21	29	9	16	13	22	21	30	21	13	32	26	8	23	24	27	29	31
7	38	20	27	21	25	39	14	20	13	15	22	38	14	17	23	18	14	15	31	26	40	40	40	31
8	16	22	15	12	22	38	12	21	21	24	40	30	3	6	21	33	9	17	40	23	56	33	44	40
9	14	14	8	13	21	35	8	14	43	37	32	30	5	12	43	26	8	12	46	33	30	39	42	36
10	9	14	13	6	6	11	9	10	43	37	37	36	2	4	53	48	5	13	46	35	31	45	46	45
11	7	13	5	5	7	11	2	7	62	55	48	29	1	2	41	55	3	3	47	55	42	26	35	38
12	8	5	0	7	2	10	0	3	90	86	46	14	0	0	49	69	4	2	48	59	27	22	26	21
Mean Rank	5.1	4.9	4.8	4.5	5.2	6.1	3.8	4.6	9.8	9.5	8.4	6.9	3.1	3.7	8.6	9.2	3.8	4.2	9.0	8.8	8.1	7.6	8.3	8.0
SD Rank	2.9	3.2	2.5	2.7	2.4	2.8	2.4	2.8	2.4	2.6	3.0	3.1	2.1	2.4	2.9	2.8	2.6	2.8	2.5	2.9	2.6	2.9	2.4	2.6
M: Std Rating	50.7	50.4	52.1	52.1	51.7*	47.9*	58.5*	56.3*	39.6*	41.6*	44.5*	49.8*	61.0*	59.2*	43.4	42.5	60.2	59.2	45.1	45.6	46.1*	47.6*	47.0	47.7
SD: Std Rating	8.5	9.5	7.6	9.1	8.4	9.7	7.9	9.3	9.3	9.6	10.6	10.8	6.4	7.0	9.8	10.4	7.6	8.0	8.9	10.9	8.9	10.0	9.0	8.8

APPENDIX 4.1
Factors for the Total Sample

(Factor 1)

Value Area	Value	Loading
M	A Normal Life	.75
P	Respect of Others	.64
P	Variety	-.30
P	A Stable Marriage	.33
M	A Feeling of Leadership	-.27
M	Emotional Support	-.24
P	A Tie to the Future	-.20

(Factor 2)

Value Area	Value	Loading
O	Prestige	-.79
O	Variety	.44
M	Prestige	-.56
O	Security	.24
M	A Helpmate	.24
M	Someone to Rely On	.21

(Factor 3)

Value Area	Value	Loading
O	High Income	-.71
O	Helping Others	.71
O	Security	-.33
O	Variety	.29
O	Leisure	-.24
M	Close Physical Relationship	-.27
M	Children	.29
M	Someone to Rely On	-.26
P	Variety	.22
P	A Stable Marriage	-.29

(Factor 4)

Value Area	Value	Loading
P	A Chance to Express Love	.30
P	Confidence as a Man or Woman	.36
P	Future Security	-.63
P	Tie to the Future	-.77
P	Friendship	.25
P	Respect of Others	.25

(Factor 5)

Value Area	Value	Loading
O	Security	.35
O	Leadership	-.80
O	Early Entry	.56
M	Feeling of Leadership	-.55

(Factor 6)

Value Area	Value	Loading
M	Emotional Support	.45
M	Prestige	-.40
M	Children	.52
M	Feeling of Leadership	-.39
P	Chance to Express Love	.42
P	Joy	.66
P	A Stable Marriage	-.21

APPENDIX 4.1 (Continued)

Value Area	Value	Loading	Value Area	Value	Loading	Value Area	Value	Loading
	(Factor 7)			**(Factor 8)**			**(Factor 9)**	
P	Accomplishment	.76	O	Leisure	-.52	M	A Helpmate	-.69
P	Sense of Pride	.75	M	Close Physical Relationship	-.52	M	A Permanent Companion	.68
			P	Variety	-.36			
P	Friendship	-.25	P	Sense of Importance	.67	M	Emotional Support	-.20
P	A Stable Marriage	-.25				M	Children	.20
P	Chance to Express Love	-.28				M	Someone to Rely On	.20
P	Confidence as a Man or Woman	-.22	O	Security	.28	P	Respect of Others	-.23
P	Future Security	-.21				P	Stable Marriage	.24
	(Factor 10)			**(Factor 11)**			**(Factor 12)**	
M	Financial Security	-.87	M	Emotional Support	-.39	O	Independence	.87
			M	Prestige	-.33	O	Leisure	-.31
			M	Children	.36			
			M	Your Own Home	.81			
O	High Income	-.28				O	Security	-.21
O	Variety	.25	O	Variety	-.28	O	Variety	.25
M	A Helpmate	.29	O	Early Entry	.27	M	Close Physical Relationship	.24
M	Permanent Companion	.26	M	A Helpmate	-.24	M	Prestige	.21
M	Children	.21	M	Permanent Companion	-.22			
M	Someone to Rely On	.25						
P	Future Security	-.24						

Value Area	Value	Load-ing	Value Area	Value	Load-ing
	(Factor 13)			(Factor 14)	
P	Variety	-.54	O	Security	-.39
P	Friendship	-.65	O	Field of Interest	.74
P	Stable Marriage	.35	M	Someone to Rely On	.40
P	Confidence as a Man or Woman	.67	P	Chance to Express Love	.30
O	Variety	-.22			
O	Early Entry	.20			
M	Children	.26			
M	Someone to Rely On	-.29			

APPENDIX 4.2
Factors for the Female Sample

Value Area	Value	Load-ing	Value Area	Value	Load-ing	Value Area	Value	Load-ing
	(Factor 1)			(Factor 2)			(Factor 3)	
P	Friendship	-.68	M	Feeling of Leadership	-.86	O	High Income	-.74
P	Confidence as a Man or Woman	.67	M	A Normal Life	.46	O	Variety	.33
P	Variety	-.59	P	Joy	.34	O	Helping Others	.31
P	Stable Marriage	.33				M	Financial Security	-.72
			O	Leadership	-.25	M	Children	.38
M	Children	-.28	M	Permanent Companion	.28	M	Permanent Companion	.35
M	Permanent Companion	-.20	M	Prestige	-.26			
P	Sense of Importance	.28	M	Children	-.28	O	Field of Interest	.22
			P	Variety	.20	P	Respect of Others	-.20
			P	Confidence as a Man or Woman	-.20	P	Sense of Importance	-.20
	(Factor 4)			(Factor 5)			(Factor 6)	
O	Prestige	.88	P	Accomplishment	-.74	P	Tie to the Future	.85
O	Variety	-.30	P	Sense of Pride	-.74	P	Respect of Others	-.50
M	Prestige	.55	P	Variety	-.34	M	A Normal Life	.37
			P	Chance to Express Love	.41			
M	Your Own Home	-.27	P	Stable Marriage	.31	P	Stable Marriage	-.23
						P	Confidence as a Man or Woman	-.29
						P	Joy	.24
						P	Future Security	.27

APPENDIX 4.2 (Continued)

Value Area	Value	Loading	Value Area	Value	Loading	Value Area	Value	Loading
	(Factor 7)			(Factor 8)			(Factor 9)	
O	Leadership	.77	M	Someone to Rely On	.75	M	Emotional Support	.73
O	Early Entry	-.72	M	Permanent Companion	.48	M	Your Own Home	-.57
P	Joy	.30	P	Respect of Others	-.36	P	A Stable Marriage	-.36
						P	Chance to Express Love	.47
O	High Income	.28	O	A Normal Life	.27	P	Joy	.24
O	Field of Interest	-.23	M	Prestige	-.26	P	Future Security	-.24
O	Variety	.20	M	Close Physical Relationship	-.23	P	Respect of Others	-.24
P	Sense of Importance	-.20	M	Financial Security	-.23			
			P	Sense of Importance	.27			
	(Factor 10)			(Factor 11)			(Factor 12)	
O	Variety	-.53	O	Field of Interest	-.48	O	Leisure	-.71
M	Helpmate	-.83	M	Close Physical Relationship	-.58	O	Helping Others	.38
M	Permanent Companion	.30	P	Future Security	.63	P	Field of Interest	.34
M	Children	.31	P	Joy	-.40	P	Sense of Importance	.54
M	Financial Security	.24	O	Variety	.21	P	Variety	-.25
			M	Normal Life	.22	P	Stable Marriage	-.28

APPENDIX 4.2 (Continued)

Value Area	Value	Load-ing		Value Area	Value	Load-ing
	(Factor 13)				(Factor 14)	
O	Independence	-.74		O	Security	-.84
O	Helping Others	.45		P	A Stable Marriage	-.34
M	Prestige	-.45				
M	Children	.33				
				O	Independence	.28
O	Variety	-.27		P	Chance to Express Love	.28
M	Your Own Home	.29		P	Future Security	.21
P	Chance to Express Love	.22				

APPENDIX 4.3
Factors for the Male Sample

Value Area	Value	Loading	Value Area	Value	Loading	Value Area	Value	Loading
	(Factor 1)			(Factor 2)			(Factor 3)	
O	Security	.55	O	Leadership	-.70	M	Permanent Companion	.73
M	Financial Security	.78	M	Feeling of Leadership	-.63	M	Your Own Home	-.64
P	Future Security	.48	P	Sense of Importance	-.49	M	Normal Life	.54
P	Variety	-.35						
			O	Early Entry	.28	M	Financial Security	-.20
M	Permanent Companion	-.22	O	Prestige	-.20	P	A Stable Marriage	.22
M	Children	-.29	M	Normal Life	.25			
			P	Variety	.29			
			P	Respect of Others	.25			
	(Factor 4)			(Factor 5)			(Factor 6)	
O	High Income	.78	P	Accomplishment	.77	M	Someone to Rely On	.62
O	Helping Others	-.76	P	Sense of Pride	.75	P	Confidence as a Man or Woman	-.80
			P	A Stable Marriage	-.34	P	Variety	.38
O	Variety	-.29				P	Friendship	.37
O	Security	.25	P	Friendship	-.27			
M	Children	-.25	P	Joy	-.26			
P	A Stable Marriage	.26						
P	Future Security	-.23						

289

APPENDIX 4.3 (Continued)

Value Area	Value	Loading
	(Factor 7)	
M	Emotional Support	.65
M	Children	.33
P	Joy	.60
P	A Stable Marriage	-.48
P	Respect of Others	-.30
P	Friendship	.29
O	Prestige	.20
O	Early Entry	-.20
M	Normal Life	-.27
P	Chance to Express Love	.22
	(Factor 10)	
O	Field of Interest	-.80
P	Chance to Express Love	-.32
P	Sense of Importance	.30
O	Leisure	.22
O	Security	.28
O	Independence	.22
M	Normal Life	.21
P	A Stable Marriage	-.20
P	Future Security	-.20

Value Area	Value	Loading
	(Factor 8)	
O	Independence	.70
O	Leisure	-.70
O	Variety	.21
O	High Income	-.21
P	Sense of Pride	.20
	(Factor 11)	
P	A Tie to the Future	.81
P	Future Security	.46
P	Chance to Express Love	-.43
P	A Stable Marriage	-.23
P	Respect of Others	-.24
P	Friendship	-.22

Value Area	Value	Loading
	(Factor 9)	
O	Variety	-.35
M	A Helpmate	-.84
M	Children	.41
O	Leadership	.27
M	Permanent Companion	.20
M	Your Own Home	.21
P	Sense of Importance	-.22
	(Factor 12)	
O	Prestige	-.60
M	Prestige	-.80
M	Children	.33
O	Security	.26
M	Emotional Support	-.25
M	Normal Life	.24
M	Your Own Home	.23
M	Someone to Rely On	.25
P	Respect of Others	.28
P	Chance to Express Love	.22
P	Joy	.24
P	Variety	-.20

Value Area	Value	Load-ing	Value Area	Value	Load-ing
	(Factor 13)			(Factor 14)	
M	A Close Physical Relationship	.72	O	Early Entry	.67
M	Your Own Home	-.31	O	Variety	-.66
P	Respect of Others	-.48	P	Variety	-.30
P	Chance to Express Love	.36	P	Sense of Importance	.31
			M	Normal Life	.29
O	Helping Others	-.29			
O	Leisure	.22			
M	Normal Life	-.21			
P	A Stable Marriage	.22			

APPENDIX 5.1
Cross Tabulation of Involvement Level and
Job-Child Orientation Scales: Total

Job-child Orientation Scale		Involvement Level Scale							Total	
		Least 1	2	3	4	5	6	Most 7	N	%
Job	1	8	6	9	15	10	8	23	79	13.2
	2	1	3	10	7	8	5	8	42	7.0
	3	1	6	4	5	5	3	7	31	5.2
	4	1	11	22	43	31	2	16	126	21.0
	5	3	7	10	25	24	20	20	109	18.2
	6	0	10	25	30	18	12	15	110	18.4
Child	7	12	19	18	23	14	5	11	102	17.0
Total	N	26	62	98	148	110	55	100	599	100%
	%	4.3	10.4	16.4	24.7	18.4	9.2	16.7		

APPENDIX 5.2
Cross Tabulation of Involvement Level and
Job-Child Orientation Scales: Females

		Involvement Level Scale							Total	
Job-child Orientation Scale		Least 1	2	3	4	5	6	Most 7	N	%
Job	1	4	3	2	13	6	4	18	50	16.7
	2	0	2	5	4	4	3	3	21	7.0
	3	0	6	1	5	4	2	6	24	8.0
	4	0	1	9	26	16	1	14	67	22.3
	5	1	2	2	14	15	12	13	59	19.7
	6	0	3	9	12	8	4	8	44	14.7
Child	7	3	3	7	10	4	3	5	35	11.7
Total	N	8	20	35	84	57	29	67	300	100%
	%	2.7	6.7	11.7	28.0	19.0	9.7	22.3		

APPENDIX 5.3
Cross Tabulation of Involvement Level and
Job-Child Orientation Scales: Males

Job-Child Orientation Scale		Involvement Level Scale							Total	
		Least 1	2	3	4	5	6	Most 7	N	%
Job	1	4	3	7	2	4	4	5	29	9.7
	2	1	1	5	3	4	2	5	21	7.0
	3	1	0	3	0	1	1	1	7	2.3
	4	1	10	13	17	15	1	2	59	19.7
	5	2	5	8	11	9	8	7	50	16.7
	6	0	7	16	18	10	8	7	66	22.1
Child	7	9	16	11	13	10	2	6	67	22.4
Total	N	18	42	63	64	53	26	33	299	100%
	%	6.0	14.0	21.1	21.4	17.7	8.7	11.0		

APPENDIX 6.1
Variables with Significant Sex X A/T Interactions
and Means for the Four Groups Based on the
Occupational, Marriage, and Parenthood Values

| | Group | | | |
| | Female | | Male | |
Variable	Atypical	Typical	Atypical	Typical
Occupational Values				
Number of children desired	2.67	3.09	2.65	2.62
Job-Child Orientation Scale[1]	3.75	4.32	4.88	4.80
Number of children in family	3.03	3.46	3.55	3.05
How good a student are you?[2]	2.39	2.61	2.58	2.52
MV - A Helpmate	46.56	48.85	48.93	46.81
MV - Permanent Companion	54.62	56.64	57.11	55.74
MV - Feeling of Leadership	42.56	39.50	39.82	43.72
PV - Variety	51.05	52.06	50.10	46.75
(N)	(106)	(194)	(107)	(193)
Marriage Values				
Number of children desired	3.14	2.79	2.46	2.74
Job-Child Orientation Scale[1]	4.32	3.98	4.45	5.10
Part-time job-work pattern	4.53	3.96	3.83	3.93
OV - Prestige	48.74	50.74	52.44	47.76
OV - Variety	52.36	50.68	47.36	49.31
PV - A Sense of Pride	50.96	52.86	53.00	51.49
PV - A Stable Marriage	45.89	43.57	47.94	51.01
(N)	(125)	(175)	(123)	(177)

1. Scores range 1-7; a higher score means more child oriented than job oriented (Coombs, 1979).
2. 1 = one of the best students, 4 = just good enough to get by.

APPENDIX 6.1 (Continued)

	Group			
	Female		Male	
Variable	Atypical	Typical	Atypical	Typical
Parenthood Values				
How good a student are you?[3]	2.75	2.40	2.35	2.65
High school grade average	5.21	5.88	5.46	4.78
Planned level of education	5.40	5.78	6.13	5.40
Occupational Level (Roe)[3]	2.65	2.32	2.33	2.56
Occupational Score (Census)	81.56	85.36	87.90	83.96
Work pattern:				
Part-time career[4]	5.61	5.98	5.47	5.22
Full-time job	4.48	4.17	4.05	4.92
Part-time job	4.40	4.08	3.63	4.04
Age at completing education	21.87	22.32	22.80	21.83
Age at marriage	23.54	24.55	26.30	25.52
Age at second child	27.72	28.46	29.39	28.90
OV - Helping Others	55.32	56.05	53.08	49.44
OV - Variety	50.80	51.72	50.15	47.55
OV - Leisure	45.59	47.05	49.28	47.50
OV - Early Entry	39.02	36.18	34.15	37.70
MV - Emotional Support	57.25	61.25	60.37	57.26
MV - A Close Physical Relationship	54.73	56.69	56.29	55.49
MV - A Normal Life	42.21	37.66	39.58	43.53
(N)	(111)	(189)	(111)	(189)

3. Variables in which the lower values indicate the "better" end of the scale, for example, 1 = one of the best students.
4. Higher scores indicate more highly desired.

APPENDIX 6.2
Means for Sex-Typical and Sex-Atypical Groups on Occupational Values with Significant Interactions (Extreme Groups Analysis)

| | Group | | | |
| | Female | | Male | |
Value	Atypical	Typical	Atypical	Typical
High Income	54.10	46.63	48.41	55.53
Prestige	51.34	48.63	46.90	51.78
Helping Others	45.56	61.46	60.81	44.36
Variety	46.37	54.17	54.95	44.23
Leadership	52.02	38.35	38.36	53.04
(N)	(61)	(133)	(67)	(139)

APPENDIX 6.3
Means for Sex-Typical and Sex-Atypical Groups on
Marriage Values with Significant Interactions
(Extreme Group Analysis)

	Group			
	Female		Male	
Value	Atypical	Typical	Atypical	Typical
Financial Security	41.20	52.67	53.17	40.02
Emotional Support	56.26	61.69	61.63	55.15
A Helpmate	51.00	46.96	45.42	50.11
Prestige	39.03	55.02	53.97	37.53
A Normal Life	42.29	37.65	36.71	45.47
A Permanent Companion	57.00	53.40	52.35	58.47
Children	55.55	50.35	50.39	55.26
Your Own Home	52.07	43.32	46.81	50.56
Someone to Rely on	57.96	51.47	51.95	57.43
(N)	(72)	(125)	(75)	(128)

APPENDIX 6.4
Means for Sex-Typical and Sex-Atypical Groups on
Parenthood Values with Significant Interactions
(Extreme Groups Analysis)

	Group			
	Female		Male	
Value	Atypical	Typical	Atypical	Typical
A Sense of Pride	49.91	53.49	52.72	50.87
Variety	43.45	55.12	54.92	42.07
Friendship	55.49	59.46	58.45	54.57
Respect of Others	42.35	39.60	40.68	43.27
A Stable Marriage	56.88	36.91	37.31	57.10
A Chance to Express Love	57.20	63.26	62.97	57.13
Confidence as a Man or Woman	46.75	41.91	41.68	44.21
Joy	57.70	61.14	60.56	58.24
A Sense of Importance	48.57	46.36	46.59	49.46
(N)	(60)	(138)	(62)	(140)

APPENDIX 6.5
Regression Analyses for Number of Years of Full-Time Work to Age 41: All Females with Occupational Values

Variable	B	Beta	Standard Error B	F (5,290)	R Each Step	R^2
IL Scale	.9680	.2901	.1832	27.93	.359	.1287
J-C Scale	-.5462	-.1920	.1681	10.56	.465	.2162
Working Pattern: Continuous-Briefly	-.8977	-.1407	.3399	6.98	.484	.2346
Career Pattern: Full-time	.0802	.1295	.0334	5.60	.499	.2490
Circle: No. Segments for Children	-.3342	-.1028	.1844	3.28	.507	.2574

(constant) 6.4574   N = 296

APPENDIX 6.6
Regression Analyses for Number of Years of Full-Time Work
to Age 41: All Females—All Values

Variable	B	Beta	Standard Error B	F	R Each Step	R^2
IL Scale	.9712	.2910	.1812	28.74	.359	.1287
J-C Scale	-.5327	-.1872	.1605	11.02	.465	.2162
Working Pattern: Continuous-Briefly	-.8032	-.1259	.3401	5.58	.484	.2346
Career Pattern: Full-time	.0821	.1325	.0336	5.96	.499	.2490
M--Children	-.0784	-.1438	.0303	6.70	.512	.2625
M--Someone to rely on	-.0670	-.1032	.0330	4.12	.522	.2729
(constant) 12.1654	N = 296					

APPENDIX 6.7
Regression Analyses for Number of Years of Full–Time Work to Age 41: White Females—All Values

Variable	B	Beta	Standard Error B	F	R Each Step	R^2
Career Pattern: Full-time	.1645	.3390	.0428	14.77	.3913	.1531
Circle: Work Segments	.7267	.2956	.2164	11.28	.5028	.2528
Working Pattern: Continuous-Briefly	-.9618	-.1744	.4786	4.04	.5343	.2855
O--Variety	-.1051	-.1844	.0507	4.30	.5537	.3065
M--A Helpmate	.1001	.1752	.0503	3.97	.5792	.3355
(constant) -2.4277						

APPENDIX 6.8
Regression Analyses for Number of Years of Full-Time Work to Age 41: Black Females—All Values

Variable	B	Beta	Standard Error B	F	R Each Step	R^2
Family Activity: Earning Salary to Support Family	-2.8789	-.3295	.7835	13.50	.3982	.1585
IL Scale	.7982	.2340	.2938	7.38	.4942	.2443
J-C Scale	-.8316	-.2961	.2481	11.24	.5456	.2976
O--Helping Others	-.0952	-.1687	.0474	4.03	.5665	.3209
Wife Responsibility to Earn Money	-.1017	-.2685	.0387	6.90	.5806	.3371
Husband Responsibility to Keep House	.0693	.2182	.0308	5.06	.6037	.3645
O--Security	.1107	.1713	.0556	3.97	.6253	.3910

(constant) 20.7566 N = 99

APPENDIX 6.9
Regression Analyses for Number of Years of Full-Time Work to Age 41: Hispanic Females—All Values

Variable	B	Beta	Standard Error B	F	R Each Step	R^2
M--Someone to Rely On	-.2075	-.3246	.0577	12.93	.2708	.0733
Work Pattern: Continuous-Briefly	-1.3061	-.2127	.5628	5.39	.3985	.1588
Career Pattern: Not Working	-.1193	-.1822	.0591	4.08	.4478	.2005
M--Children	-.1270	-.2184	.0534	5.67	.4817	.2321
IL Scale	.7742	.2323	.3057	6.41	.5219	.2724
M--Your Own Home	-.0195	-.1572	.0517	3.13	.5442	.2961
(constant) 36.1101	N = 100					

APPENDIX 7.1

Frequency and Percentage of Total Sample Responses to Activities for Families with Children [1]

Activity	Only a Woman's responsibility 1		Mainly a Woman's responsibility 2		Could be either person's responsibility 3		Mainly a Man's responsibility 4		Only a Man's responsibility 5		Missing - no response 0		Mean
	N	%	N	%	N	%	N	%	N	%	N	%	
Cleaning the house (dust, vacuum)	27	4.5	179	29.8	393	65.5	1	-	1	-	1	.2	2.61
Mending clothes	84	14.0	332	55.3	182	30.3	1	.2	1	.2	1	.2	2.17
Managing family money	2	.3	14	2.3	400	66.7	159	26.5	24	4.0	1	.2	3.32
Repairing household appliances	-	-	7	1.2	177	29.5	335	55.8	80	13.3	1	.2	3.81
Mowing the lawn	-	-	2	-	185	30.8	267	44.5	144	24.0	2	.3	3.92
Planning color scheme for home	25	4.2	126	21.0	441	73.5	5	.8	2	.3	1	.2	2.72
Reading to children	4	.7	17	2.8	570	95.0	7	1.2	2	.3	1	.3	2.98
Taking out garbage	-	-	2	-	343	57.2	204	34.0	50	8.3	1	.2	3.50
Washing the family car	-	-	4	.7	337	56.2	184	30.7	72	12.0	3	.5	3.54
Washing clothes	72	12.0	305	50.8	222	37.0	-	-	-	-	1	.2	2.25
Caring for baby	39	6.5	185	30.8	376	62.7	-	-	-	-	-	-	2.56
Taking children to doctor	18	3.0	75	12.5	501	83.5	4	.7	2	.3	-	-	2.83
Earning salary that supports family	-	-	2	.3	238	48.0	241	40.2	69	11.5	-	-	3.63
Doing family's food shopping	33	5.5	200	33.3	353	58.8	10	1.7	2	.3	2	.3	2.58
Deciding when car needs tune-up	-	-	1	.2	194	32.3	280	46.7	125	20.8	2	-	3.88
Teaching children sports	-	-	1	-	324	54.0	205	34.2	66	11.0	4	.7	3.56
Cooking meals	72	12.0	245	40.8	278	46.3	5	.8	-	-	-	-	2.36
Fixing a broken lamp	-	-	2	.3	207	34.5	311	51.8	78	13.0	2	.3	3.78
Deciding to move to another city	-	-	2	-	526	87.7	58	9.7	14	2.3	1	-	3.14
Helping children with homework	2	.3	21	3.5	573	95.5	2	.3	1	.2	1	.2	2.96
Staying home from work if a child is sick	53	8.8	224	37.3	316	52.7	3	.5	3	.5	1	.2	2.46
Deciding to buy a large item: color TV, washing machine, etc.	4	.7	8	1.3	540	90.0	40	6.7	7	1.2	1	.2	3.06

1. Adapted from Eagly and Anderson (1974).

APPENDIX 7.2

Means for Activities with Significant Sex, Ethnic, or SES Group Differences

	Group means						
	Sex		Ethnic			SES	
Activity	F	M	W	B	H	M	L
Cleaning the house	2.7	2.5	2.6	2.7	2.6	2.7	2.6
Managing family money	3.2	3.4	3.3	3.3	3.4		
Repairing household appliances	3.7	3.9	3.7	3.8	3.9	3.7	3.9
Mowing the lawn	3.7	4.1	3.8	4.0	4.0		
Taking out garbage	3.4	3.6	3.4	3.6	3.5		
Washing the family car	3.4	3.7	3.5	3.7	3.5	3.5	3.6
Washing clothes						2.3	2.2
Taking children to doctor	2.8	2.9				2.9	2.8
Earning salary that supports family	3.4	3.8	3.8	3.5	3.6	3.6	3.7
Deciding when car needs tune up	3.8	4.0				3.8	4.0
Teaching children sports	3.3	3.8				3.5	3.6
Cooking meals						2.4	2.3
Fixing a broken lamp	3.7	3.9	3.7	3.9	3.8	3.7	3.9
Deciding to move to another city	3.1	3.2	3.0	3.1	3.1		
Deciding to buy large items	3.0	3.1					

APPENDIX 7.3
Factors and Activity Item Loading—Total Sample[1]

Activity	Loading
Factor 1	
Repairing Household Appliances	.69
Mowing the lawn	.54
Deciding when the car needs tune up	.62
Teaching children sports	.44
Fixing a broken lamp	.74
Managing family money	.31
Washing the family car	.30
Factor 2	
Cleaning the house	.65
Mending clothes	.69
Washing clothes	.72
Doing family food shopping	.44
Cooking meals	.67
Staying home from work if a child is sick	.42
Factor 3	
Managing family money	.61
Planning color scheme for home	-.35
Earning salary that supports family	.59
Teaching children sports	.49
Deciding to move to another city	.65
Factor 4	
Caring for baby	.62
Helping children with homework	.83
Staying home from work if a child is sick	.45
Factor 5	
Reading to children	.62
Taking children to doctor	.73
Doing family food shopping	.48
Factor 6	
Mowing the lawn	.43
Taking out garbage	.74
Washing the family car	.36

1. N = 579.

APPENDIX 7.4
Frequency Distributions for Ages at Which All Students Expect Major Events to Occur

Code/Age	Age Finishing H.S. F	%	Age Completing Education F	%	Age of Marriage F	%	Age at 1st Child F	%	Age at 2nd Child F	%	Age at 3rd Child F	%
Missing/O	-	-	-	-	26	4.3	26	4.3	56	9.3	323	53.8
16	24	4.0	1	.2	-	-	1	.2	-	-	-	-
17	289	48.2	13	2.2	-	-	1	.2	-	-	-	-
18	254	42.3	32	5.3	5	.8	1	.2	-	-	-	-
19	33	5.5	32	5.3	6	1.0	4	.7	1	.2	-	-
20	-	-	40	6.7	14	2.3	8	1.3	-	-	-	-
21	-	-	125	20.8	32	5.3	10	1.7	4	.7	3	.5
22	-	-	141	23.5	46	7.7	16	2.7	8	1.3	4	.7
23	-	-	48	8.0	70	11.7	33	5.5	12	2.0	6	1.0
24	-	-	69	11.5	77	12.8	45	7.5	15	2.5	10	1.7
25	-	-	42	7.0	122	20.3	80	13.3	40	6.7	13	2.2
26	-	-	29	4.8	64	10.7	88	14.7	46	7.7	24	4.0
27	-	-	11	1.8	48	8.0	77	12.8	67	11.2	31	5.2
28	-	-	12	2.0	25	4.2	75	12.5	72	12.0	29	4.8
29	-	-	1	.2	23	3.8	36	6.0	75	12.5	42	7.0
30	-	-	-	-	23	3.8	41	6.8	71	11.8	34	5.7
31	-	-	1	.2	-	-	30	5.0	43	7.2	24	4.0
32	-	-	2	.3	5	.8	12	2.0	33	5.5	17	2.8
33	-	-	-	-	1	.2	5	.8	30	5.0	19	3.2
34	-	-	1	.2	1	.2	-	-	10	1.7	11	1.8
35	-	-	-	-	5	.8	7	1.2	7	1.2	5	.8
36	-	-	-	-	1	.2	1	.2	3	.5	2	.3
37	-	-	-	-	1	.2	1	.2	5	.8	1	.3
38	-	-	-	-	-	-	-	-	-	-	2	.3
39	-	-	-	-	1	.2	-	-	2	.3	-	-
40	-	-	-	-	2	.3	2	.3	-	-	-	-
Mean	17.5		22.2		25.0		26.7		28.6		29.9	
SD	.7		2.5		3.1		3.1		3.1		3.2	

APPENDIX 7.4 (Continued)

Code/Age	Started Full Time Work F	%	Resumed Full Time Work F	%	Started Part Time Work F	%	Ended Part Time Work F	%	Started Part Time Work F	%	Ended Part Time Work F	%
Missing Cases	17	2.8	469	78.2	177	29.5	209	34.8	550	91.7	553	92.2
16	–	–	–	–	29	4.8	4	.7	–	–	–	–
17	1	.2	–	–	34	5.7	5	.8	–	–	–	–
18	22	3.7	–	–	114	19.0	16	2.7	–	–	–	–
19	25	4.2	–	–	93	15.5	22	3.7	–	–	–	–
20	36	6.0	–	–	15	2.5	52	8.7	–	–	–	–
21	49	8.2	2	.3	11	1.8	70	11.7	2	.3	1	.2
22	88	14.7	–	–	10	1.7	36	6.0	–	–	1	.2
23	106	17.7	4	.7	13	2.2	40	6.7	4	.7	3	.5
24	53	8.8	3	.5	7	1.2	25	4.2	4	.7	2	.3
25	73	12.2	1	.2	11	1.3	28	4.7	3	.5	1	.2
26	37	6.2	3	.5	6	1.0	9	1.5	2	.3	3	.5
27	28	4.7	5	.8	11	1.8	13	2.2	3	.5	1	.3
28	17	2.8	3	.5	8	1.3	8	1.3	4	.7	4	.7
29	12	2.0	11	1.8	9	1.5	10	1.7	7	1.2	3	.5
30	10	1.7	9	1.5	6	1.0	2	.3	3	.5	3	.3
31	4	.7	9	1.5	6	1.0	8	1.3	4	.7	4	.5
32	2	.3	6	1.0	5	.3	5	.8	7	1.2	3	.7
33	5	.8	8	1.3	4	.7	6	1.0	3	.5	2	.3
34	2	.3	10	1.7	6	1.0	2	.3	1	.2	3	.5
35	6	1.0	20	3.3	9	1.5	4	.7	5	.8	2	.3
36	–	–	9	1.5	2	.3	–	–	1	.2	–	–
37	2	.3	8	1.3	2	.3	4	.7	2	.3	1	.2
38	2	.3	6	1.0	4	.7	–	–	2	.3	3	.5
39	–	–	1	.2	4	.7	4	.7	2	.3	3	.5
40	3	.5	13	2.2	4	.7	20	3.3	3	.5	16	2.7
Mean	23.8		32.8		21.5		24.9		32.1		34.7	
SD	3.6		4.7		5.8		5.4		4.5		5.0	

309

APPENDIX 7.5
Frequency Distributions for Part-Time Work Expectations
for Females and Males

	Age started part-time work				Age ended part-time work			
	Female		Male		Female		Male	
	F	%	F	%	F	%	F	%
Missing/								
0	77	25.6	101	33.7	95	31.7	114	38.0
16	8	2.7	21	7.0				
17	13	4.3	21	7.0	2	.7	2	.7
18	46	15.3	67	22.3			5	1.7
19	44	14.7	49	16.3	8	2.7	8	2.7
20	8	2.7	7	2.3	10	3.3	12	4.0
21	7	2.3	4	1.3	24	8.0	28	9.3
22	6	2.0	4	1.3	27	9.0	43	14.3
23	7	2.3	6	2.0	21	7.0	15	5.0
24	5	1.7	2	.7	13	4.3	27	9.0
25	5	1.7	6	2.0	10	3.3	15	5.0
26	5	1.7	1	.3	13	4.3	15	5.0
27	11	3.7			5	1.7	4	1.3
28	6	2.0	2	.7	6	2.0	7	2.3
29	8	2.7	1	.3	6	2.0	2	.7
30	4	1.3	2	.7	9	3.0	1	.3
31	5	1.7	1	.3	2	.7		
32	5	1.7			7	2.3	1	.3
33	3	1.0	1	.3	5	1.7		
34	4	1.3	2	.7	6	2.0		
35	9	3.0			1	.3	1	.3
36	2	.7			2	.7		
37	2	.7			4	1.3		
38	4	1.3						
39	4	1.3			4	1.3		
40	2	.7	2	.7	20	6.7		
41								
Mean	23.3		19.4		26.7		22.9	
SD	6.6		3.9		6.5		2.8	

AUTHOR INDEX

SUBJECT INDEX

*italics indicate title of a test

ABOUT THE AUTHOR

Carol Kehr Tittle is Professor in the School of Education, University of North Carolina at Greensboro, and a member of the faculty for the M.Ed. program in Educational Research and Evaluation. She received her Ph.D. from the University of Chicago and has been active in research related to women and their educational and career development, as well as in research in the measurement and evaluation areas. She is currently on the editorial board of *Sex Roles: A Journal of Research* and is coauthor with Elenor Rubin Denker of *Returning Women in Higher Education: Defining Policy Issues.* She also coedited the *Handbook of Vocational Education Evaluation.* She previously held positions at Queens College and the Center for Advanced Study in Education of the Graduate Center of the City University of New York.

DATE DUE			
7-6-82			
MAR 2 9 '85			
8·17·95			
GAYLORD 234			PRINTED IN U.S.A.